Southern Living.
1995
Garden Annual

Southern Living
1995
Garden Annual

ISBN: 0-8487-1409-1
Manufactured in the
United States of America
First Printing

Southern Living®
Garden Editor: Mark G. Stith
Senior Writer: Stephen P. Bender
Senior Photographer: Van Chaplin
Associate Garden Editor:
   Linda C. Askey
Associate Projects Editor:
   Julia Hamilton Thomason
Assistant Garden Design Editors:
   Rebecca Dell Bull,
   Joann Catherine Kellum
Assistant Garden Editor:
   Charles Thigpen
Production Manager: Kenner Patton
Assistant Production Manager:
   Vicki Weathers
Editorial Assistant: Tena Z. Payne

Oxmoor House, Inc.
Editor-in-Chief: Nancy J. Fitzpatrick
Senior Homes Editor:
   Mary Kay Culpepper
Senior Editor, Editorial Services:
   Olivia Kindig Wells
Art Director: James Boone

Southern Living 1995 Garden Annual

Editor: Rebecca Brennan
Designer: Eleanor Cameron
Editorial Assistant:
   Catherine Barnhart Pewitt
Copy Editor: Jennifer K. Mathews
Production and Distribution Director:
   Phillip Lee
Production Manager: Gail Morris
Associate Production Manager:
   Theresa L. Beste
Production Assistant: Marianne Jordan

Cover: *Zinnias*

page 22

page 190

page 154

Nowhere is the love of gardening more passionate than in the South. It's evident in the plants we have grown for generations—azaleas, camellias, dogwoods, live oaks, magnolias, and gardenias—to name a few. These mainstays of the Southern landscape are firmly entrenched in the images most people conjure up when they think of the South.

The last several years have seen a broadening of the palette of plants grown by even the most casual gardeners. Interest in native plants, heirloom flowers and vegetables, and new introductions has never been keener. Hopefully, this book, a compilation of gardening articles from *Southern Living* magazine, will reacquaint you with some old favorites, as well as introduce you to some delightful new plants to try. In either case, I hope that this book inspires you to get out there and garden.

Mark G. Stith
Garden Editor

BASIC TO

BEAUTIFUL

Project Timeline

1 *Established what owner wanted and needed*

2 *Determined the existing condition of yard*

3 *Planned what to do*

4 *Removed steps and driveway (stockpiled flagstone from drive for reuse)*

5 *Built new stone front steps*

6 *Poured new driveway*

7 *Added new parking area (back)*

8 *Built stone walls (front)*

9 *Built stone walkway and landing (front)*

10 *Removed sweet gum trees (front & back)*

11 *Planted front yard*

12 *Corrected downspout problem*

13 *Built deck and storage area (back)*

14 *Laid flagstone path and terrace (back)*

15 *Planted & sodded backyard*

16 *Decided front yard needed more light: trimmed trees, ground stump, patched sod*

Time hadn't been kind to this older home. But with a major makeover, it now has a fresh new look.

magical Makeover

Wait a minute! Is the plain-Jane house in the upper lefthand corner of the page the same one as the cute little cottage below? (Feel free to compare them before answering.) Yes, it's the same. What's going on here? Smoke and mirrors? A little magic?

No, there's no magic, although the effect is magical. What has taken place is a major landscape renovation to both the front and back. In this special section, we take you through a "Basic to Beautiful" transformation. No matter how big or small, young or old your house is, we think you'll come away with some good ideas for adding delights and solving dilemmas in your own landscape.

Let's be fair—the house wasn't that bad. It was actually rather charming. The landscape, however, looked a little scary. The flagstone driveway was a rough ride. The old steps on the side of the front porch challenged visitors to find them. And those overgrown shrubs around the front of the house and porch offered about as much impact as a parsley sprig on a plate of spaghetti. The backyard? A yawn of a lawn, chain link fencing on one side and along the back . . . you get the idea (see "before" photo on page 8).

This is a story about realizing the potential of this place, a small cottage among cottages on a busy two-lane street. It's also about updating and personalizing a landscape to suit the homeowner's needs.

The owner bought the house about

A new driveway, a pull-in space for guest parking, and relocated front steps transformed this small cottage from an eyesore into a sight for sore eyes.

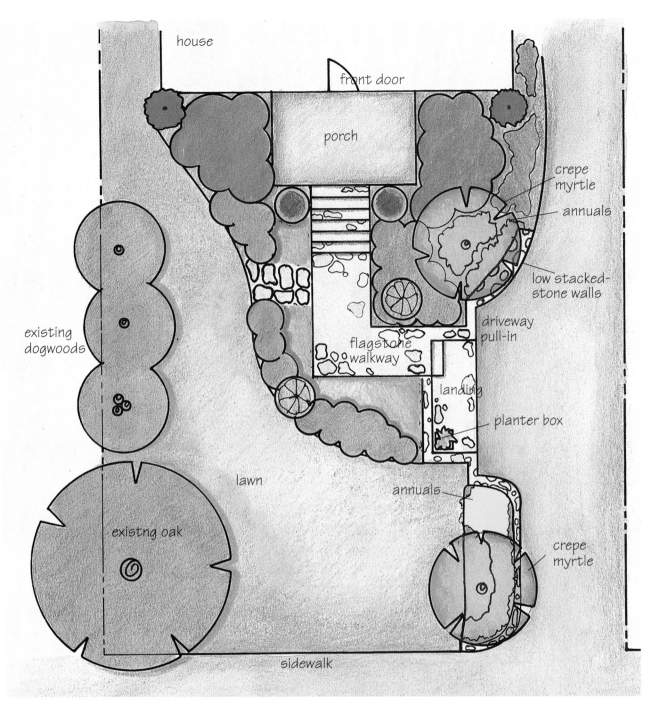

house

front door

porch

crepe
myrtle

annuals

low stacked-
stone walls

driveway
pull-in

landing

planter box

flagstone
walkway

existing
dogwoods

lawn

annuals

existng oak

crepe
myrtle

sidewalk

FRONT PLAN

six years ago. "I first saw the house in November of '88," she recalls. "The leaves were down, and the house was all dark. It seemed to have a real need for a new life."

She wanted a small house (and yard) convenient to her work. "The inside wasn't large, but it was livable and usable space," the owner says. The owner also liked the neighborhood, which has lots of old-fashioned charm. Sidewalks parallel the tree-lined street, and neighbors wave as they stroll by. But the old-time charm had to come face-to-face with modern realities.

The once-quiet row of houses on the street is now surrounded by a city that grew up around it. An apartment complex looms just behind the alley in back of the house. Privacy? Forget it. Visitors park at streetside? Downright dangerous. Back the car out into the street? No way.

Essentially, the landscape had to take a giant leap forward from the 50s into the 90s. Because we knew the owner, the Garden staff of *Southern Living* offered to update the landscape. She eagerly agreed, but was quick to point out her needs. Basically, our design had to create a look she could manage and enjoy. And it had to fit her budget. Read on as we relate the stories behind making a landscape fit the dreams of the owner, given the real-world constraints of time, money, and the site.

Laying the Welcome Mat

Front steps should be in the front. It's just that simple. Originally, the steps were hidden at one end of the porch. Guests couldn't see the front door as they approached; the side steps brought people alongside the house instead of leading them to it.

Sledgehammers and crowbars eliminated that problem. With the offending side steps out of the way, we built flagstone steps where they should be: in the front. "I was very pleased when the suggestion was made to move the steps to the front. It gave a more formal balance," explains the owner.

Centered between the porch columns, the new steps direct attention straight to the front door. To further emphasize the door, we painted it dark green to contrast with the white vinyl siding.

After: A stone landing framed by dry stacked walls creates a welcoming entrance.

Putting the steps in the front had another advantage. The original plain concrete walk had to hug the house to connect the driveway to the side steps. With the steps now in the front, there was room for entry embellishment.

We kept two requirements in mind as we designed the new entrance: convenience and hospitality. For easy access from the car to the porch, we added an L-shaped walkway. An inviting stone landing borders a pull-in for cars, which was added during the driveway renovation. Two steps up, the wide and comfortable flagstone walk turns to meet the new front steps.

Because the front yard slopes, we cut into the grade to level the pull-in and landing. Low, stacked-stone walls retain the soil, making plants look as if they are nestled in raised planters. The walls lean backward into the slope, so mortar is not needed. This came in handy when an unfortunately placed downspout began washing mulch away. We solved the problem by connecting a buried PVC pipe to the downspout. Because water can seep through the stones in the wall, there is no problem with accumulated water.

The cost of all the stonework—walls, steps, walk, and landing (together with removal of the steps)—was under $3,000. Broken stone salvaged from the old driveway was used as filler in walls and steps, but we purchased prettier pieces for the top layers. The investment has quite an impact; the new entrance is like a welcome mat for the house.

Originally, the front steps weren't in the front. They led to the porch from the side.

(Above) *The low end of the walk needed a double layer of flagstone to level the surface.*

(Right) Top: *New stacked-stone steps lead directly to the front door.* Bottom: *The downspout dumped too much water in the planting bed. We added a buried pipe to solve the problem.*

(Below) *Mortaring stone to the ground is not a good idea because frost can cause cracks. For a firm foundation, we poured concrete.*

Dressing Up the Driveway

The original flagstone driveway was rough and inconvenient. Because there was no room to turn a car around, the owner had to back out onto the busy street. Because the drive was as unattractive as it was impractical, we opted to demolish it and start over. But the old drive did have something going for it—the stones themselves weren't ugly, just misplaced.

To make way for a new drive, we asked the contractor to remove and stockpile the flagstone. Every bit of salvaged stone was used: We laid large pieces in the landing and back terrace, while broken pieces were ideal for edging (see page 26) and for filler in the walls and steps.

The new drive has some custom features. Because the only place to add parking was in the backyard, we decided to make a pull-in spot for cars in the front. The pull-in creates easy access to the front

(**Left**) *The flagstone in this bumpy drive was saved to build a terrace and other projects.* (**Below**) *Adding a pigment to the new concrete toned down the impact of the driveway.*

(Above)
We cut into the slope to build a stone landing and a pull-in for a car. After leveling the landing, we built stacked-stone walls to hold the soil.

(Right) *We spent $2,750 on the new driveway. This included materials, as well as the labor to remove the existing drive, stockpile the old stone in the backyard, and pour the new concrete driveway.*

door without completely blocking the narrow drive. The crushed stone parking in the back makes it possible to turn a car around, so the owner no longer has to check her life insurance policy every time she ventures onto the busy street.

Most driveways are made of glaring white concrete, often marred by oil stains. Coloring the concrete can lessen both of these problems. Although existing concrete can be stained, aging and chipping may expose the white concrete beneath the tinted surface, making the drive look pockmarked.

Because we were starting over with a new drive, the pigment was mixed in before the concrete was poured. Known as an integral color mix, the pigment tints the concrete all the way through, so chipping is not a concern. Although color mixes are available in just about any hue you can dream up, you can keep costs down by starting with standard-gray portland cement, instead of more expensive white cement. We used a dark-gray pigment, which only cost $100 more than regular, untinted concrete. The color fades during the curing process and in the hot summer sun, so choose a color a little darker than what you ultimately want.

Start Small, Save Money

Smaller plants allowed us to do the planting ourselves, saving lots of money. The shrubs we chose provide year-round interest, frame the steps and walkway, and guide visitors to the door. And they'll never block the porch or windows.

Plant	Letter	Quantity	Unit Price	Total
Crepe myrtle	**A**	2 5 gallon	$25	$50
Nellie R. Stevens holly	**B**	2 2'-3' B&B	$50	$100
Wintergreen boxwood	**C**	2 3 gallon	$25	$50
Schipkaensis cherry laurel	**D**	12 15"-18" B&B	$20	$240
Gumpo azalea	**E**	21 1 gallon	$6	$126
Japanese aucuba	**F**	7 2 gallon	$10	$70
Dwarf Japanese andromeda	**G**	7 1 gallon	$6	$42
Cameo flowering quince	**H**	2 1 gallon	$6	$12

Back in the winter of 1988, when the homeowner bought the house, a row of gnarly, old shrubs lined up against the front. Wonder what happened to them? They are now prime, Grade A mulch. We gave them the ax because they served no real purpose. There wasn't an exposed foundation to hide. The only things hidden were the front steps behind them. So out they went in favor of a better planting scheme.

The new entry planting accomplishes four objectives. First, it establishes a backbone of evergreens to give the garden interest in every season. Second, it frames the walk and landings with massed plants to guide visitors to the front door. Third, it doesn't hide the porch and windows behind a bunker of overgrown shrubs. Finally, it leaves plenty of room for lots of seasonal color to catch your eye from the street.

We chose Nellie R. Stevens holly, Schipkaensis cherry laurel, Wintergreen boxwood, gumpo azalea, Japanese aucuba, and dwarf Japanese andromeda to satisfy the first three objectives (see plan below). These evergreen shrubs grow at a moderate pace and won't swallow the house. They need pruning no more than once a year. In addition, all grow in sun or shade and pests don't bother them.

Seasonal color, the final objective, arrives in spring with the flowers of gumpo azaleas. The crepe myrtle follows with gorgeous pink blooms in summer. But the lengthiest show comes from annuals. To read more about year-round color from annuals, see page 17.

Not counting the annuals, the entry plants cost $690 (see plant chart), excluding tax. We kept expenses down by choosing smaller plants whenever possible. Sure, these plants look a little puny at first. But they'll fill in nicely within two years. We also cut costs by resisting the temptation to jam small shrubs together for immediate impact. Doing so would have simply meant ripping out overcrowded plants a few years later. We spaced all massed shrubs at least 2 feet apart.

Now let's talk about labor costs. On a job like this, if a contractor buys and installs the plants, you'll likely pay double the retail price of the plants for the entire job. In other words, if the plants cost $100, plants plus planting will run you about $200. So hiring a contractor to complete this job would have cost approximately $1400.

However, because we used small plants, we could plant them ourselves. This saved approximately $700. Sometimes it's better to start off small. Who can't use the extra money?

A changing
display of
flowers
shows off
the beauty
in each new
season.

Up Front With Flowers

Flowers around the entry give the home a cheerful look. They say welcome before you even open the door. By limiting the area for flowers to a container and a few small beds, we found that a continuous display of color was affordable, both in terms of time and money.

Because Southern winters are mild, cool-weather annuals can be planted in fall and will bloom for months. Pansies are the hardiest of them all, blooming from October until late spring, when they wane with the first warm days. Then summer annuals carry the color through the hot season.

By the time autumn leaves reach their peak of color, summer's annuals are usually tired and will be overwhelmed by the vivid leaves around them. That's the time

for chrysanthemums. They're bright enough to make a statement, and they also complement fall foliage. Then as their blossoms fade, it's back to the cool-weather annuals.

Changing the color three times each year requires a couple of afternoons for pulling out the old, freshening the soil with organic matter, and planting the new. And there are a few hours involved in bringing home the plants and supplies.

In terms of cost, we estimate up to $300 per year for plants, depending on how dense you want them and where they are purchased. That does not include labor if you hire someone to do the work. We needed about six flats of annuals ($10 to $13 each) to cover the area, with plants

Pansies and foxgloves planted in the fall provide a spectacular spring display.

spaced 6 to 8 inches apart. Some seasons we used less. Wax begonias, blue salvia, foxgloves, and lantana were spaced 12 inches apart. The chrysanthemums required more than a third of the annual budget. Gardeners who want to cut costs can grow their own transplants from seeds.

In addition to seasonal changes, varying the choice of plants from one year to the next provides a kind of playground for the gardener. It's fun to try something new; go to the garden center with an open mind and a curious eye. For example, wax begonias were excellent, but for the sake of interest, we tried lantana the next year, and we liked it even better. However, some plants are not as successful. When we planted narrowleaf zinnia, it did not live up to our expectations, probably due to

insufficient light. Although blue salvia and lantana will be perennials in some regions and foxgloves are reseeding biennials, a complete change between seasons allows for greater impact in confined areas. Incidentally, foxgloves are set out in fall with the pansies.

Matching plants to the growing conditions requires some observation. When the trees lose their leaves in the winter, these beds are in full sun. In the summer, they get sun in the morning and midday, but they are shaded in the afternoon by tall trees to the west.

COLOR COMBOS

Because the house is white and, with the exception of the pink crepe myrtle in summer, the framework of the garden is a neutral green, we were free to experiment with color combinations. However, if the home were redbrick, for example, our choices would have been more limited. We would have wanted to be cautious when using reds and pinks. Depending on the shade of brick, the colors could clash.

We also learned that, as much as we like blue flowers in the garden, they have limited impact at a distance. And without another color to serve as a spark, blue fades into the landscape like a mist. So when we planted blue salvia, we used a lot of it combined with yellow lantana.

(Above) *For a blast of autumn color, chrysanthemums cannot be beat. They bring out the delicate colors in the stonework, yet they are strong enough to show up when fall leaves are at their peak.*

(Right) *Wax begonias provide a nonstop display through the summer months. The white flowers seem cool in the heat while the bronze foliage brings out the color in the stone.*

Taming the Backyard Beast

The backyard was unused and over-looked—the kind of yard where you slip out the back door to plop the trash in the can and then hurry back inside. There was nothing to look at and nowhere to sit. To make matters worse, the sloping lot dipped down into a low damp spot near the back door.

Architect Kent Campbell designed a deck to change all of that. Built at the same level as the floor inside the house, the deck eliminates the need for back steps. It also spans most of the change in elevation, so the rest of the yard doesn't seem to be high above the back door.

"The back door used to open onto what was essentially a drainage swale. The deck hides that low area without altering the flow of runoff," Campbell says. An enclosed storage area built off the deck hides garbage cans, firewood, and yard tools. A contractor built the deck and storage area for $1,250.

Because the deck is only 120 square feet, there isn't a lot of room for furniture. To save space, Campbell designed a backless bench to double as the railing. Beyond the bench, a collection of plants, selected to thrive in the shade of a large oak tree, helps set a getaway mood. To make the most of her new oasis, the owner replaced a bedroom window with a French door opening onto the deck.

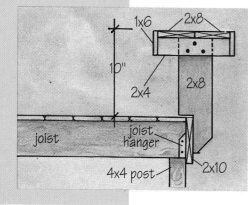

DECK BENCH
(Side View)

1x6 *2x8* *10"* *2x4* *2x8* *joist* *joist hanger* *4x4 post* *2x10*

Backyard Beautiful. A cozy deck makes the backyard a favorite spot.

(Right) *For a neat look, the deck planks were cut to fit inside the 2 x 10 facing instead of letting the edges overlap. The 2 x 10 facing also hides the underside of the deck.*

(Far right) *Notched 2 x 8 bench supports are attached with joist hangers to the finished deck. At the corners, we mitered the pair of 2 x 8s that form the bench seat.*

But the makeover doesn't stop with the deck. A flagstone path leads to a new parking area. "I never used the back entrance before," says the owner. "Adding space for parking has changed the whole way of going and coming from my house." One load of crushed gravel at $125 was plenty for the parking area. A sunny spot to the left of the path was especially appealing, so we used stone salvaged from the old driveway to build a small terrace.

Each of these projects—the deck, the parking area, and the terrace—met specific needs. Planning the overall backyard design before beginning work helped us tame the backyard beast.

(Above) *The barren backyard was uninviting.*

(Right) *A much-needed parking area made of crushed gravel doubles as a turn-around. A flagstone path leads from the car to the terrace and deck.*

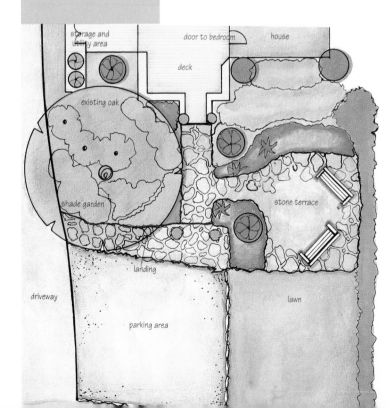

Nestled beneath an oak, the deck is a perfect place for entertaining.

Disappearing Act

See this trash can? We hid it in a wooden box.

Part of the plan for creating a pleasant backyard involves hiding a rather unattractive necessity—the trash can. A 3- x 9-foot wooden enclosure made of double gates is the solution for this home. Not only is there room to hide the trash can, but there's also space left over for storing the garden hose, tools, firewood, and lawn sprinkler.

Several touches make this storage area a bit more clever than your average, hide-a-can screening fence. There are actually four gates—two on each long side—that allow convenient access from both the kitchen door (for tossing the trash) and the driveway (for fetching the hose). As with the front steps and parking area, the challenge here was to make the structure blend in. This was achieved by building both the deck and the enclosure out of the same size and type of lumber.

A thoughtful plan and matching materials have produced a storage area that fits in well and functions just right. That's a pretty flashy performance for something with such a plain-Jane purpose.

The storage area combines the look of an attractive fence with practicality and convenience. The enclosed area and deck were designed as a unit for a more pleasing appearance.

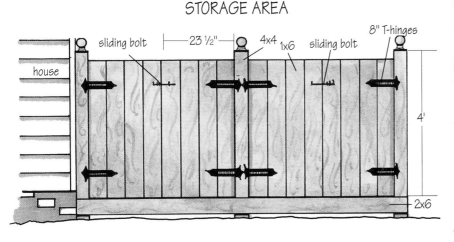

STORAGE AREA

house

sliding bolt   23 ½"   4x4   1x6   sliding bolt   8" T-hinges

4'

2x6

CROSS SECTION

4x4 set in concrete

decking   ledger

2x6   2x6

To ensure they would swing open and closed properly, each gate panel was checked for fit and clearance before it was attached to the inside of the 4 x 4 post. To add strength and to prevent warping, the backs of the panels were braced with 1 x 6 boards.

(Left) *Amid the textures of leafy Lenten roses, columbine, and hosta, caladiums bring a spark of color.*
(Above) *Even pots can be planted with shade-loving plants. Pink caladiums add color in a garden filled with white, while asparagus fern delicately cascades.*

Shaded Opportunity

Nothing is more welcome on a hot Southern day than cooling shade. This home is fortunate to have a mature oak tree to shelter the deck, stone terrace, and parking area. But shade also presents a special challenge when it comes to planting.

When the owner moved in, there was already a rock-filled bed that sloped down from the upper area toward the house. Columbine and ferns grew among the stones. Once the deck, walk, and parking area were completed, other perennials were added. Lenten roses provide evergreen foliage and early-spring flowers. Rohdea and mondo grass are also evergreen and furnish a dark-green background to the light-green maidenhair ferns.

Because this shaded garden is so rich with foliage, the texture created by the leaves draws attention to the plantings. Big leaves mixed with small ones and round leaves combined with linear ones provide textural contrast, which creates interest.

For example, hosta grown in the bed of mondo grass combines a big leaf with a small one. In addition, there is a difference in the shades of green, and that underscores the contrasting textures.

But this shaded area is not without color, and impatiens, coleus, and caladiums are a shade gardener's best friends. Caladiums are grown as annuals in all but the Coastal South, where their underground tubers survive winter. The owner will have to replant them each spring, but they are an inexpensive way to introduce color.

Because the stones were not mortared in place but set on a bed of sand and gravel, we had the opportunity to grow small plants in the cracks between the stones. Some of the most successful were reticulated iris, Callaway ginger, and galax.

Sometimes it takes a year or two to learn the pattern of sunlight in a garden. Even though the backyard appears totally shaded, one corner of the terrace catches enough midday sun to burn shade plants. Here melampodium was a good choice, and now it reseeds itself from one year to the next. We also found there was not enough sun for gomphrena or sweet alyssum.

Containers were handy in bringing interesting color and texture into the garden. A pair of large concrete pots was filled with caladiums and asparagus fern. Not only were the caladium leaves colorful, but they were big, bold, and upright in combination with the lacy fern cascading over the edge of the pots. On the deck, ivy topiaries, ferns, and favorite houseplants spend the summer outdoors.

DRY-LAID STONE PATIO

Flagstone—If bought, about $450, not including delivery

Soil—If bought, about $25 for a pickup truck of sand or topsoil that you haul

Time—About two days if ground is fairly level and no demolition is needed

Equipment—Shovel, garden rake, soil tamper (optional)

Cost of hiring a professional—About $500, not including materials

ITEMS NEEDED FOR LAYING STONE EDGING

6- x 12-inch stone sections
Short-handled mattock
   (digging tool)
Garden hose
Wooden stakes (optional)
Carpenter's level (optional)
Rubber or wooden mallet (optional)

INSTALLING STONE EDGING

Whether it's made of brick, stone, wood, or other materials, edging neatly defines the separation between grass and flower beds. In this backyard, we used stone pieces recycled from the old driveway to edge the centipede lawn.

First came the outline for the edge, which was a broad curve defining the oval-shape lawn. We used a garden hose to form the curve. (If it's cold outside, you may need to set the hose in the sun for awhile to give it more flexibility.)

Using a short-handled mattock, we dug a trench. To keep a creeping grass like centipede out of the beds, the trench had to be at least 4 inches deep. We left about an inch or two of the stone above ground to define the curve and to keep the grass from growing over it. Because the pieces were irregular, each had to be loose-set first to check for fit and level. After adjustments were made, each stone was placed in the trench, and soil was packed firmly around it. (A rubber or wooden mallet might come in handy for tapping the stones into place.)

We saved a lot of money (about $300 in materials) by recycling small stone pieces from the dismantled driveway and patio. Most of the stones were about 12 inches long and 6 to 8 inches wide—perfect for setting on edge. The entire edge (about 120 feet) was set in an afternoon; you'd probably need to budget an entire day for the project if you had to go buy the stone.

And speaking of budget, flagstone doesn't come cheap: Prices in this area varied from $2.75 to $3.25 a square foot. But if you can recycle old stone as we did, it's a much more practical consideration. You may want to see if a local excavating or highway construction company has any loose stone you can carry off from a job site.

Edging prevents warm-season grasses from creeping into beds. You'll probably have to loose-set each one to make sure it is level with the adjacent one. Remove the stone and make adjustments to the trench, as needed.

Place the stone in the adjusted trench, and firmly pack soil around the stone to keep it in place. If you're laying the first stone, set it about 4 inches deep, and leave a few inches above ground level.

1 *A stump grinder removed the 4-foot-wide stump and roots left after the sweet gum was cut down in the front yard. The grinder reduced the stump to chips in less than 20 minutes.*

2 *To repair the gaping hole left in the front lawn, the hole was first filled with commercial soil mix and lightly tamped.*

3 *A thin layer of coarse sand allowed for precise leveling; centipede sod patches were then set in place and watered.*

Troubled Trees Need Expert Help

When we took a hard look at the redesign of this yard, we came face-to-face with a couple of knotty problems. Two large sweet gum trees—one in the front and another in the back—had to be cut down.

The sweet gum in the front yard leaned precariously over power lines that ran above the sidewalk. The one in the backyard had a couple of strikes against it. First, it was growing too near a large oak tree, which provides shade for the new deck. Both trees were suffering as a result. Second, the sweet gum was in the way of the proposed rear parking area.

Because of the size and location of both sweet gums, we knew that cutting the trees down was better left to a professional. We didn't hire just any person with a pickup truck and a chain saw, however. We contacted a licensed and insured tree service. Not only are such outfits licensed to do that type of work, but also their employees and your personal property are insured in case of an accident. You may also see the

term "bonded" in a company's advertising. Without delving too deep into the "legalese," that means that you may be able to demand compensation if one of their employees should steal from you while on the job (provided that their coverage extends to job sites).

But back to our sweet gums. Having two trees cut down and hauled away cost $500. That may seem steep, but considering the size of the trees and their precarious locations, it was money well spent. If you're in the market for a tree service, try to get several estimates. You may be able to get a break on the cost by going in with a couple of neighbors. One final word of advice: If you've got a good-size tree or two that are in trouble, get a professional's opinion as to what should be done. The alternative—that a sudden storm may send one toppling on your roof—is a bad gamble at best.

Pruning or cutting down a large tree is better left to professionals with the know-how and equipment to do it safely.

STUMPED? GET A PRO

After the sweet gum tree was cut down in the front yard, we thought we'd just leave the stump. The tree service had cut it almost flush with the ground, and it really wasn't a hazard to mow around. But after a while, we reconsidered. For one thing, the stump was big—about 4 or 5 feet across, counting the anchor roots. And for another, it was right on the front slope, so it stuck out like a blemish on your forehead.

So we contacted our licensed and insured tree service once more to have the stump ground up. Out they came, with a gnarly looking piece of machinery that ate the

In just a few weeks, the sod patches grew together.

stump like it was a baked potato. It cost us $100 to have a stump this size ground up and hauled off. (You can expect to pay anywhere from $1 to $2 per inch of stump for this type of service. Sometimes you can get a price break if you have several stumps to grind up, or go in for a "package deal" with neighbors.)

Once the stump was gone, there remained a gaping hole. Because the stump was in the middle of a centipede lawn, we decided to fill in the hole and patch it with spare pieces of sod left over from sodding the backyard. The process took the better part of an afternoon. To look at the front yard today, you'd never guess that a huge sweet gum once loomed overhead where a neat lawn now grows.

Maintaining Your Garden—
A Beginner's Guide

JANUARY
• Use a rake or mower to remove leaves and other winter debris from the lawn.
• Plant spring bulbs in the Coastal South.
• Defend your intention to watch all the bowl games by pointing out that many are named for flowers.

FEBRUARY
• Prune summer-flowering trees and shrubs.
• Trim off the old foliage from liriope.
• Apply lime to lawn and garden beds, if indicated by soil test.
• Improve your cardiovascular conditioning by leafing furiously through seed catalogs for 20 minutes a day.

MARCH
• Plant and fertilize trees, shrubs, perennials, and ground covers.
• Sow seed to thicken up cool-season lawns.
• Patch dead spots in lawn with new sod.
• Ponder whether "March Madness" refers to the NCAA basketball tournament or the urge to set out annuals just before a killing frost.

APRIL
• Set out summer annuals after your frost-free date.
• Plant caladiums, gladioli, cannas, and other summer-flowering bulbs.
• Fertilize the lawn with slow-release fertilizer.

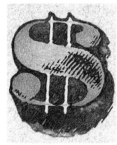

• Use your spouse's tax refund to throw a lavish garden party.

MAY
• Plant summer annuals.
• Sow seed for warm-season lawns.
• Mulch trees, shrubs, and flowerbeds to reduce summer watering.
• Bribe Mom with a bouquet on Mother's Day to get out of weekend yard work.

JUNE
• Fertilize warm-season lawns. Use weed-and-feed to control dandelions, clover, ground ivy, plantains, and other broadleaf weeds.
• Prune spring-flowering trees and shrubs.
• Feed annuals with slow-release fertilizer.
• Give Dad a new mulching mower on Father's Day. Escape to the mall while he struggles to start it.

JULY
• Mow lawn ½ inch higher than normal in hot weather.
• Be sure to give lawn an inch of water per week. Water in early morning to reduce evaporation.
• Thoroughly water newly planted trees and shrubs twice a week.
• Cut back leggy annuals to encourage more blooms.
• Buy a houseplant so you can garden indoors where it's air-conditioned.

AUGUST
• Plant colchicums, autumn crocus, and other fall-blooming bulbs.
• Remove spent flowers from annuals to keep new flowers coming.
• Keep watering lawn, shrubs, flowers, as well as trees.
• Thank the Almighty that August lasts only 31 days.

SEPTEMBER
• Replace tired summer flowers with cool-weather annuals, such as pansies or flowering cabbage and kale.
• Apply pre-emergence weedkiller to lawn to control annual bluegrass.
• Fertilize cool-season grass.
• Place beautiful potted mums by your front door. Check your pulse as your child's football smashes one.

OCTOBER
• Buy spring bulbs early for best selection. Store in cool, dry place.
• Dig and store tender bulbs, such as caladiums and gladioli.
• Clean plant debris from flower and vegetable gardens.
• Bring tender potted plants indoors.
• Plant or transplant trees and shrubs.

• As the Braves lose the World Series once more, admire autumn's colors.

NOVEMBER
• Plant spring bulbs in Upper and Middle South.
• Refrigerate spring bulbs in Lower and Coastal South.
• Clean and store garden tools.
• Plant or transplant trees and shrubs.
• When leaves rain down from the trees, introduce your teenagers to their new friend, Mr. Rake.

DECEMBER
• Plant spring bulbs in Lower South.
• In Coastal South, keep refrigerating spring bulbs.
• Mulch trees, shrubs, and perennials after a hard freeze.
• Water evergreens thoroughly every two weeks if rainfall isn't regular.
• Ask Santa for a garden that looks beautiful with absolutely no attention.

January

Gerbera daisies, freesia, larkspur, mums, and pansies

CHECKLIST FOR JANUARY

BARE-ROOT PLANTS

Roses and fruit trees are arriving in garden centers and home-center stores with their roots in plastic packages filled with sphagnum moss. Make your selection as soon as plants go on display so they will not grow in the store. Unwrap the roots and soak them overnight in water. Cut off any broken roots.

BREAKING NEW GROUND

Wear heavy shoes or boots when using a fork or other tool to break  ground for a new garden (or rework your existing garden). The work will go much easier with less wear and tear on you and your feet. Leather gloves can help protect your hands from painful blisters, too.

BULBS

If mild temperatures coax your bulbs into bud somewhat early, do not worry about cold snaps. The closed flower buds of tulips and narcissus are quite hardy. Even when blooming, early-flowering bulbs, such as crocus and snowflake, can withstand freezing temperatures.

CACTI

Water cacti and succulent houseplants sparingly during the next few months. Winter is their natural period of dormancy; water only when plants begin to shrivel. Overwatering can induce rot.

CITRUS

In Florida, leave unripened fruit on the tree even if a freeze is predicted. Citrus does not improve in flavor once it is picked. Fruit that freezes but remains on the tree is still edible and good for juice. Do not harvest fruit that freezes and then falls to the ground.

COLD DAMAGE

Wait until spring to trim cold-damaged plants. Pruning too early may encourage new growth that could be damaged in subsequent cold snaps. In Florida, even tender ornamentals, such as bird-of-paradise, should come back after a hard freeze if dead foliage is undisturbed until spring.

EVERGREENS

Don't forget that evergreens need water in winter, too. Water them thoroughly whenever a prolonged freeze is forecast. Once the soil has frozen, plants will have to survive on the moisture already absorbed. Broadleaved evergreens are particularly vulnerable in the Upper South.

FREEZES

Protect tender plants if severe cold weather is predicted. Makeshift covers, such as cardboard boxes, bedspreads, and plastic, work well. If you use plastic, be sure to remove it before morning sun hits the plants. Mulching around trees and shrubs with pine bark can also help.

GRAPES

In Texas, a good selection of white grapes to plant now is Aurelia, which will do well in all areas except the coast. Orlando Seedless is recommended for East and Central Texas only. For black grapes, try Lenoir (Black Spanish) or Champanel, which do well everywhere but South Texas.

HOUSEPLANTS

In winter, you may need to water indoor plants more often than normal. The heated air from many forced air systems is often quite dry, which can dry out containers more quickly than at other times of the year. There are several reasons that leaves turn yellow or drop. The most common is too little light. Plants that summer outdoors may drop leaves once they've been indoors for a little while; give them the sunniest spot in your home. Also, be careful not to water too much or too little. Most plants like to get slightly dry between thorough waterings. Also look for spider mites, scale, and mealybugs. If found, spray houseplants with a horticultural oil or insecticidal soap as directed on the label.

LAWNS

If rains have been infrequent, water overseeded warm-season lawns thoroughly. Dry turf is much more susceptible to cold damage than moist. Even dormant warm-season grasses can be hurt by cold and drought.

MULCH

After the last of the lingering leaves have fallen, vacuum them off the lawn with a bagging mower or rake them into shrub beds or the compost bin. Add a fresh layer of pine straw mulch over fallen leaves in the beds and border for a tidy appearance.

NEW LAWNS

Lay sod to establish new lawns now. To seed or sprig, wait until warmer, wetter months. Such conditions enhance seed germination and root growth.

NEW PLANTING

In Florida this month, plant cold-hardy plants, such as hollies (but wait until late March in Central and North Florida before planting tender tropicals).

PEACHES

Prune peach trees this month before buds begin to swell. Remove up to one-third of the past season's growth for optimum fruit production. Small limbs should be thinned to develop an open, spreading canopy.

POINSETTIAS

In Florida, plant leftover holiday poinsettias outside after the risk of freezing weather has passed. Plant in a sunny location and cut stems to within 12 to 18 inches of the ground.

PRUNING

A pruning saw or bow saw is best to remove dead or damaged limbs. If the limb is less than 6 inches in diameter and within reach, remove it yourself (otherwise, contact a professional). For branches several inches in diameter, make three cuts. First, make a small cut on the underside of the limb, about 15 inches out from the main trunk. Then cut the branch from above, slightly beyond the undercut. Make your final cut close to the trunk, leaving a small "collar."

SCALE

White, crusty deposits on the underside of mottled leaves are a sure sign of scale insects. Camellias, hollies, and euonymus are these pests' favorite prey. Spray the foliage with dormant oil; be sure to coat the undersides of the leaves. Make sure that temperatures will stay above freezing for 48 hours before and after spraying.

SEEDS

It's time to buy vegetable, herb, and flower seeds for the spring and summer garden. Whether you purchase them locally or through a mail-order catalog, be sure to try out a few new plants as well as old favorites. If you are just starting to garden, call your local Extension office. It usually has lists of selections recommended for your area.

SOIL SAMPLE

Whether you are starting a new garden or refurbishing an old one, test your soil with a kit from your state agricultural Extension service. Former agricultural land or garden soil that has been fertilized for several years usually has plenty of phosphorus. And if you have been diligent about adding compost, your soil may not need nitrogen.

STRAWBERRIES

Measure the amount of water your strawberry plants are receiving by setting out a few cans among the plants. Strawberries need an inch of water every week. A 2- to 3-inch layer of pine straw mulch will help retain soil moisture.

TRANSPLANTS

Dig and move established shrubs now. Get as much of the root ball as possible when transplanting. Prune by one-third (if deciduous) or two-thirds (if evergreen) to compensate for root loss. Water thoroughly after planting, and mulch to prevent moisture loss and protect the roots from cold weather. While many trees are dormant, take time to rearrange or improve your landscape. Transplant badly placed small trees before new growth begins. Soak the roots before digging a root ball about 18 inches deep and 1 foot wide per inch of trunk diameter. Water newly moved trees regularly for the next few months.

TREES

In Texas, plant shade trees now. When choosing the best spot, consider overhead or buried utilities. Large shade trees should be planted at least 15 feet from the house. Good shade trees for all parts of Texas include Chinese pistachio, red oak, lacebark elm, and Texas ash.

VEGETABLES

In the Lower South, set out transplants of cabbage and its relatives (broccoli, cauliflower, kale, collards, turnips, Chinese cabbage, and kohlrabi) during the last half of the month. Also sow seeds of radishes and carrots. Spray or dust your transplants with *Bacillus thuringiensis* (Bt) to prevent damage from cabbage loopers and imported cabbage worms. In Texas, start seeds of cool-weather vegetables, such as broccoli, cauliflower, and Brussels sprouts, indoors. From Austin southward, asparagus, cabbage, and onion transplants can be set out in the garden after mid-month.

January Notes

TO DO:
- Clean and have your power lawnmower serviced if needed
- Prune grapes, leaving about four leaders per vine
- Root hardwood cuttings from plants such as azaleas, camellias, and hollies
- Till leaves, compost, and other soil amendments into vegetable and flower gardens
- Spray deciduous shrubs and fruit trees with dormant oil

TO PLANT:
- Seeds of hardy perennial herbs indoors
- In Middle, Lower, and Coastal South, trees and shrubs
- In Coastal South, cool-weather annuals and vegetables

TO PURCHASE:
- Flowering houseplants for winter color

_____

_____

_____

_____

TIP OF THE MONTH

When you root cuttings in water, the roots absorb oxygen directly from the water and rarely develop the root hairs necessary for growing in soil. To stimulate the growth of root hairs, gradually add a little soil each day to the water. In about 10 days, the cuttings should be ready to transplant.

Deb Roebuck
Pontotoc, Mississippi

clay, sand particles resist compaction, drain quickly, and till easily. Trouble is, water and nutrients pass through them like grain through a goose. So unless you enjoy watering and feeding every hour on the hour, most plants grown in sand will be chronically starved and thirsty.

Now you might think that by blending equal parts of clay and sand, you could achieve loose, moist soil that's easy to work. Not so fast, warns Brent Heath of The Daffodil Mart in Gloucester, Virginia. "Sand mixed with certain types of clay produces bricks," he reminds us. The best way to loosen clay or enrich sand is to incorporate copious amounts of the same ingredient—organic matter, the garden's black gold.

Organic matter consists of the decaying remains of plants and animals. Peat moss, compost, manure, pine bark, and rotting leaves typify some of its forms. Organic matter benefits soil by storing nutrients and moisture. It also binds clay particles together, permitting free passage of water and air. Plentiful organic matter attracts abundant soil organisms—earthworms, bacteria, fungi, protozoa—which break this matter down, releasing its nutrients. As an added bonus, these organisms also loosen and aerate the soil.

BETTERING BAD SOIL

Your first step to bettering bad soil is getting a soil test. Ask your county cooperative Extension service or local garden center for a soil test kit. The results will tell you which kind of soil you have (sandy loam, clay loam, etc.), its pH and nutrient content, and how much fertilizer and lime to add. Next, use a garden fork or tiller to loosen the existing soil to a depth of 12 to 18 inches. This will dramatically improve drainage and aeration, whether you're reworking an entire bed or just preparing a small spot in which to plant a few bulbs.

Finally, work in heaps of well-decomposed organic matter, preferably several different kinds, along with fertilizers recommended by the test. Add an equal amount of organic matter next year and again every year after. Accompanied by sufficient organic matter, even clay will work for you, augmenting the soil's nutrient and water-holding capacity while allowing excess water to drain.

In some cases, existing soil will be so bad (pure red clay) or so unsuited to what you want to grow (azaleas in Southwestern soil) that you can't use it. Then you'll need to build a raised bed filled with 10 inches or so of new soil. Equal parts of topsoil, coarse builder's sand, and organic matter make a good, general-purpose mix.

Well, it's time to get to those recipes. Each is a version of the general mix, fine-tuned to suit specific plants. We hope this article has whetted your appetite for gardening, and that our recommendations aren't too hard to swallow. But if we've bitten off more than we can chew, undoubtedly we'll receive our just desserts. ◇

PHOTO STYLING: LESLIE BYARS

PERENNIAL PARFAIT

1 part organic matter, preferably more than one kind
2 parts existing soil

• **Combine** as above, incorporating lime and 13-13-13 fertilizer or cottonseed meal as specified by test.
• **Mulch** with several inches of composted pine bark. The surface should end up several inches above existing grade.   *Bill Welch, Extension Landscape Specialist*
College Station, Texas

AZALEAS À LA BILL

1 part humus, preferably composted oak leaves or
**   pine straw**
1 part finely ground pine bark
1 part coarse builder's sand or pea gravel

• **Combine** as above. In alkaline soils, adjust pH to between 5.5 and 6.0 by adding garden sulfur as specified by test.
• **Mulch** with 3 to 4 inches of pine straw. Replenish mulch every other year. Plants need little fertilizer. This mixture also suits rhododendrons, hollies, camellias, dogwoods, and other acid-loving plants. Finished bed should be several inches above existing grade.
Bill Storms, Cardinal Nursery
State Road, North Carolina

BULB SOIL JUBILEE

1 part finely ground pine bark or compost
1 part coarse builder's sand
1 handful of sharp gravel over each bulb at planting
**   to discourage voles and other rodents**

• **Combine** pine bark and sand.
• **Mix** in amounts of bone meal, superphosphate, or slow-release bulb fertilizer specified by soil test. Do not add fresh organic matter, such as grass clippings or uncomposted manure. (This recipe suits tulips, daffodils, hyacinths, crocuses, lilies, irises, and other fleshy-rooted plants.)   *Brent Heath, The Daffodil Mart*
Gloucester, Virginia

ROSE RÉMOULADE

6 parts finely ground pine bark
3 parts topsoil
1 part peat moss

• **Combine** as above, adding lime and fertilizer specified by test.
• **Mulch,** after planting, with 3 inches of pine straw. Replenish every year.   *Joseph Edwards, Rosarian*
Tallahassee, Florida

An attractive half gate serves as an appealing entry; a vine-covered trellis frames the view to the rest of the property.

Two Gates From One Design

Orlando architect Richard Barrette created a sense of continuity in this garden by modifying one design to build two garden gates.

The taller gate was planned for privacy; its size matches the adjacent 6-foot-high stucco walls. The shorter half gate provides access through low garden walls to the rest of the yard beyond. Topping this low gate, a vine-covered trellis gives the illusion of a garden doorway.

Barrette intentionally kept the gates similar despite their different purposes. "The cross bracing on both gates is structural, and also reflects a British style that the owners liked," he says. The gates' gently rounded tops repeat a "lazy arch" found in the architecture of the home. These easily identifiable shapes (along with the same paint color) emphasize the gates' similarities, resulting in a sense of continuity in the garden.

If you need two or more gates for your own garden, you can adapt this idea to reflect your own personal style. Paint colors, hardware, and picket shapes are a few details you can repeat.

The details of this tall wooden gate are reminiscent of the half gate above, yet its 6-foot height continues the privacy of the stucco wall.

Arrange for *Flower Elegance*

By Julia H. Thomason
Photography Van Chaplin

*The moss in this wire basket creates a base
for an assortment of flower-filled vases.*

*Are you short on time but really want to open
your home to the flowers of the season? Bud
vases offer a perfect solution.*

One bud vase allows you to display a single spectacular blossom. But clustering six or seven of the vases offers a quick way to assemble a large flower arrangement. These versatile containers are also perfect for displaying dried flowers and cuttings of foliage.

For these arrangements you'll need three to seven bud vases. Use some you have or purchase a few at a florist's shop, crafts store, or gift shop. Classic cylinder vases are versatile and cost about $3 each. For an even more creative look, collect vases in different shapes, sizes, colors, and materials, such as porcelain, cut crystal, or silver.

With a large wire or wicker basket, you can easily create an opulent arrangement. Line the basket with green sheet moss, add several water-filled vases, and insert flowers into each one. You can also use a tray or platter to unify a grouping of vases.

To display your flowers at varying heights, simply elevate the bud vases on books or boxes. Or mix several colorful blossoms in one vase and feature it in a prominent location.

For a quick centerpiece, arrange flower-filled vases on a piece of mirrored glass placed in the center of a dining table, or group the vases on a mantelpiece for an attractive flourish of color.   ◇

*Identical glass bud vases
hold Dutch iris, freesia, and
asters. A hand-carved
wooden tray unifies the
grouping.*

*Leaves, dried flowers, and twigs fill these bud
vases. Books elevate the arrangements.*

Hot on
TheTrail of
New
Plants

*Come with us as we visit these
unique plant nurseries. They're out
of the way and out of the ordinary.*

We Southerners learn about plants pretty early in life.
Many of us picked peas before we could recite our ABCs,
or delighted in huff-puffing a dandelion into a hundred
white parachutes while still diaper-bound.

For more than a few people, these early afflictions and
affections for plants escalate as they grow older. The mild
hobby becomes a serious business, or, in some instances,
a wonderful mix of the two. Such is the case with the
dozens of small, specialty nurseries scattered throughout
the South.

So hop aboard, and join us for a whirlwind tour of these
nurseries.

There's a
whole world of
bamboo that folks
are just starting to
learn about. The
Bamboo Age is just
now dawning.

—Steve Ray, Sr.

PHOTOGRAPHS: VAN CHAPLIN, SYLVIA MARTIN

Against a backdrop more reminiscent of Cambodia than Alabama, Steve Ray, Jr., and Steve Ray cultivate rare bamboos. Some, such as Pleioblastus viridi-striatus *(far left), flaunt handsome, variegated foliage.*

WAY DOWN YONDER IN THE BAMBOO PATCH

Talk about an image problem. When it comes to bamboo, most gardeners talk about how to kill it, not how to grow it. Its bad-boy reputation as a destroyer of gardens is something firefighter Steve Ray seeks to change. And as you ramble with him through acres of bamboo forest on his farm near Pell City, Alabama, you feel yourself slowly coming around to his way of thinking.

Steve caught bamboo fever 35 years ago as a youngster romping through a bamboo grove. From the first type he grew—Japanese timber bamboo (*Phyllostachys bambusoides*)—his collection gradually expanded to the more than 100 selections now offered in his catalog. To unbelievers, he points out bamboo's incredible variety of forms. They include dwarfs that top out at 12 inches tall, as well as giants that tower 60 feet. Some sport striking, variegated leaves. Others flaunt canes of rose, burgundy, yellow, orange, gray, or black.

Bamboo's propensity for spreading faster than rumors at a boarding school causes many people to fear it. Steve feels this trepidation is misplaced. "It's a misconception that when you plant bamboo, it'll immediately take over," he declares. "It just doesn't do that." The canes, called culms, generally sprout only from March through May, unless you disturb the roots. Steve controls the spread by mowing and also kicking unwanted culms over.

For smaller gardens, Steve suggests Japanese palm tree bamboo (*Semiarundinaria fastuosa*) and arrow bamboo (*Pseudosasa japonica*). The first grows 25 feet tall with canes that turn purple or rose in full sun. The latter grows 18 feet tall, features large, dark-green leaves, and spreads aggressively. For large gardens, try Henon bamboo (*Phyllostachys nigra* Henon), which grows 60 feet tall; and snakeskin bamboo (*P. n.* Bory), whose brown-, purple-, and pink-spotted culms reach 45 feet.

In addition to his farm, Steve also grows more than 100 bamboos in gardens beside the Birmingham home he shares with wife, Janie. Each week brings visitors, many from out of state. Some seek elusive rarities, such as black bamboo (*Phyllostachys nigra*).

"Visitors are always fascinated by what they see," observes Steve. "We like to give them a glass of iced tea, walk the grounds with them, and talk bamboo." Steve, Jr., also a firefighter, often accompanies his father.

Steve Ray, Sr., bamboo evangelist, believes prejudice against his favorite plant must surely wane as people discover its obvious merits. "There's a whole world of bamboo that folks are just starting to learn about," he asserts. "The Bamboo Age is just now dawning."

Steve Bender

Steve Ray's Bamboo Gardens, 909 79th Place South, Birmingham, AL 35206. Catalog is $2. Tours by appointment only, call (205) 833-3052.

RHODIES OFF THE BACK ROADS

Willis Harden looks, talks, and acts like the northeast Georgia country gentleman that he is. But at first impression, he does not look, talk, or act like someone who can rattle off the scientific names and origins of rhododendrons like they were kinfolk. "I'm in the gasoline business," he says. But spend some time visiting Homeplace Garden Nursery, and you will come away greatly impressed by the person and the place. This country gentleman knows his rhododendron business, too.

Case in point: Willis, accompanied by his Jack Russell terrier, Pooch, is leading us through his nursery and past neat rows of containerized rhododendrons, set under the scattered light of tall pines. It's early spring, and the plants are in various stages of bloom. We pause to ooh-aah at a beautiful, white-flowered rhododendron. "That's Dora Amateis," Willis offers. "It's a cross between our native Carolina rhododendron, *R. carolinianum,* and *R. ciliatum,* a fragrant Chinese species." And he goes on like that—every plant has a story, and Willis can tell it with authority and experience. He grows about 120 varieties of rhododendrons, plus a host of other woody ornamentals.

The 450-acre property that contains the nursery operation is also home for Willis and his wife, Betty. Beyond the confines of the nursery grow such garden gems as a 25-year-old specimen of Temple Belle rhododendron in full, perfect-pink bloom. A walk around the 10-acre pond takes you over carpets of moss, and past clumps of wildflowers and other native plants.

Like many owners of specialty nurseries, Willis admits that it's a hobby that got a little out of hand. And it doesn't hurt that he grows all of his plants with loving care and attention. "I'm convinced that rhodo-

> I'm convinced that rhododendrons, including azaleas, are the best flowering shrubs you can grow in the South.
>
> —*Willis Harden*

The cheerful, pink trumpets of Temple Belle rhododendron show off to proud papa Willis Harden, who planted this prize 25 years ago on his 450-acre property near Commerce, Georgia.

dendrons, including azaleas, are the best flowering shrubs you can grow in the South." If you saw Homeplace Garden Nursery, you'd be a convert, too.

Mark G. Stith

Homeplace Garden Nursery, P.O. Box 300, Commerce, GA 30529. Catalog is $2. Nursery open April, May, and October; call (706) 335-2892. Garden tours by appointment only.

AMAZING TOMATOES

Angora. Dinner Plate. Garden Peach. Dad's Mug. Pink Grapefruit. You probably never would have guessed that these are selections of tomatoes.

For the most part, tomato seeds are what Vince and Linda Sapp, of Fort Myers, Florida, say keep their business, Tomato Growers Supply Company, growing. It's difficult to believe that a company could make a go of it by selling only tomato seeds and related paraphernalia. Well, it doesn't —Vince and Linda also sell some pretty cool-sounding sweet peppers, as well as some smokin' hot ones, too. Habañero: "20 times hotter than Jalapeño!" the catalog reads.

Vince was confident the idea would work. "What I did was look at what gardeners grow," he recalls. "Nearly all of them grow tomatoes, and lots of them grow peppers, too." Tomato Growers Supply Company (which is 10 years old this year) is an example of filling a niche that no one else had nabbed.

Unlike the other specialty nurseries we visited, there are no demonstration gardens to admire, plant-filled greenhouses to ogle, or acres of container plants to wander through. "We've got a 1,000-square-foot office with a plate glass window," Linda says with a laugh.

And the "test garden" is the Sapps' own backyard plot.

And where do they find all these exotic tomato varieties? "We work with the Seed Savers Exchange, small, independent growers, as well as commercial vegetable breeders," Linda says.

The catalog is a tomato—and pep-

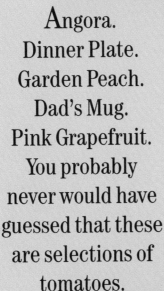

Vince and Linda Sapp, owners of Tomato Growers Supply Company in Fort Myers, Florida, grow many of the tomatoes offered in their catalog.

per—grower's delight. Listen to these descriptions: "Pineapple Tomato: Unique red and yellow striped tomatoes that grow to a huge 2 pounds. Watermelon Beefsteak: Very large oblong tomato features a shape reminiscent of a watermelon. . . ."

Somebody knows how to talk tomatoes here. Maybe some exaggeration for effect? Fine with us. A little boasting elevates someone who fishes to a fisherman, and someone who grows tomatoes to a tomato grower. Well, tomato grower, you're at the right place. *Mark G. Stith*

Tomato Growers Supply Company, P.O. Box 2237, Fort Myers, FL 33902. Catalog is free. No tours. Call (813) 768-1119.

FILLED WITH DELIGHTS

Stamped in red on the 1993 Plant Delights Nursery catalog is "WARNING: THE HORTICULTURE GENERAL HAS DETERMINED THAT OPENING THIS CATALOG MAY BE HIGHLY ADDICTIVE." Inside, it states that the catalog "should be viewed only by professionals or . . . certified plant crazies."

Both descriptions fit Tony Avent. Recently retired as the landscape director of the North Carolina State Fair, his passion for plants grew all around him—at work and at home.

The nursery began as a yard sale in the most literal sense. "The nursery started 15 years ago in our first garden, but we didn't sell anything," Tony explains. "We gathered plants from all over the country and trialed them in our garden. It was always open for people to visit, and then, before we moved, we had a few yard sales just to get some plants sold."

That was five years ago. Tony and his wife, Michelle, moved to a 2½-acre property in Juniper Level, a community 18 minutes south of downtown Raleigh. There they put up their first greenhouse and printed their first catalog. Their focus: "the best, the newest, and the strangest in perennials."

If there is any doubt that their perennials perform, just visit the nursery. The Avents have gone beyond the requisite neat rows of potted perennials. Their display garden covers at least 2 acres with ideas and inspiration—and more than 3,000 different plants. Open to the public several days each season, gardeners see catalog offerings grown to maturity.

One group of plants that they have targeted for improvement is hosta. "No one has done any controlled crosses in the South," observes Tony, "so we are taking the opportunity to breed hostas that will take our heat. And we are doing a lot of testing for hostas that will tolerate sun when given adequate moisture."

Among the new hostas to look for in the 1994 catalog is Redneck Heaven, which has "the reddest petiole of any hosta we have grown." Another is Bubba, "because he's short, fat, and has a little red neck."

Linda C. Askey

Plant Delights Nursery, 9241 Sauls Road, Raleigh, NC 27603. Catalog is $2. Open days in 1994: April 30, May 1, 7-8, July 9-10, 16-17, Sept. 10-11, 17-18; call (919) 772-4794.

YAHOO! IT'S YUCCA DO

The next time your garden turns into toast during a rainless summer, John Fairey and Carl Schoenfeld of Waller, Texas, want you to think of them. Their company, Yucca Do Nursery, specializes in plants native to Texas and Mexico that thrive in torrid air and parched soil.

"These plants are quite adaptable to abusive weather," comments John. "Many can go through extreme droughts, months with no water at all." Moreover, those indigenous to the Mexican mountains exhibit excellent cold hardiness, withstanding near-zero temperatures.

Since 1986, these men have led 50 expeditions into the Sierra Madre Mountains of northeastern Mexico to collect seed and cuttings. Travel in the Mexican back country can be extremely rugged.

"Sometimes the driving is so intense, it'll take a full day to go 30 miles," declares John. "You'll find yourself on a one-way logging road with a 1,500-foot drop on your left

> **Warning: The Horticulture General has determined that opening this catalog may be highly addictive.**
>
> *—Plants Delight Nursery*

In Raleigh, Tony and Michelle Avent offer the newest and best perennials through their catalog for Plant Delights Nursery. In their display gardens and greenhouses, they grow more than 3,000 plants to perfection.

and a sheer cliff on your right."

Urgent issues such as overgrazing and development threaten many of the plants they target for propagation. Carl recalls a unique yellow-flowered salvia they discovered on one trip. "The original plant now no longer exists. It was trampled by goats and burros," he notes. "If we hadn't brought back cuttings and introduced it, it would have been lost forever."

After securing samples of a promising plant, John and Carl grow and test it in their gardens near Hempstead. If it's deserving and propagates easily, they list it in their catalog. They also send samples to botanical gardens and institutions around the world for further evaluation and eventual distribution.

"We want people to know that these plants exist, that they're worthy of cultivation and should be preserved," explains John.

These days, John and Carl are particularly enthusiastic about Mexican mockoranges and oaks. "The blooms of these mockoranges have exceptional fragrance," John remarks, "a wonderful combination of orange, honey, and cinnamon. If you're driving by, the scent will make you stop the car."

As for the oaks, John points out that while the entire United States harbors approximately 50 native oak species, Mexico contains more than 400. Not only are most Mexican oaks evergreen, but their foliage typically flushes pink in the springtime, then changes to glossy deep-green or blue-green by summer. "The Mexican oaks have great potential for the Southeast," he suggests. "They adapt well to most soils, and their forms, colors, and textures are wonderful."

John and Carl's contributions appear all the more impressive when you consider that neither boasts a horticultural background. John was trained as a painter; Carl as an architect. In these disciplines, each learned to look at things intently, to discern the minutiae others might miss. It's a skill that serves them well—for if they overlook a rare or endangered plant, they know they may not get a second chance.

Steve Bender

Yucca Do Nursery, P.O. Box 655, Waller, TX 77484. Catalog is $3. Open 10 a.m. to 5 p.m. Monday through Friday. No plants sold on premises. No telephone orders. Visits by appointment only; telephone (409) 826-6363. ◇

> # Many [of these plants] can go through extreme droughts, months with no water at all.
>
> —*John Fairey*

At Yucca Do Nursery, in Waller, Texas, John Fairey admires a Mexican bee balm (Monarda pringlei). *This evergreen, mildew-resistant perennial blooms spectacularly in spring and early summer and tolerates heat, drought, and cold.*

February

Yoshino cherries

CHECKLIST FOR FEBRUARY

ANNUALS

In Florida, trim overgrown petunias, wax begonias, and impatiens by a third to increase flowering. Add dianthus, snapdragons, dusty miller, and calendula to annual beds.

BIRDS

Continue feeding birds; we'll have some of the coldest winter weather this month. This is a good time to start a list of the birds at your feeder. Several inexpensive field guides are available at local bookstores. The winter birds will soon be joined by waves of migrating species heading north.

BLUEBERRIES

Plant blueberries now; you'll need two selections to cross-pollinate the flowers and produce fruit. Recommended selections include Tifblue, Woodard, Climax, Premier, and Brightwell. Blueberries do best in acid soils. Be sure to add plenty of organic material when planting. Space plants about 8 to 10 feet apart for maximum fruit production.

CABBAGE LOOPERS

Control these slender, green caterpillars before they damage your harvest. These green caterpillars form a "loop" as they crawl and feed on leaves. Handpick when possible, or spray the foliage with Dipel, Thuricide, or Sevin to control large infestations.

DAFFODILS

Soak the stems of freshly cut daffodils or paperwhites in their own container of water for 6 to 8 hours before arranging them with other flowers. Otherwise the sap will clog the stems of surrounding flowers.

FORSYTHIA

Cut a few branches to brighten the indoors. Dormant buds will open quickly in the warmth of the house. Arrange by making a fresh cut and placing the branches into warm water.

FRUIT TREES

Prune your tree for better fruit and a healthier tree. Cut dead branches and sprouts from the base. Remove crossed or crowded limbs. Prune out water sprouts, those long branches that grow straight up. If the tree is too large to spray or reach all the fruit, reduce the height by removing tall branches; do not chop off the top.

GLADIOLUS

For longer-lasting displays, make several plantings of gladiolus corms about a week or two apart. Set the corms about 4 to 6 inches deep and 6 to 8 inches apart in well-prepared soil in a sunny location.

GRAPES

Prune bunch grapes to a single trunk with two to three canes on each side to train along a trellis. Trim canes, leaving 8 to 12 buds per cane. Prune muscadines to a central trunk with two opposite branches. Allow spurs to grow on each branch with two to three buds per spur.

HERBS

For strong plants, sow seeds of dill directly where you want the plants to grow. In Middle and Lower South gardens, parsley probably stayed green all winter. Go ahead and use all you want. As soon as the weather gets warm, the plants will go to seed and die. Start seeds of parsley and basil indoors for setting in the garden after the danger of frost has passed.

HOUSEPLANTS

Give your plants a shower to wash away dust and discourage insects. Drench the soil in each pot; then let it drain well before moving plants back into place. Gently clean the foliage with a damp cloth to remove dust; remember to wipe the underside of the leaves. Feed indoor plants with a water-soluble fertilizer such as Miracle-Gro or ProSol.

ICE

When ice makes your driveway or walkway hazardous, use sand or cat litter to roughen the slick surface. Avoid using salt where it will wash into beds and damage plants. Along salted streets, hose residue off foliage.

LAWNS

Fertilize cool-season grasses this month in the Middle South; wait until next month in the Upper South. Warm-season lawns should be fed about two weeks after they begin to turn green. Apply pre-emergence fertilizer immediately in the Lower and Middle South. Read the label carefully to be certain it is recommended for your type of lawn. In North Texas, fertilize cool-season fescue lawns with 16-4-8 or a fertilizer of similar analysis. The same formulation can be used to feed annual or perennial ryegrass overseeded on dormant warm-season lawns. In either case, apply fertilizer at the rate of 5 pounds per 1,000 square feet. Water thoroughly after spreading fertilizer; always use a drop spreader or other measured applicator. Never apply fertilizer to the lawn by tossing handfuls. In Florida, apply a weed-and-feed fertilizer to nourish lawns and stop weeds before they sprout. Central and South Florida homeowners should spread fertilizer by midmonth, but North Florida gardeners should wait until early March.

NANDINA

Prune nandinas now to keep plants from becoming leggy. Don't wait until flowerbuds appear or you will cut off next year's holiday berries. Remove one-third of the canes each year; be sure to stagger the heights at which you cut the canes, leaving the youngest ones to grow.

ORNAMENTAL GRASSES

In Florida, cut fountain grass to within 3 to 6 inches of the ground. Leave a foot of stubble when cutting back pampas grass. Use loppers or hedge shears, and wear gloves; many grasses have serrated edges. If you're adding ornamental grasses to your landscape, try pairing them with an evergreen ground cover, such as Asian jasmine, for year-round appeal.

PRUNING

Cut back overgrown or misshapen summer-flowering shrubs now. Don't prune spring-flowering shrubs, or you'll remove potential blooms.

In Florida, be sure to prune summer- and fall-flowering shrubs at the end of the month, when new growth signals the arrival of spring. Early pruning helps promote flowering in plants that bloom on new growth. These plants include hibiscus, thyrallis, plumbago, glossy abelia, and oleander.

ROSES

Set out rosebushes now. Choose a sunny spot in the garden with well-drained soil. You don't have to create a bed dedicated only to roses. Consider planting them with perennials or flowering shrubs so they become a part of the garden. In Texas, set out either bare-root or container-grown rosebushes now. For the best flowers and healthiest plants, choose No. 1 grade plants. A sunny spot with well-drained soil is best; if soil is poor, consider building raised beds 10 to 15 inches high. In Florida, plant roses now throughout the state. If you live in a coastal area, your soil is probably too alkaline for roses, so be sure to add ½ cup of wettable sulphur to your soil mix before planting. Water newly planted

roses every day for the first two weeks; then reduce watering to every other day for the remainder of the month.

SOIL

A warm weekend is a good time to turn the garden soil and get ready for spring planting. Mix in last fall's leaves from your compost bin. If your soil is heavy or poorly drained, add an extra measure of organic material and some sand as well. If the soil is wet, wait until it dries enough to crumble easily. If adding fresh manure to your garden soil, wait 45 days before planting. The addition of manure raises soil temperature and releases by-products that may damage seedlings.

TOMATOES

Start your own transplants 6 to 8 weeks before you want to plant. Order seeds of favorite selections or those that you may not be able to find locally. Fill individual containers with seed starting mix, moisten, and sow 2 to 3 seeds in each one. Cover seeds with about ½ inch of soil mix. Cover with plastic or a sheet of glass to keep them moist until they sprout; then move the seedlings to your sunniest window to encourage strong growth. Set out tomato transplants in South and Central Florida. To reduce bacterial wilt problems, remember not to plant tomatoes, peppers, or eggplants in the same spot each year.

VEGETABLES

In Texas, plant broccoli, collards, cabbage, turnips, and cauliflower now in South and East Texas. Wait until the end of the month to plant cool-weather vegetables outdoors in North Texas. Sugar snap and English peas can be direct-sown in gardens throughout the state.

COLOR
in the
COLD

Crocuses

Lenten rose

Paperbush

Algerian iris

Japanese flowering apricot

John and Billie Elsley with Winston

BY LINDA C. ASKEY
PHOTOGRAPHY
SYLVIA MARTIN

January 31, 1993. Winter. Cold. But John and Billie Elsley told us this was one of the best times of the year in their garden, and so we found ourselves pulling up in front of their home in Greenwood, South Carolina.

And what a show we saw.

Lenten roses and daffodils, crocuses and snowdrops, fragrant daphne and delicate witch hazel—glorious, colorful abundance in the depths of winter.

How do they do it?

Well, his being horticultural director for Wayside Gardens—and having the resources to locate and obtain cold-weather beauties—certainly doesn't hurt. But even horticultural beginners can triumph over winter.

For most Southerners, the signatures of winter have long been the broad-leaved evergreens—camellias and mahonias and such. The Elsleys simply build on their beauty.

"It's remarkable what a wide range, not only of evergreens but of flowering plants, you can use at this time of year," John says.

He and Billie favor bulbs, especially the crocuses and snowdrops that bloom from fall throughout the winter months. Cyclamen also bloom through the cold season, beginning with *Cyclamen hederifolium,* which offers fall flowers and winter foliage. In early spring, *C. Coum* unfurls its blooms.

One of the showiest small trees is Japanese flowering apricot (*Prunus mume*). But their favorite for this time of year is *Prunus subhirtella autumnalis,* which blooms from late October through the winter.

In addition to winter flowers, fragrance abounds, and winter daphne (*Daphne odora*) is foremost. But John also recommends *Daphne bholua.* This is a rare one that is adapted to Southern gardens but seldom available through nurseries. John's working on that.

The most dominant plants are the masses of Lenten rose (*Helleborus* x *hybridus*). The Elsleys also grow the Christmas rose (*Helleborus niger*) that can be so challenging. John's advice: "It needs to be planted from a

Cyclamen

Prefix daffodils

Snowdrops

well-established, container-grown plant, never bare root. And it needs a little more protection. Once you get it growing, it will do well."

But there's more to this winter garden than just picking the right plants and growing them correctly. Anyone wishing to take inspiration from the Elsleys' experience should first compare their situation to a climate where there's a real winter with temperatures that occasionally reach into the teens.

But on any property, microclimates are created by cold air settling in low areas, or draining away from high places. Plants protected from drying wind or morning sun are less prone to winter damage, as are those planted near a wall or foundation.

Billie emphasizes that their garden is located on elevated ground under a canopy of tall oaks. Consequently, they have more moderate temperatures than gardens only a couple of miles away. Take all that into consideration when estimating a plant's hardiness.

In addition, excellent soil preparation gives deep-rooted, vigorous plants that are very hardy. The Elsley garden covers almost an entire acre, but its expanse has not deterred John from painstaking soil work. He has vigorously turned and amended the soil—so much so that he wore 2 inches off his stainless steel spade blade.

"Basically you build the soil up by adding organic matter," John explains. "In this part of the world you have to irrigate, and with the [summer's] high temperatures and humidity, the organic matter is consistently breaking down. You've got to get that initial good drainage, so what you are doing is really raised bed gardening."

The Elsleys let the annual windfall of oak leaves remain in the beds to nourish the soil. While the trees shelter the garden in winter and summer, they come with a price. "The hardest thing to grow is grass," says Billie, referring to the turf paths that meander between the beds.

John and Billie's year-round approach to gardening is simply a matter of outlook. They knew that they could, so they did. And best of all, with little more than desire and a plant list, you can have flowers in winter, too.

PHOTOGRAPHS: VAN CHAPLIN

James Baskin is shaping the Bonica hedge. Notice the height after four years of growth.
Removing stray canes is the only pruning required.

Roses Either Way

James Baskin is quite a rose gardener. He does everything right. He sprays every week, he fertilizes on a regular schedule, he deadheads regularly, and he spends all of his work hours tending roses.

I, on the other hand, am a gardener with little time and a diversity of interests. My roses lack proper, by-the-book care. But with a new group of roses called landscape or shrub roses— especially the Meidiland family selections—I can have roses that may not look as good as James's but give me a lot of bloom for a little effort.

One of my favorites, the pale-pink Bonica is the first shrub rose to win All-America rose honors. Others in this family include Sevillana (red), Alba Meidiland (white), Scarlet Meidiland (bright scarlet), and Pink Meidiland (rich pink).

As you can see from the photographs, Bonica is a profuse bloomer. But don't expect long stems like the hybrid teas. Bonica has short stems with clusters of blooms. Mine bloom most of the year, from late spring till frost in the fall. Once frost hits the

Unlike the popular hybrid teas, shrub roses have clusters of blooms and flower all season.

plant in a good year, the shrub rose will have a prolific crop of colorful orange-red fruit (hips) that provide a subtle show through fall. They can also be used in decorative projects.

While I don't have a regular spray-and-groom program for my roses like James does, I fertilize them with 16-4-8 at the rate of ¼ cup per plant in early spring and again in mid-summer. If you don't spray, don't expect the foliage of these roses to be beautiful the entire growing season;

they are susceptible to all the common rose pests. However, when it comes to things like black spot, they are not nearly as susceptible as hybrid teas.

Now is the time to purchase and plant roses. While some garden centers are beginning to carry the selections, the most reliable source is mail order. But check with your garden center first.

Take a cue from the photo, and use these roses as a living hedge or in mass. To achieve this effect, space about 3 feet apart and prune only to retain the desired height and shape.

If you are ever in Birmingham, stop by Dunn Rose Garden at the Birmingham Botanical Gardens, and enjoy the beauty of James's labor. Be sure to see the glorious hedge of Bonica that has been grown and cared for the *right* way. *John Floyd*

Rose hip

The Birmingham Botanical Gardens, located at 2612 Lane Park Road, is open daily until sunset. Call (205) 879-1227.

Mossy Containers

With our quick tips, you can make these good-looking accessories at a fraction of retail cost.

BY JULIA H. THOMASON
PHOTOGRAPHY
VAN CHAPLIN,
COLLEEN DUFFLEY

Decorative containers for plants are easy to make, using a hot-glue gun to attach moss to an inexpensive basket, wooden box, or clay pot. You'll need green sheet moss, available from a florist or well-stocked crafts store. You can also use fresh moss collected from the garden.

If you need to make a large container for several plants, select a wooden box or basket to serve as a base for the moss. Use a hot-glue gun to attach one piece of moss at a time, covering the exterior and lining the interior. Fill the box or basket with small plants, first placing a wa-

(**Top, right**) *To make an exotic surround for this phalaenopsis orchid, floral designer Jon Martinez of Birmingham hot-glued fresh moss onto a plastic pot. Bamboo adds support.*

(**Above and right**) *Wrap pots containing ferns and candles with dried green sheet moss purchased from a florist or crafts store. Use a piece of string or sisal to hold the moss in place.*

terproof saucer beneath each one. You can also glue moss directly to a plastic or clay pot.

For making naturalistic plant containers and candle holders, simply wrap clay pots of various sizes with moss; then tie the moss with strands of raffia to hold it in place. Insert plants in the larger pots, and place votive candles in the smaller ones, arranging the group on a tray to make a centerpiece.

If the moss gradually begins to turn brown, mix a few drops of green food coloring with water. Use a spray bottle to apply to the moss. ◇

(**Left**) *Floral designer Jon Martinez picked fresh moss for this distinctive arrangement. He removed loose dirt and hot-glued the moss to a basket, using dried pomegranates as accents. After lining the basket with a plastic trash bag, Jon inserted small pots of ivy and used a kalanchoe for added color.*

(**Left and above**) *Cover a small wooden crate or box with moss, making a container for a group of small plants, such as these bromeliads. Use scissors to cut green sheet moss to size. Using a hot-glue gun, attach the moss to the box. Also line the interior of the box with moss. Use broken twigs to cover places where the pieces of moss meet.*

Together, this mailbox and post create a custom look. Brass numbers add a finishing touch.

Easy and Elegant Mailbox

BY JO KELLUM / PHOTOGRAPHY VAN CHAPLIN

You can always tell where the artistic people in your neighborhood live. Their mailboxes are works of art, individual expressions of creativity that just happen to have mail shoved into them every day. Here's a simple way to jazz up your own mailbox without

going to a lot of trouble.

Start with one of those ready-to-assemble wooden mailbox posts, available at most home centers. Usually, these posts extend too high above the box, giving it an awkward look. You can improve the propor-

tions with just one cut (honest). Although it only takes a few minutes to trim the top of the post, you'll be surprised at what a difference it makes.

Here's how to figure out how much of the post to cut off. Lay the post on the ground with the arm in place (see photo A). Position the mailbox on the arm so you can see how they will look together. Topping off the post with a prefabricated finial is an easy way to create a custom look. Lay the finial on the ground beside the post to visualize the finished height. Usually, trimming the post to within 4 or 5 inches of the top of the box will do the trick. Draw a line across the post before making the cut with a circular saw.

Most posts come with a chunky support piece. There's an easy way to deal with this piece—just throw it away. Instead, use an 8-inch metal corner brace to secure the post and arm together (see sketch). You'll paint over the metal brace later. You can use four lag bolts through the arm for additional support. Countersink the heads and cover with wood putty so you can paint over those, too.

Since the fasteners make it unnecessary to brace the arm from beneath, you can substitute a decorative bracket. Prefabricated pieces available from lumberyards or catalogs take the work out of this step. Next, drill a small hole in the center of the top end of the post to insert the finial. Prime the whole thing and give it a couple of coats of glossy white paint. Using just one color on the post, bracket, and finial makes everything look as if it were made to go together.

Now you need a mailbox worthy of the post. Transform a plain white mailbox into your own custom creation by sponge-painting an ivy leaf pattern across the top and along the edges. It's easier than you think.

Step 1: Trace around ivy leaf on a flat, dry sponge (see photo B). Cut out with household scissors.

Step 2: Drop the sponge in water; squeeze to remove excess water.

Step 3: Dip the surface of leaf-shaped sponge into green paint. Blot once on the paper surface of your work area to prevent dripping.

Step 4: Make sure the surface of the sponge is still covered with paint after blotting; then press it against the mailbox (see photo C). Press harder around the edges than in the center to get a texturized appearance.

WHAT YOU'LL NEED

A cedar or pressure-treated post, unassembled (about $15)
Decorative bracket (about $60)
Wood finial
One quart of white, latex, gloss exterior paint
Small can of primer
Paint remover for cleanup
3-inch-wide brush
8-inch metal corner brace
Wood screws
Lag bolts (optional)
White mailbox (about $5)
Several pop-up sponges for painting the leaves
English ivy leaves, various sizes and shapes
Small can exterior enamel paint, hunter green
Pencil
Scissors
Source: Decorative bracket (Corbel No. 708) available from The Old Wagon Factory, 1-800-874-9358.

HELPFUL TIPS

■ Before you paint, nail a 1-inch-thick board to the top of the post arm to attach the mailbox easily.

■ Set the mailbox on this piece with the back end against the post, and mark the locations of two or three screw holes for each side.

■ Remove box, and predrill the holes. Spray paint the screw heads white, and attach finished mailbox.

■ When collecting ivy leaves, pick a whole sprig to use as a guide. Leaves should face each other at the base, with the tips pointing outward at various angles. End with small leaves. Don't worry about a stem; the pattern itself suggests a vine.

■ Continue your pattern across the top of the box and around the edges. Add a few leaves on the door for a finishing touch.

■ Don't paint leaves in the area that will be covered by the flag when it's down. Preserving the white space keeps the pattern looking neat.

■ Make several leaf-shaped sponges by tracing around leaves of varying sizes and shapes. Practice on paper first, and then use the two or three best sponges for the mailbox. ◇

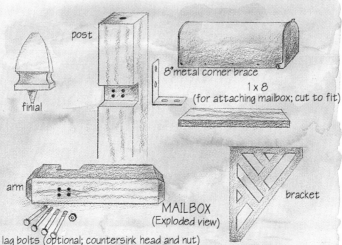

post
finial
8" metal corner brace
1 x 8
(for attaching mailbox; cut to fit)
arm
MAILBOX
(Exploded view)
bracket
lag bolts (optional; countersink head and nut)

Some of the most fascinating garden ornaments await you in unexpected places.

OWNER/DESIGNER: MICHAEL HOPPING, BATON ROUGE

OWNER: AMASA SMITH, BIRMINGHAM

fabulous finds
For the Garden

BY JULIA H. THOMASON
PHOTOGRAPHY SYLVIA MARTIN, EMILY MINTON

Explore flea markets and junk shops to find time-worn baskets and wooden boxes that will make handsome containers for plants and flowers. Shop yard sales and secondhand stores for a collection of old rakes and hoes to cluster on a fence or on an exterior wall of your home. Rummage through salvage yards for ironwork and architectural fragments to display like statuary in a planting bed. Check your own garage or attic for a favorite personal memento, such as an ancient bicycle or wagon, to feature imaginatively as sculpture in your garden.

Old pieces often have finishes that are less than perfect, but flaws only enhance their appeal. With every

(**Right**) *Ornaments often add a welcome note of humor or whimsy to the garden.*
(**Far right**) *Silhouetted against an exterior wall, a rusty fragment of an old gate finds a new calling as a garden ornament.*
(**Top**) *An architectural tie-rod plate caps a doorway. Long nails hold it securely in place.*

DESIGNERS: DON MORRIS AND HARRY WHITE, SAN ANTONIO

(Left) *This open expanse of wall displays a garden trophy, an assemblage of old tools and clay pots arranged in a decorative way. Use several long-handled tools positioned so that their handles appear to radiate from a central point. Wire each object to long nails hammered into the wall. Fill the arrangement with small garden-related items, including clay pots that serve as containers for ivy and flowering plants.*

(Above) *An old wooden shoeshine box becomes a decorative container for pots of artemisia, blue salvia, and dianthus. The box rests on a porch where its worn paint finish is somewhat protected from the elements.*

season, the weathered surfaces of metal, wood, and paint will add a sense of timelessness and a patina of age to the garden. If the item you select is not durable enough to withstand wind and rain, display it on a porch or other sheltered area.

Both wall-mounted objects and freestanding pieces are useful as focal points. Place them at the end of a garden walk or at the foot of steps. You can nestle an architectural element into a flowerbed or position it beside a pathway. Give any special object a place of honor, such as a spot beside a garden entrance that you use frequently.

Now is the time to unearth your own garden treasures, and then find just the right spot for them. Remember that, like a room inside your house, almost any spot in the outside room of your garden can be brightened by just the right piece. ◇

A terra-cotta architectural fragment nestles beside a rustic stone wall, adding warm color and sculptural form to this garden setting.

A quartet of lovely Yoshino cherries shelters a quiet sitting area in this Wilmington, North Carolina, backyard.

Shade in Less Than a Lifetime

"I'll be dead before I can enjoy them." How many times have you heard this lament applied to the planting of trees? Fifteen years ago, Richard Tomes and John Croley of Wilmington, North Carolina, must have faced similar doubts when they planted four small Yoshino cherries in the middle of a neglected backyard. But today, the trees extend a comforting canopy over a restful sitting area.

The trees went in long before the benches and fountain. For years, refurbishing the 1844 Greek Revival house demanded nearly all of the owners' attention. The only gardening was maintaining the cherry trees and a privet hedge to establish a framework for a future garden.

The planning paid off. A decade-and-a-half later, the trees and hedge have grown dramatically, providing both canopy and backdrop for a tiny, formal garden. Slate pavers lead from the back porch to a trio of concrete benches and a splashing fountain ringed by flowers. So delightful is the setting that several years ago the garden earned a spot on the city's Azalea Festival garden tour.

This garden teaches two lessons. First, if you can implement your design only one part at a time, start with the part that takes longest to develop. Second, large shade trees aren't the only source for shade and structure. Ornamental trees, like these cherries, can supply both to a small area—and they won't take a lifetime. *Steve Bender*

PHOTOGRAPHS: VAN CHAPLIN

The iron fountain was added more than a decade after the trees. By then, the cherries had attained sufficient size to shade and define the new garden "room."

March

Iceland poppy and Professor Blaauw Dutch iris

CHECKLIST FOR MARCH

ANNUALS

When it comes to buying transplants, bigger isn't always better. Choose the branched plant that is well-proportioned, not the tall one that has become rootbound. The transplant without flowers will perform better, and a young, healthy plant is a better bet than an older, stressed one. Watch out for signs of insects or diseases. In Texas, plant flowering annuals, including ageratum, dusty miller, lisianthus, Madagascar periwinkle, pentas, petunias, geraniums, and salvia in sunny areas of the garden.

APHIDS

Curling leaves are a clue that these sap-sucking pests have arrived. Tender new leaves often attract aphids. Many plants will outgrow the problem, or predators, such as ladybugs and praying mantis, may intervene for you. Spray as soon as possible with an insecticidal soap; sometimes just a blast of water from the garden hose will do the trick. Check again in a few days. If they return, spray with malathion for control.

BLOSSOM-END ROT

Before planting tomatoes, add calcium to the soil to help prevent blossom-end rot. Use a testing kit from your local Extension agency to determine your soil pH. Tomatoes thrive in soil with a pH of 6.5. Add dolomitic lime at a rate of 2 to 5 pounds per 100 square feet if your soil pH is too low, or mix gypsum into the soil if you need to bring the pH level down. A pound or two of gypsum per 100 square feet of bed is usually adequate.

CAMELLIAS

In Florida, spray camellias with Volck oil while the temperature is cool to smother insects before they can inflict serious damage. Tea scale feeds on camellias from spring through fall. Infested leaves will appear mottled and yellowish and have crusty white deposits on their undersides. Spray large infestations with Cygon, Orthene, or Di-Syston.

GARDENIAS

In the Middle and Lower South, trim plants that are overgrown or ones that turned brown after severe cold. Remove entire branches at their point of origin to avoid a pruned look. Then feed the plants with a slow-release fertilizer that contains iron as well as other minor elements, such as zinc, boron, and manganese.

LAWNS

If you haven't already fed your lawn, it's time. Apply fertilizer as recommended on the label; amounts will vary with formulation. Fertilize warm-season lawns about two weeks after they begin to turn green. Feed cool-season grasses as soon as possible in the Middle South and anytime this month in the Upper South. In Florida, starting in mid-March, seed to establish new lawns throughout the state. Use a drop-type or rotary spreader for uniform distribution. For very small seeds, such as centipede or bahia, mix seeds with equal parts sand for easy spreading. Rake seed into the soil, and mulch with straw (one bale covers about 1,000 square feet). Keep the soil moist by watering lightly two or three times a day until sprouts appear. In Texas, fertilize cool-season lawns in North Texas with a 15-5-10 or similar granular fertilizer; wait until later in the month to fertilize warm-season lawns. Gardeners in warmer parts of the state can fertilize lawns now. Apply at a rate of 6 pounds per 1,000 square feet; use a drop spreader to apply evenly, and water after application. Don't apply a weed-and-feed fertilizer to newly seeded lawns.

LETTUCE

It's not too late to enjoy lettuce in the spring garden. Leaf or semi-heading types do better than those that make a tight head. Set out transplants now.

NASTURTIUMS

These annuals are easy to grow and will bloom all spring. Soak seeds in a saucer of water overnight; then plant them directly in the garden approximately a foot apart or in containers outdoors. They will germinate in a week.

PARSLEY

Even if this herb remained green through winter in your garden, you can't count on it for long. As soon as the weather gets warm, parsley will grow tall, bloom, and go to seed. Set out transplants when frost is no longer a danger. Pick from last year's plants as long as possible so the new ones can get established. In Florida and Texas, don't pull up parsley plants that have survived the winter; wait until they have gone to seed. To collect seeds for next fall, herb enthusiast Brandon Brown recommends picking the entire stem and seedhead after the flowers have fallen off and the seeds begin to turn brown. Hang the stems upside down indoors over a box. As the seeds begin to dry, they will fall into the box.

PEAS

Sow seeds of edible-podded and English peas, such as Sugar Snap and snow peas, directly into prepared garden soil. Lower South gardeners should hurry to plant before the middle of the month so peas will have time to mature before the weather gets too warm.

PERENNIALS

Gardeners in Central and South Texas can set out transplants of Shasta daisy, fall salvia, candytuft, gaillardia, and blazing star by mid-month. Choose a sunny location with well-drained soil. Before planting, till the soil to a depth of 12 inches; add plenty of organic matter.

ROSES

Prune hybrid tea roses as soon as possible by cutting away dead canes. Secondly, remove the small and weak canes that are crossed or growing toward the center of the plant. Leave four to eight healthy canes that are spaced evenly around the plant, and prune them back to 18 to 24 inches, making your cut in living wood just above an outward-facing bud. In Texas, if your roses had trouble with black spot last year, begin spraying with Funginex as soon as the new foliage appears. Funginex also helps prevent other rose diseases, including powdery mildew and rust. Treat after every rain or overhead watering.

SHRUBS

Apply 12-6-6 or similar granular fertilizer to shrubs at a rate of ½ tablespoon per foot of plant height. Spread fertilizer evenly beneath shrubs and several inches beyond the dripline to include feeder roots. In areas with alkaline soil, use a fertilizer specially formulated for those acid-loving plants in the garden. In Texas, use 16-4-8 granular fertilizer and water thoroughly after application. In Florida, apply 15-5-15 fertilizer and in South Florida, use 8-8-8 complete with minor elements to offset the high soil pH.

STAGHORN FERN

In Florida, propagate new staghorn ferns by separating pups from a mature plant. These tiny ferns transplant easily to a bed of damp sphagnum moss. Set each pup in the moss, covering roots.

STRAWBERRIES

In Florida, leave the stem and cap on each berry you pick to help fruit last longer. If slugs are damaging your harvest, set out halves of grapefruit rinds among the plants. Position rinds with the peel side up so slugs will collect beneath. Slide a piece of paper beneath the peel to trap the slugs; then discard.

TANGELOS

In Florida, plant bare-root trees in early March; plant container-grown trees as soon as warm weather is here to stay. Keep a 3-foot circle around each tree free of grass. Fertilize young trees with a citrus blend, such as 14-7-10, as soon as new leaves sprout.

TENT CATERPILLARS

Be on the lookout for the large, white webs of these caterpillars in apple, cherry, peach, elm, maple, oak, and willow trees. To control these hairy, blue-and-black pests, spray with *Bacillus thuringiensis* (Bt) or malathion, or remove the webs with a long stick in early morning or late evening.

TOMATOES

It's time to plant tomatoes in the Lower South; wait until next month in the Middle South and May in the Upper South. If transplants are tall, you can either set them on their side in a shallow trench with only the topmost leaves showing, or dig a deep hole with a shovel or posthole digger to set the transplant straight down. Either way, you should enrich the backfill soil with compost. Set out transplants now in South Texas; wait until the end of the month in North Texas and the Panhandle. Good selections for the state include Celebrity, Carnival, President, Quick Pick, First Lady, and Super Fantastic. Pick off lower leaves, and set plants deeper than they grew in their original containers. Dig a trench, and lay the root ball and stem so that remaining leaves are just above the soil.

TREES

In Florida, feed palms, citrus, dogwoods, and redbuds with a granular fertilizer blended especially for them, such as Marico. It contains magnesium sulfate and manganese sulfate, which are beneficial to these trees. Follow recommended rates on the label.

March Notes

TO DO:
■ Trim overgrown or uneven hedges
■ Fertilize houseplants with a water-soluble fertilizer
■ Fertilize warm-season lawns
■ Cut back tired fronds of evergreen ferns
■ Begin spraying roses with fungicide as soon as first leaves appear
■ Set out bedding plants after last frost

TO PLANT:
■ Trees and shrubs
■ Perennials
■ Sow seeds of warm-weather vegetables

TO PURCHASE:
■ Seeds
■ Vegetable transplants
■ Fertilizer

_____
_____
_____
_____
_____
_____

TIP OF THE MONTH

Here's a good way to keep insects off your cabbage plants. Wait until your plants are wet with dew; then sprinkle wood ashes on them.

Adelyne Smith
Dunnville, Kentucky

Clematis heracleifolia

The Undiscovered
Clematis

BY LINDA C. ASKEY

The name "clematis" brings to mind the hand-size blossoms that festoon mailboxes across the South. But the species from which they were bred are not as big or as uniform. They have a wide range of forms: evergreen or deciduous, climbing or shrubby, fragile or robust. And for the gardener, they are proven perennials that are filling new niches.

Behind all big mailbox clematis are their parents, smaller in flower but delightful in character.

Southerners usually like to keep plants separate, planting them so they don't touch and then pruning them if they do. But as garden designer Jimmy Stewart of Decatur, Georgia, suggests, the species clematis are much more at home scampering up a small tree or shrub or scrambling through a perennial border than just adorning a lamppost. "We have just begun to see the im-

A young vine of Clematis montana rubens is already making a splash in a Richmond garden.

portance of these growing *through* roses, hydrangeas, and Japanese maples,'' Stewart says. While this practice could cause crowding with more vigorous vines, most of this group are gentle companions, and their blossoms are even more interesting when they're shown off against a background of foliage.

The evergreen, bamboo-like foliage of **armand clematis** (*Clematis armandii*) makes a perfect backdrop for the pure white, 2-inch flowers in early spring. Dependably hardy in the Lower South (and worth the risk in the Middle South), a temperature of -5 degrees will knock it back to the ground, but it will return. In shaded settings, this vine blankets walls, fences, or pergolas.

C. montana rubens has escaped any simplified nicknames and goes by all three of its Latin names. Of the species clematis, it has some of the larger flowers, pink blooms 3 inches across. *C. montana grandiflora* is a white form with 4-inch flowers. Both are deciduous.

Not all of these species are tame. *C. montana rubens* and *C. armandii* are energetic growers, leaping 10 feet in a single growing season when happily situated. These should have their own location, for they are covered in an abundance of blossoms in spring. And both have a lovely, sweet fragrance.

From Texas comes a rare native, ***C. texensis,*** whose red, bell-shaped flowers have given rise to some of the best selections for the South, including Gravetye Beauty, Duchess of Albany, and Etoile Rose. They have larger flowers with more open bells. These gentle climbers also bloom in spring.

Clematis serratifolia

Clematis texensis

Clematis integrifolia

C. integrifolia is a delight to some gardeners and a puzzle to others. Perhaps the difference lies not in the plant's performance but in the expectations of the gardener. Unlike most clematis, this one does not climb but rambles on the ground. It does not produce one spectacular show of enormous flowers, but instead gives a sprinkling of blue bells mingled with fuzzy seed clusters. It is particularly effective when mixed with more thickly flowered plants.

John Elsley, at Wayside Gardens in South Carolina, is excited about ***C. x durandii,*** a hybrid between *C. jackmanii* and *C. integrifolia.* Like its parents, *C. durandii* reblooms through the season, and the 5-inch, four-petalled blue bells are stunning.

Another non-climbing species is ***C. heracleifolia.*** Clusters of blue blooms decorate upright stems that reach 3 feet each season, then die back to the ground in winter.

Other favorites among the species clematis include: ***C. viticella*** for blooms through summer; ***C. cirrhosa*** for fall and winter flowers; ***C. chrysocoma*** for dogwood-like blooms in late spring; and ***C. serratifolia*** and ***C. tangutica*** for yellow flowers in summer.

For best results, grow clematis where the roots are shaded and the leaves are in sun. Stewart explains, "We've always known to keep the roots cool, but if you can get the vines started growing up on something and get the leaves out into the sun, it really makes a difference." Because clematis tends to climb by twining, sometimes it needs a little support and guidance to get started going in the right direction. ◇

An Initial Approach to Gardening

The closest most kids come to gardening is being rooted to the floor in front of the television. If hour after hour of *Teenage Mutant Ninja Turtles* has you crawling into a shell, it's time to get your children involved with something else that's green—plants.

Growing a vegetable garden can teach young minds valuable lessons about how the natural world works. But in order to keep children interested, you must remember the Three Golden Rules of Kids' Gardening. *Rule #1—Make it easy. Rule #2—Make it fun. Rule #3—Make it fast.*

Select a sunny, well-drained spot for the garden. Adults should do any necessary tilling, raking, and weed-pulling. Then let the kids do the planting. Show them how deep and far apart to plant the seeds. Choose "can't fail" vegetables—leaf lettuce, radishes, peas, spinach, carrots—that have easy-to-handle seeds that sprout quickly. Challenge your brood to a contest to see who can spot the first seedling or harvest the first mature vegetable.

Young attention spans are short, so the more fun you can inject into the proceedings, the more dedicated gardeners you'll have.

The children shown here are Henry, Vandiver, and Sarah Chaplin, offspring of Lois and Van Chaplin. Van came up with the idea of having his kids plant their initials in leaf lettuce and radishes. The H for Henry turned out all right, but somehow Vandiver's V got changed to an A. "Oh well," says Van, "first let's master gardening; then we'll work on spelling."   *Steve Bender*

Kids will love planting their initials in radishes and lettuce, and watching them grow.

Sarah drops the seeds; then Henry and Vandiver press them into the soil.

These Potatoes Are Basket Cases

In our efforts to create the perfect world for our plants, we gardeners sometimes go to lots of trouble. Often, there's a quicker, easier, and better way to grow them. Take potatoes, for example.

The time-honored method: Plant the potato pieces. See the leaves come up. Pile up some straw and rich soil or compost around the leaves. Then pile some more. What fun. What a great big mess that takes up lots of space in your garden. Dig through the dirt and straw with your garden fork when potatoes are ready. Accidentally spear and ruin half the potatoes with your garden fork.

The clever, basket method: "We plant the seed potatoes or 'spud buds' about an inch or two deep in late February or early March," says Lucinda Mays, who came up with the idea. "Then we set an old bushel basket with a hole cut out of the bottom over the potatoes." Check your local farmers market for a good supply; they're about $3 new. If you don't have a bushel basket, a couple of old tires or a large plastic garbage bag works, too. Just don't go any taller than knee high with your stack. When the sprouts are several inches high, add a generous amount of well-rotted compost and sand right on top of the foliage. (If you've got sandy soil, just add compost.) Leave a little bit of the tops showing. Water

Old bushel baskets make great space-saving containers for growing potatoes. Just cut the bottoms out of the baskets, and set over the potatoes. Shovel compost and sand on top of the plants every few weeks until the baskets are full.

when needed, but don't add any fertilizer. "That will cause lots of leafy growth and fewer potatoes," Lucinda advises.

Continue the process until the basket is full. When the tops yellow, just pull the basket up. "The basket won't be full of potatoes," Lucinda says. "Just the lower third and in the ground. But you don't have to risk injuring the potatoes by using a digging fork."

Because of their high moisture content, **new** potatoes should not be stored. But after harvesting **mature**

potatoes, brush off the dirt, and store them in a cool, dry place. Don't leave potatoes in the sun to dry, or they will turn green and become inedible. Another advantage to this space-saving basket method is that you can plant around them with other cool-weather crops, such as lettuce. "The baskets help shade the lettuce, and you can enjoy fresh lettuce at least two weeks later into summer," Lucinda says.

Lucinda Mays is curator of Victory Garden South, Callaway Gardens.

Starting warm-weather plants from seeds grown inside is a great way to get them off to a good start before you transplant them outside. You can even enjoy the plants indoors in small containers until it's time to set them out.

Starting Seeds Indoors

If you think a small child waiting for his birthday to come is impatient, just witness a gardener waiting for the last frost to pass so he can plant something. But many folks outwit the season by starting their seeds indoors. If you have the time, growing seeds indoors can really be quite profitable in terms of getting the most fruit, flowers, or foliage for the buck. Here's a beginner's guide to starting plants from seed.

Seed needs. Okay, so maybe we're starting out a bit too obvious, but there are some things you should know about these little plants-in-waiting. Buy selections that you know will do well in your area. How do you know that? The seed packet will sometimes tell you, or check with a gardener friend, nearby botanical garden, local gardening book, or county Extension service.

Trays, pots, and whatnots. There is a huge assortment of paraphernalia for growing seeds indoors, from exotic "miniature greenhouses" to simple plastic trays left over from all those begonias you set out last year. It all boils down to this: If you want to improve the odds that your seeds will make it past the cute little sprout stage, those clear plastic-covered seed trays (greenhouses) are relatively expensive but hard to beat. If you've got a large quantity of plants you want to set out, and will fuss over your sprouts like newly hatched chickens, the inexpensive, plastic flat is the way to go.

Now, about the media. The soil media, that is. Again, you've got several choices. You can use ordinary, sterile potting soil to start many seeds, but it's hard to beat the water-holding capacity of vermiculite. Some mail-order companies sell special soil media "blends" that are especially suited for starting seeds.

Sowing lessons. You've got your pots, or trays, potting media, and seeds—now it's time for them to take the plunge. Not too deep—follow the planting depths recommended on the packet. It's a common mistake to set the tray full of seeds in a sunny window. Instead, seeds need warmth to germinate. Put them on top of the refrigerator or other warm place (not on a heating vent—that's a little too warm). And be sure to keep the soil moist at all times.

They're up! What do I do? When the magic moment arrives—from a few days to several weeks, depending on the plant—and the seeds germinate, move the tray near a sunny window. Young seedlings can dry out quickly, so keep tabs on the soil's dryness. You may have to water twice a day if you keep your home warm and dry when the weather is cool. Wait until the plants are up a few inches before watering them with a liquid fertilizer.

Out they go. So the weatherman says no more freezes. Can you take your babies out? No, not just yet. Plants raised indoors have led a pampered life, and may need to be gradually introduced to the great outdoors. Try setting them outside, out of direct sunlight, a few hours for a couple of days. Some gardeners set their plants out in cold frames, shallow boxes with hinged lids containing plastic or glass panels. After a week or so in the cold frame, the plants are put in the ground.

Maybe all this sounds like a lot of trouble. But ask an avid gardener if it was worth the bragging rights to be the first one in the neighborhood to slice into a homegrown tomato. And expect a smile and a nod every time.

Mark G. Stith

Symphony of *Spring*

By Jo Kellum

Photography Van Chaplin

Trey and Valerie Vaughan are true gardeners. How many people would remodel the garden before the house?

—Landscape architect Dan Franklin

Lewis M. Vaughan, Sr., built the original pond in the 1930s.

It's the kind of garden where the flowers sing. Petals compose a symphony that plays from dawn until dusk: Yellows, pinks, blues, and violets swell in a crescendo of color. And like a lone cello, the white blooms are always the last notes fading into night.

Trey and Valerie Vaughan are the maestros of this Atlanta garden, coaxing and cajoling the best performances each season. The Vaughans and their friend, Dan Franklin, orchestrated the garden's rebirth.

A Legacy

The garden and the house that looks over it originally belonged to Trey's grandparents. In the early 1930s, his grandfather built a round pond in the backyard. Two generations later, this perfect circle of water proved irresistible to the engineer in Trey.

The pond's old concrete-and-stone bottom had settled and cracked, but the Vaughans persisted. "I remember that pond from when I was a kid," Trey says. "My grandfather had this concrete frog that spit water into the pond. I remember being scared of that frog." Eventually, fear turned to affection, and so the project first focused on saving the pond.

Trey tried to patch the original pond, but finally built a new one on top of it. To make it watertight, he chose to have the pond's new sides and bottom coated with Shotcrete, a type of concrete that is sprayed into place. To cut costs, Trey hired a swimming pool contractor in the spring, before the busy pool-building season began.

Because the old pond was not dug up, the new one built above it is about 2 feet higher. "The sides of the

(**Left**) *A bench beneath the saucer magnolia is a peaceful spot in the garden.*
(**Inset**) *Trey saved the wheelbarrow his father used as a boy to move topsoil from nearby woods to the garden.*

Favorite Perennial Performers

Forget-me-nots. Valerie: "Sow seeds in the fall or in spring after the last frost."

Happy Returns daylily. Trey: "This is the best daylily I have ever seen. It's yellow, and it blooms all summer long. Really, *all* summer long."

Coneflowers. Valerie: "These bloom throughout the summer, too."

Monch aster. Trey: "It blooms early for an aster (mid-summer), and it's easy to grow."

Nippon daisy. Valerie: "This is a small shrubby plant with fall blossoms similar to Shasta daisies. It's worth the search."

Siberian iris. Trey: "These are easy; they'll bloom their first year in the garden."

Liatris (blazing star). Valerie: "You can't kill it. My friend forgets to water hers for a couple of weeks and it still looks great."

Phlox. Trey: "You gotta have phlox. Miss Lingard and Mount Fuji do well."

Cosmos. Valerie: "This is a good tall plant for background, like foxglove."

Shirley poppies. Valerie: "These are like little bushes. On one plant you may have a red flower blooming, a hot-pink one, and a white one edged in red."

Fall

English daisies, ⎫ Plant now
delphinium, violas, ⎬ for spring
foxgloves, tulips ⎭

Sow seeds: forget-me-nots,
Shirley & Oriental poppies

Plant pansies & snapdragons
for winter color

Winter

Trim and mulch snapdragons
to get more blooms next spring.

Deadhead pansies and violas

Spring

Plants to buy and set out:
Canterbury bells, lupine,
larkspur, astilbe, trillium,
candytuft and Iceland poppies

Don't forget to sow seeds:
Queen Anne's lace,
bachelor's-buttons

Summer

Replace pansies with
Madagascar periwinkles
or petunias

Replace foxgloves with
cosmos or cleome

Plant zinnias & miniature
sunflowers

new pond just stuck up out of the ground," Trey remembers. "I had to bring in two tandem [double] loads of soil to raise the grade of the whole area around the pond."

To hold it all, Dan Franklin designed stone retaining walls that stairstep down the backyard slope. Because the original stacked-stone walls had crumbled, Franklin mortared the new stones in place. The curving walls echo the pond's shape.

Trey studied walls throughout Atlanta in search of just the right style for the new garden. He discovered what he was looking for in Chastain Park. The irregular granite face and caps have an old-fashioned air about them that suits this young garden rooted in personal history. Salvaged cobblestones, found by Trey's brother, edge the garden with a touch of the past.

Random Order

The walls' geometric shape gives the garden a formal symmetry. But instead of confining the planting to ordered rows, the Vaughans grow a glorious profusion of flowers.

Bound by curves of stone, flowerbeds border a carpet of putting green-perfect grass. In contrast with the smooth Emerald Green Zoysia lawn, the beds seem like a chorus of color—and it's no accident. The Vaughans plan ahead each year to achieve a random cottage-garden look. To determine where each plant belongs in the garden, Trey and Valerie carefully consider blossom and foliage color, plant size, texture, and season of bloom. A valuable aid in planning is Valerie's garden journal, a record of the garden's changes through the year.

Valerie fine-tunes the composition seasonally. The daughter and granddaughter of gardeners, Valerie continues her family traditions. "My grandmother had a little nursery in Ocilla, Georgia, and my mother gardened, too," she explains. "I learned from them." Dan Franklin also shares his gardening know-how and plants

(Left) *Curving stone walls divide tiers of flowers.*
(Inset) *Valerie's secret to profuse pansies is to spend a few minutes in the garden every day, removing spent blossoms.*

April

Japanese roof iris

CHECKLIST FOR APRIL

ANNUALS

Start summer flower beds now. Choose from a variety of hot-weather annuals including coleus, dusty miller, impatiens, periwinkle, marigold, red salvia, rudbeckia, and zinnias. Filling a bed with a single color is a dramatic way to add color to your landscape. In Texas, it's not too late to set out seeds of summer-flowering annuals, including globe amaranth, cosmos, marigolds, portulaca, flowering tobacco, zinnias, and cleome. Sow the seeds in well-prepared flower beds, and water them thoroughly. When seedlings have grown 2 to 3 inches high, thin the plants to the spacing that is recommended on the seed packet.

AZALEAS

Prune erratic growth on azaleas as soon as they finish blooming. If you wait, you may cut off next year's blossoms. Don't use electric clippers on azaleas. Instead, remove overgrown branches with hand pruners to keep azaleas naturally shaped.

CALADIUMS

Don't plant caladiums until after the danger of frost has passed in your area and soil temperatures have warmed. Gardeners in the Lower South can plant this month, but wait until May in the Middle South and late May or early June in the Upper South. North and Central Florida gardeners can still plant tubers until May. Set out containerized plants throughout the state. Caladiums thrive in rich, organic soil; work peat moss or composted cow manure into sandy soils. Plant caladiums in filtered shade where they will

receive morning sun. In Texas, plant tubers about 12 inches apart and 1 inch deep for masses of beautiful foliage; space fancy-leaved selections 6 inches apart. Wait until later in the month to set out caladiums in North Texas.

CEDAR-APPLE RUST

Prune to remove swollen brown spots, known as galls, from juniper foliage. Cedar-apple rust often appears as orange gelatinous masses on galls in the spring. This disease requires a nearby alternate host, such as apple, crabapple, hawthorn, pear, or quince, and may cause damage to the fruit.

COMPOST

Recycle oak leaves, which fall in the spring just before new leaves appear. Some cities collect leaves to compost for use in parks. If your town participates, bag your leaves in clear bags, or attach labels for pickup. Or add leaves to your own compost pile. To hasten decomposition, turn the pile once a week to expose new material to warm temperatures inside the pile.

DAYLILIES

Dig up each clump, and separate into small clusters of roots and foliage. Replant divided daylilies 18 to 24 inches apart, at the same depth the plants were originally growing. Cut back leaves to within 6 to 8 inches of the ground. Keep the soil evenly moist until the daylilies are well established.

DOGWOODS

A good small tree throughout the South, these trees are sensitive to fluctuations in soil temperature, so don't plant dogwoods near paving, which can heat up quickly. Dogwoods grow best in filtered shade and moist soil rich in organic matter. Avoid dense shade, which can discourage flowering.

EASTER PLANTS

Easter lilies perform beautifully in the garden. Do not cut them back; plant them in a well-drained, sunny bed outdoors. Chrysanthemums should be divided, planted, cut back, and fertilized. They will bloom in fall,

but selections bred for the garden will give a superior display. Plant hydrangeas and azaleas in the garden, keeping their colors in mind.

FERTILIZE

Hanging baskets of ferns, impatiens, petunias, and geraniums respond well to weekly applications of water-soluble fertilizer, such as Miracle-Gro, Peters, or Vigoro. Remove spent blooms of flowering plants for continued flower production.

FRUIT TREES

Reduce insect and disease problems on fruit trees by spraying every 10 to 14 days with a combination insecticide and fungicide spray, such as malathion and benomyl. For good-size peaches, thin fruit on the branches to one peach every 6 inches or so.

HERBS

After frost, set out transplants of pineapple sage, lemon grass, and basil. Even hardy perennials such as oregano, winter savory, thyme, rosemary, and lavender are best when planted after frost if they are fresh from a greenhouse. Gardeners in South Florida and Texas should protect herbs from afternoon sun. Plant anise, lemon balm, tarragon, lemon verbena, summer savory, sage, and thyme. Herbs require good drainage to thrive; if your soil doesn't drain well, plant them in raised beds or containers. In Texas, if you can't find transplants at your local garden center, it's easy to grow some herbs from seeds. Basil, borage, summer savory, and dill are a few that you can start directly in the garden or in containers.

HIBISCUS

For a flowering shrub to fill a large container, Chinese hibiscus is a good choice. Although hibiscus can be grown in the ground as annuals, most gardeners plant them in pots and bring them indoors when the temperature dips below 34 degrees. In Florida, prune hibiscus for full, healthy plants. Remove overgrown branches, cutting the stem just above a bud. Although hibiscus may reach 10 feet, they look best when kept 3 to 5 feet tall. Regular pruning encourages the plant to produce abundant foliage and  profuse flowers. In Texas, set out tropical hibiscus now, either in large containers or directly in the garden. They need almost a full day's sunlight to flower well. Fertilize monthly with a water-soluble fertilizer that has a low-phosphorus formula.

LAWNS

If you haven't already done so, feed lawns of St. Augustine, Zoysia, centipede, Bermuda, and bahia now. Choose a 16-4-8, slow-release fertilizer that will feed your lawn gradually; if it's not slow release, much of the nitrogen will just wash away. Be sure your mower blades are adjusted to cut your grass to the correct height. Mow hybrid Bermuda and Zoysia ½ to 1 inch, centipede 1 to 2 inches, St. Augustine 2 to 3 inches, and buffalo grass 2 inches high. Turf-type fescue should be cut about 2½ inches high.

PERENNIALS

In Texas, plant or divide established chrysanthemums, Mexican mint marigold, perennial salvia, and other perennials now for a colorful fall show. When dividing established mums, be sure to take only healthy plants from the edge of the main clump.

PLANT LABELS

When setting out new perennials, be sure to put the label beside the plant for future reference and to mark its spot during its dormant season. For a massed annual planting, simply put a couple of plant labels in the ground and staple one label to a page of your garden journal. Remove or loosen any tags on new trees and shrubs that have the potential to cut into a growing stem.

PRUNING

Now is a good time to shape up spindly or overgrown shrubs, including pyracantha, ligustrum, and elaeagnus. Cut away any dead limbs that didn't green up this spring. Prune evergreen hedges to a lampshade shape to allow sunlight to reach lower branches and keep the plants full-looking from top to bottom.

STAKING

Use strips of old panty hose to gently secure tomato plants to a stake, cage, or trellis. These ties are as strong as twine and more resistant to weathering. They stretch as the stem grows, yet hold it in place without injury.

SLUGS

Silvery trails among ravaged leaves are a sure sign these pests are present. To get rid of them, late in the evening set out shallow bowls filled with beer or even lay down small strips of cardboard for the slugs to crawl under. The following morning, collect and remove the slugs. Repeat until they are under control.

TOMATOES

Choose selections for every purpose. For the first ripe tomatoes, plant Early Girl or First Lady. Then grow selections for both large fruit (Park's Whopper or Burpee's Supersteak VFN Hybrid) and medium fruit (Heinz 1350 and Homestead 24F). And don't forget cherry tomatoes, such as Super Sweet 100. If you grow tomatoes for canning or sauce, try LaRoma VF Hybrid or Red Pear.

Getaway
Garden

Surrounded by the

flowers and countryside

they love, the Welches

find delight at each

week's end.

Most Friday evenings, Diane and Bill Welch leave behind their faculty positions at Texas A&M University and retreat to Cricket Court, their weekend home in rural Washington County near Round Top. From the porch and gardens of their 1906 Victorian cottage, they enjoy country quiet and open vistas.

Picket fences enclose gardens on each side, providing flower-filled views from inside the home. Those flowers are Bill's passion. He combs the South in search of heirloom plants. In his role as a professor and Extension landscape horticulturist, he has introduced old-fashioned plants to Texas nurserymen, Master Gardeners, and Extension agents. As a lecturer and author, Southerners have come to know Bill as an expert on perennials and roses that can take the heat.

In the course of his travels, Bill has befriended gardeners from Texas to the coast of the Carolinas. As garden-

ers typically do, they swap plants, so he brings home little treasures in plastic bags from every trip.

Gardens connect not only friends but also generations, so some of the most prominent plants of the Welches' garden are hand-me-downs from Diane and Bill's families. Examples include a cloverlike Oxalis (*O. crassipes*) that lines the beds at Cricket Court, and the Maggie rose that is becoming popular across the South. Both plants came from the garden of Diane's grandmother in northeast Louisiana. From Bill's mother's family in Yoakum, Texas, came German red carnations and Dutchman's-pipe vine.

The herb garden holds special charm for Diane. "It's a serenity point when I look out the bedroom window," she says. As a member of the Pioneer Herb Society in the Round Top area, she uses this bit of ground—just as Bill does the rest of the garden—as a place to test new plants and learn how they grow and

BY LINDA C. ASKEY
PHOTOGRAPHY SYLVIA MARTIN

(**Left**) *The late-Victorian cottage is nestled between gardens on either side with open vistas all around.*

(**Below**) *Bill Welch's favorites include pinks, old-fashioned petunias, and Texas bluebonnets gathered around a Victorian urn filled with yucca and Mexican sedum. Climbing Old Blush rose festoons the fence and German red carnations grow over the path.*

Roses and perennials mingle in beds of harmonious color. Trellises and fences offer support for favorite roses while buffalo grass provides a fine-textured Texas lawn.

perform in their area.

The garden, however, does not have the hodge-podge appearance of a testing ground. In fact, the color combinations and architectural details make this 3-year-old planting look like the accomplishment of many seasons. Bill credits the quick growth of roses and perennials with the overall effect, but there is more to it than that.

The structure of the garden is the result of a collaboration between Bill and landscape architect Nancy Volkman. Picket fences wrap the gardens in cottage style, while gateway arbors echo the gables of the house. "I wanted a lot of fence space to display flowering vines in addition to climbing roses," Bill explains. So the fences and arbors serve not only to enclose the garden but also as trellises.

Bill describes the garden as a contemporary interpretation of a Texas cottage garden. Because of his fondness for antique flowers, many of the plants are true to the period of the house. But personal preference takes the garden beyond any re-creation. Just like a house furnished with cher-

BILL'S CHOICES FOR HARDY SOUTHERN PERENNIALS

Louisiana iris (*Iris* x *hybrida*)

Downy phlox (*Phlox pilosa*)

Hinckley's columbine (*Aquilegia hinckleyana*)

Powis Castle artemisia (*Artemisia* x Powis Castle)

Aromatic Aster (*Aster oblongifolius*)

Milk-and-Wine lilies (*Crinum* sp.)

Gaura (*Gaura lindheimeri*)

Hardy gladiolus (*Gladiolus byzantinus*)

Summer snowflake (*Leucojum aestivum*)

Grand Primo and Campernelle narcissus (*Narcissus tazetta* Grand Primo and *N.* x *Odorus*)

Tuberose (*Polianthes tuberosa*)

Mexican bush sage (*Salvia leucantha*)

White swamp lily (*Zephyranthes candida*)

ished belongings, this garden is filled with horticultural favorites. And it is not beauty alone that earns a plant favor; they also have to be sturdy.

"It's a relatively low-maintenance garden because it has to be—because it's ours," he says. They don't spend every weekend working in the garden; they frequently have company. "Sharing with other people is part of the fun," says Bill.

The plants that help make these weekends possible include a buffalo grass lawn and hardy, long-lasting perennials (see box at left). The roses are those that require little or no pesticides. Old-fashioned petunias spring up from the seeds that fell last year. These plants have survived the generations because they are tough. They take care of themselves, leaving Bill with time to do what he always intended—to simply enjoy them.

Books by William C. Welch include *Antique Roses for the South* and *Perennial Garden Color for Texas and The South*. Both are available from Taylor Publishing Company. ◇

A fast-growing evergreen, loropetalum reaches an imposing size in just a few years and blooms for two to three weeks each spring.

Burgundy, a new, pink-flowered selection, offers an exciting break with the past.

Fleecy, cream-colored flowers are most commonly found.

Alluring Loropetalum

Question: What is loropetalum?

(A) A pernicious fungus from southeast Asia that turns your eyebrows green.

(B) An ancient Roman city that gave birth to the raisin industry.

(C) A highly ornamental, flowering shrub that's the subject of this article.

Yes, of course, the answer is (C)—you're much too smart for us. The only way to appear even smarter is to plant a loropetalum (pronounced lore-o-PET-a-lum) in your garden.

What does this weird-sounding shrub, *Loropetalum chinense*, have to offer? For starters, it's evergreen—an endearing quality all Southerners respect. Second, it grows fast—a 1-gallon plant can easily reach 5 feet tall in three or four years. Third, this Chinese import left its enemies behind—no domestic bugs or diseases plague it. Finally, when loropetalum, which is also called Chinese Fringe, blooms in spring, it literally stops traffic.

Chances are, you haven't seen flowers quite like these. Each blossom consists of four straplike petals three-quarters of an inch long. Creamy white is the usual color, but a pink-flowering form recently appeared on the scene. Pundits say this new selection, called Burgundy, will take the gardening world by storm.

As you can see from the photo, loropetalum looks great planted on the corner of the house. Don't plant it in front of your porch or first-floor windows unless you're hiding from the authorities. You can trim off the lower branches and convert the shrub into a small, multitrunked tree. Or use a row of loropetalums as a tall screen to block unwanted views.

Don't faint when you first see loropetalum at the nursery offered in a 1-gallon pot. A young plant grows nearly flat at first, looking prostrate like many cotoneasters. But it stands up straight before long. If your local garden center doesn't carry loropetalum, we can supply a list of mail-order sources. Just send a self-addressed, stamped, business-size envelope to Loropetalum, P.O. Box 830119, Birmingham, AL 35283.

We bet you're feeling smarter already.

Steve Bender

LOROPETALUM AT A GLANCE

Size: 10 to 15 feet high and wide after 10 years

Light: Full sun or light shade

Soil: Moist, acid, well drained, lots of organic matter

Pests: None serious

Prune: In late spring soon after flowers fade

Propagation: Take cuttings in July

Range: Middle, Lower, Coastal South. Hardy to about 5 degrees.

A New Walk You Can Build

Sometimes it's easier to replace than to repair. The narrow walk and uneven landing at this home necessitated a start-from-scratch project. The sunken landing also exposed the foundation of the bottom step, making renovation difficult.

The concrete walk and no-slab brick landing were easy to remove with a few blows of a sledgehammer. For the new walk, we used interlocking pavers—individual rectangles of brick-shaped, precast concrete. Pavers have a tiny lip on the bottom edge that helps lock them together. Unlike real bricks, which are sized to leave room for mortar between each row, pavers are available in an even 4- x 8-inch size. This makes it easy to create patterns in the walkway.

GETTING READY

The trick is avoiding having to cut the pavers. A quick sketch before getting started made this easy. By sticking with dimensions that were divisible by 4, we made sure that the new walk could be built entirely of whole pavers.

After breaking up and hauling away the original walk and landing, we measured the shape of the new walk on the ground. To mark the measurements, we sprayed small dashes with bright-orange marking paint, then connected the dashes with a straight line of paint. Because it was critical to line up the new walk with the front steps, we started at that end.

At the foot of the steps we planned a square landing. Because the bottom step was 67 inches long (a number not divisible by 4), we could not build the landing the same size without cutting pavers. The solution: build a slightly smaller landing—but only 64 inches wide.

To keep the old steps and the new landing from looking odd, we centered the landing on the bottom step. Starting from the center point of the step, we measured 32 inches in each direction. The small size difference

(Left) *Before: This walk was old, narrow, and ugly.*
(Above) *After: The new paver walkway has a spacious landing at the steps and allows plenty of room for two people to walk comfortably side by side.*

between the step and the landing is unnoticeable, especially with plants framing the steps.

After outlining the shape of the landing with paint, we marked the connection between the landing and the walkway. First, we marked the center of the landing where it faces the drive. That gave us a center point for a 40-inch-wide walk, enough for two people to walk comfortably side by side.

BUILDING THE WALK

After outlining the walk and landing, we carefully removed the sod between the painted lines and replanted it in soil left bare by the removal of the original walk. Daily watering

made the transplantation successful.

We raked the soil to level it, then framed the walk using No. 1 grade wolmanized 2 x 6 lumber, suitable for ground contact. To hide the exposed step foundation, we used 2 x 10s to build that frame.

We filled the frames with a 3-inch bed of sand. Compacting the sand helped keep pavers from settling later. A 12-inch-square board nailed to the bottom of a 4 x 4 post is a useful tool for pounding the sand in place.

Next, we set the pavers in the sand-filled frame. We began at the driveway end to make sure the two surfaces were flush. But instead of just ending the walk at the driveway, we created a small rectangular land-

Step 1: *Lay a pair of garden hoses on the ground to check measurements before beginning your work.*

Step 2: *Outline the new walk on the ground with marking paint.*

DESIGN TIPS

If your new walk will line up with red brick steps, don't choose a red paver. The shades can vary and may end up clashing. Use a neutral color instead.

To avoid having to cut pavers, use 4- x 8-inch brick-shaped pavers and size your walk so that all dimensions are divisible by 4. Instead of curves, use only straight lines and 90-degree angles.

Match paver pattern to dimensions of your walk. A quick sketch can show you where adjustments need to be made.

ing to give the entrance a welcoming touch. The landing required four additional rows of pavers, with eight pavers to each row.

To finish the project, we shoveled more sand on the walk's surface and swept it into the cracks between pavers, repeating this process several times. This will help prevent settling.

Our total material cost was $430. We used six 16-foot 2 x 6s, 2½ cubic yards of sand, and 800 brick pavers. Your costs may vary, depending on the length of your walk.

It's good to remember that pavers are as forgiving as they are attractive. If you make a mistake, just pull them up to rearrange.   *Jo Kellum*

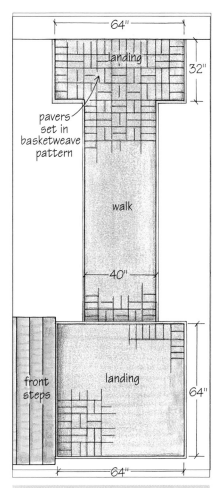

MARKING PAINT

Some regular spray-paint cans won't work when you hold them upside-down to paint an outline on the ground. Marking paint in inverted cans is available at paint stores for about $8 a can.

Step 3: *Frame the walk, and fill it with sand. A board is a handy tool for leveling the sand.*

Step 4: *Use a hand level and rubber mallet to level the walk's surface while setting pavers in place.*

Step 5: *Sweep sand into the cracks between pavers to help keep them from settling.*

Baby-Blue-Eyes: *An Annual Delight*

Some flowers just plant themselves. These beauties bloom on their own, wanting only neglect. It's odd that we take them for granted and coddle the more demanding types. In fact, as gardeners, we should be wanting more blooming plants of this independent sort, especially baby-blue-eyes.

Like spring in the South, these annuals are beautiful, and then they are gone. Baby-blue-eyes (*Nemophila phacelioides*) grow wild in the dappled shade of woodlands, streams, and prairies in Southeast and Central Texas, Oklahoma, and Arkansas.

We found the plant blooming at the Antique Rose Emporium in Brenham, Texas. Owner Mike Shoup remembers, "It came with the property, and it comes back every year. It does better in the shade on the northeast side of the house. It's planted there by a big cistern, so the soil is typically moist. Ferns grow well there, too. We've had it spread to other parts of the cottage garden, but it never does quite as well as it does there."

Foot-tall baby-blue-eyes are usually in full bloom during the peak of the roses and spring wildflowers. Then the flowers fade and the seeds set, turning it into an attractive green ground cover that leads into summer. The seeds fall to produce next season's plants, and then the dying plants can be pulled out of the garden and tossed on the compost pile.

Although baby-blue-eyes are not available commercially, gardeners in areas where they are native should note wild stands and return to gather ripening seeds (and remember to leave some for nature). Scatter them in an area that is partially shaded and moist, but well drained. Seedlings should appear in late fall and bloom the following spring.

Gardeners in all areas can grow a similar form of baby-blue-eyes (*Nemophila menziesii*) from seeds for sale in local garden centers and mail-order catalogs. Sown in fall or early spring in well-prepared beds, this form has clear, azure-blue blossoms that are spectacular with spring bulbs. Fall-sown seedlings will begin to bloom as early as February in the Middle South, starting to show color when they are only a few inches tall. Then they will continue to flower into May when they will have reached about 12 inches. Let the plants linger in the garden and they may reseed.

Linda C. Askey

Baby-blue-eyes flower unattended beneath a Rêve d'Or rose in full bloom

PHOTOGRAPHS: SYLVIA MARTIN

PHOTOGRAPHS: GEOFFREY GILBERT, MARY-GRAY HUNTER

The flowers may be pink, rose, blush, lavender, or violet. One-inch blooms appear atop the plant in April and May.

Plant a True Geranium

How would you like to be the first in your neighborhood to grow geraniums? Sounds unlikely, doesn't it? After all, just about every gardener you know has filled a flowerbed or planter with geraniums at one time or another. Or have they? In fact, the colorful annuals sold in this country as geraniums aren't true geraniums at all, but South African natives known as *Pelargonium hortorum*. True geraniums, most of which are perennial, are ironically seldom grown. One of these is a native Southern wildflower called wild geranium (*Geranium maculatum*).

In nature, you'll often spot wild geranium growing along stream banks, the forest floor, poking out from between rocks, or sunning itself in open fields and meadows. Growing 12 to 20 inches tall with a loose, open habit, the plant sports deeply lobed leaves that develop white spots as they age. For this reason, some people call it "spotted geranium."

Clusters of one-inch blooms appear atop the stems in April and May. Pink is the most common color, but you'll also see blush, rose, lavender, and even violet flowers. The plant blooms in midspring, along with other wildflowers, such as blue phlox (*Phlox divaricata*), trillium, and foamflower (*Tiarella cordifolia*), as well as native azaleas and dogwood. After the flowers of wild geranium fade, its foliage persists until midsummer, then withers and disappears. The plant hasn't died, but simply gone dormant until the next spring.

Laura Martin, author of several books on wildflowers, is fond of massing clumps of wild geranium in woodland gardens, rock gardens, and waterside plantings. "I would definitely plant it in groups of three or four," she says. "The flowers are really delicate and airy, and you don't get the same mass of color you get from annual geraniums or pansies."

She finds that drifts of wild geranium blend well with those of blue phlox, particularly the white-flowered form of blue phlox.

You'll sometimes see wild geranium growing in light shade on the woodland floor.

Wild geranium prefers moist, well-drained, organic soil with a pH between 6 and 7. Although the best flowering for the plant occurs in the dappled shade of tall pines and hardwoods, you can also grow the plant in full sun if you strive to keep the soil moisture constant.

The easiest way to propagate the plant is by division in spring, because the seeds are tiny and hard to handle and may take two years to germinate.

Steve Bender

If you would like a list of mail-order sources of this plant, send a self-addressed, stamped, business-size envelope to Wild Geranium, *Southern Living,* P.O. Box 830119, Birmingham, AL 35283.   ◇

The simple, unadorned look of the fence, deck, terrace, and steps reflects a subtle Oriental influence.

Getting Past the Parking

If your idea of an elegant evening on the terrace doesn't include resting your drink on the car parked beside you, you can sympathize with Jim Dice and Duward Somner.

They moved into a home in Washington, D.C., beset by several problems. For one thing, to get from the street to the front door, they had to navigate around the end of a large brick wall, squeeze by the car, then traverse the parking area. Upon arriving at the terrace, which doubled as extra parking, they looked out on a hodgepodge of garden features that didn't fit together well.

To chart a new course, Jim enlisted local garden designers Tom Mannion and Louise Kane. The two made several important changes, beginning with the entry. Now, you no longer arrive with the cars. Instead, you open a gate and enter an outdoor foyer wide enough for two people to walk side by side. A brick wall and cedar fence screen the foyer and garden from a separate parking area.

Next, they turned their attention to the garden. Taking advantage of a slight slope away from the house, they divided the area into two level surfaces connected by stone pavers at one end and wooden steps at the other. The first surface, a deck, sits beside the house in front of sliding glass doors. The second surface, a flagstone terrace, accommodates dining and entertaining.

Perhaps the greatest improvement centered around a small fish pond in a corner of the terrace. Mannion and Kane reset the coping, giving it an overhang to cast a shadow line on the water, and painted the inside of the pond black to create the illusion of depth. They added water plants, such

The entry and parking area are now separate, making it easier to find your way into the garden and house.

Before

as dwarf papyrus. Finally, they constructed a low stone wall to hide the exposed concrete blocks. Low shrubs and perennials planted between the wall and blocks integrate the pond into its surroundings.

The last major change involved the steps that lead from the terrace to a side yard below. Large native stones were set into the slope to replace the former railroad-tie steps. The stones rise unevenly, a deliberate ploy to make you slow down and appreciate the quiet interplay of shade-loving plants.

You probably didn't notice at first, but this garden reflects subtle Oriental influences. All of its hard surfaces—deck, terrace, steps, wall, fence—are simple, straightforward, and unadorned. Bright colors are absent, and there is no lawn. As you wander through, you discern the myriad forms, textures, and shades of green supplied by ferns, hostas, epimedium, liriope, and diminutive alpine plants.

Today, Jim's garden is a pleasant, contemplative spot from which cars are forever exiled. The only parking allowed is when you take your coffee in one hand and morning paper in the other and park yourself in a comfortable chair.   *Steve Bender*

Mannion and Kane renovated the fish pond by resetting the coping, painting the inside black, and hiding its exposed concrete block sides behind a low stone wall and lush plantings.

(**Left**) *Large, native stones took the place of railroad-tie steps. Their uneven height forces a slow pace for close inspection of plants below.*

Before

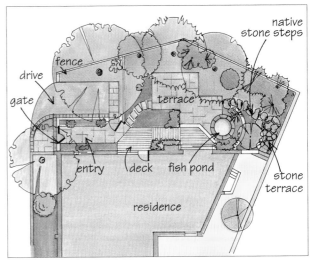

Put the Sting on Fire Ants

Have you found fire ants in your yard? Or have they found you? Unfortunately, the surest way to know is by being stung. A fire ant sting burns and later forms an itchy, swollen pustule. In most cases fire ant stings on healthy adults are a nuisance about as irritating as a horsefly bite. However, because fire ants swarm and sting over and over again, you must protect small children and the elderly, who can't quickly brush or hose off the ants. And anyone with an allergy to insect bites must beware—a few people die every year from a severe reaction.

Fire ants were accidentally imported from their native Brazil around 1918 via a cargo ship docked in Mobile. Having no natural enemies here, the small, reddish-brown ants easily marched off the boat and through the South; they now infest South Carolina, Florida, Georgia, Mississippi, Alabama, Louisiana, and parts of Texas, Oklahoma, Arkansas, Tennessee, and North Carolina. And they aren't finished. Fire ants likely will spread to all areas where winter temperatures remain above 10 degrees and where at least 10 inches of rain falls each year.

Like many other ants, fire ants live in mounds and underground tunnels. Two or three tunnels go down to the water table, but most radiate laterally within the top 18 inches of soil. When the weather is too hot, too dry, or too cold, the ants move into the deeper tunnels where it's more comfortable. When the weather is mild, they move near the surface.

Each fire ant nest has a queen that lays the eggs and keeps the populace growing. Without her, the colony would die. If you wanted to kill just one ant, it should be the queen. When she survives, the colony just moves to another spot.

Fire ants don't like to be bothered. As too many of us know firsthand, the slightest disturbance sends them

In undisturbed areas fire ants build big mounds; in the yard their mounds may be smaller.

swarming and stinging. If a mound is upset by a lawnmower, a forceful sprinkler, or even an incorrectly applied pesticide, the ants will move beside a walk, under a covered outdoor light, or to any other protected spot.

GETTING RID OF FIRE ANTS

Baits sprinkled around the mounds make the best fire ant killer. Foraging worker ants carry the baits into the nest to feed to the young and the queen. Although slower acting than pesticides poured on the mound, baits are more effective because they usually reach the queen. One bait, Amdro, contains a poison which the ants feed to each other and the queen. It works in one to four weeks, again depending on the time of year. If it's too hot or too cold, the ants will be slow to gather the bait.

Choose a fresh bait because fire ants ignore rancid food. A sealed package stays fresh about two years if kept in a cool, dark, dry place. Never leave a package open or in a hot, humid environment, such as an outdoor toolshed.

Although most experts agree baits are the surest way to eliminate fire ants, if there's a mound by your back steps, you want immediate control. Fire ant killers containing Orthene, Dursban, or Diazinon kill the ants in a nest on contact, but those out foraging won't re-enter. Instead, elsewhere in the yard they'll build satellite mounds that survive for several weeks, even without a queen.

To increase your chances of killing most of the ants, and doing so quickly, apply a bait, and allow two to three days for the ants to distribute it through the mound. Then treat with a fast-acting contact insecticide to eliminate the stinging workers quickly. Contact killers in dust form bear a slight edge over a drench for two reasons: They don't disturb the mound, and they're carried to the depths of the colony on the body of the ant. But don't overapply because it's against Federal law.

Lois Trigg Chaplin

A SUMMARY OF TIPS FOR CONTROL

■ The ideal time to treat a mound is on a sunny day when the temperature is between 60 and 80 degrees and the ground is moist. That is when the ants are near the surface.

■ Do not stir up a mound before sprinkling baits or dusts, or pouring a drench. This will increase the number of ants that escape.

■ Buy bait in small packages, and use within three months after opening. Ants reject stale or rancid bait.

■ Stop new nests by scattering bait about the yard in spring, summer, and fall when winged queens make migratory mating flights. Put the bait in flower-and-shrub beds, by electric lamps, and in other undisturbed places.

PHOTOGRAPH: VAN CHAPLIN

This classic screen is designed to provide a sense of enclosure without completely blocking the house. It helps make the adjacent courtyard feel like a space all its own.

When a Screen Is The Thing

A stucco wall provided privacy for the courtyard at John and Linda Jenkins's home in Jackson, Mississippi. But the area between the courtyard and their traditional home also needed some attention.

Landscape architect Overton Moore of Jackson summed up the problem this way: "They needed something to act as a veil. We tried to soften the house with two identical open screens. They're semitransparent, but also elegant."

Such a screen, built of clear heart redwood and hung from pressure-treated pine 6 x 6s, might give your garden just the effect of seclusion it needs. The Jenkinses' screens are 6 feet tall, and each section is 6 feet wide. (You could modify these dimensions to suit the particular needs of your own project, however.) Short returns at each end of the screen add stability and also enhance the sense of enclosure.

A substantial cap, built up from a redwood 2 x 10 and 2 x 8, gives the screen both strength and a classically stylish look. At the base, a 2 x 6 laid flat and a 2 x 4 laid upright support and finish the grids of 2 x 2s. Redwood stops (1 x 1s) finish the edges where the grids meet the posts, cap, and base of the screen.

Moore chose to paint the screens with colors in keeping with the Jenkinses' home. Though a similar screen could be left to weather naturally, the redwood and pine would eventually have a slightly different appearance.   *Bill McDougald*

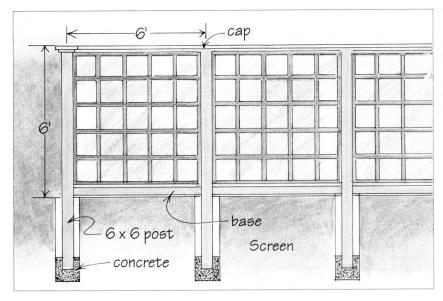

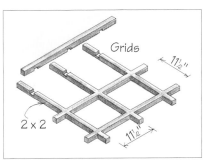

Be a Mustard Master

Has your garden challenged you enough this week? Are you ready to try a sure thing? Here's a vegetable so easy to grow even your neighbor's pet chimpanzee could master it. It's that old Southern favorite, the mustard green.

You may wonder what relationship this vegetable bears to the spicy, yellow condiment you slather on hot dogs and ham sandwiches. That tangy stuff comes from the crushed seeds of pungent, black mustard (*Brassica nigra*)—the mustard cited in the Bible—and tamer-tasting, white mustard (*B. hirta*). However, the greens we value for salads and cooking belong to India mustard (*B. juncea*).

To start mustard greens this spring, you'll need little more than reasonably fertile soil and a sunny spot. Sow seeds ½ inch deep two to four weeks before your last frost. Plant in straight rows, if that suits your sense of order, or in a block to make the most efficient use of space. Seedlings emerge fast; you'll be harvesting in just three to five weeks. A second sowing, two to three weeks after the first, extends the harvest. When hot weather arrives in late spring, mustard greens invariably turn bitter and form flowers, then go to seed. Into the compost bin they go. Plant again in late August to early September for a fall crop.

But don't overdo it. It looks like Julia Anderson (pictured above) grows enough mustard in her Poplarville, Mississippi, garden to feed the National Guard. Truth is, growing gourmet vegetables is her business. For a family of four, however, a 3- x 6-foot patch is plenty.

You can choose from a half-dozen selections. Two that Julia highly recommends are Red Giant, a handsome, red-leaved mustard; and green-leaved Savanna. Within 25 days of sowing, these mild-tasting

As Julia Anderson can tell you, growing mustard greens is a snap. From sowing to harvest takes just three to five weeks.

Tired of all-green vegetable gardens? Try Red Giant, a handsome, cold-tolerant mustard with burgundy-red leaves.

This bright-green mustard, called Savanna, produces baskets of mild-tasting, nutritious leaves in early spring.

greens produce succulent leaves brimming with vitamins A, B, and C.

Mustard belongs to the same family as cabbage and broccoli, so keep an eye out for voracious cabbage worms. To control these pests, spray with *Bacillus thuringiensis* or use floating row covers. Lastly, for the sweetest greens, pick only young leaves, and don't let the soil dry out.

That's it—you're all set. A guaranteed gardening triumph awaits you. But if at any time you feel uncertain how to proceed, don't lose confidence. Just ask the chimp next door.

Steve Bender

PHOTOGRAPHS: VAN CHAPLIN

The Right Tiller for the Job

"Plant in well-tilled, enriched soil." You often read that sentence in our garden articles and checklist every month. Just what does that mean? Hopefully, you'll recall Steve Bender's excellent piece on enriching your soil ("Recipe for Perfect Soil," January 1994, page 34). Now let's talk about that "well-tilled" part.

Putting it simply, tilling the soil fluffs it up, making it easier for roots to grow and develop. And depending on the types of plants you have, that can mean more flowers, fruit, or quicker growth.

But going to your local equipment dealer can be pretty intimidating—which size tiller is right for you? Would you be better off renting one? And what about those new lightweight tillers? Here's a quick rundown of what's on the showroom floor these days.

Rear-tined. These are the big boys of the tiller world. One step up from these and you're sitting on a tractor. As the name describes, the tines—those gnarly things that chew up the soil—are located in the rear. Usually powered by a 5½- to 7- or 8-hp. gasoline engine, these heavy-duty machines are perfect for tackling hard-packed, clay, or rocky soils that smaller machines will just bounce over. Rear-tined tillers sit on top of a pair of large, air-filled tires. Because of their weight, these tillers are almost always self-propelled. If you're breaking new ground and it doesn't want to be broken, this is the machine for you. Expect to pay somewhere between $1,000 and $1,400 for a shiny, new one.

Front-tined. This includes most tillers with gasoline engines from 2½ to 5 hp. The tines are located either directly under or slightly in front of the engine, hence the name. Many models in this category will have a single stabilizing rubber wheel in front or back. "The smaller, front-

Gear-driven 2½ hp.

Lightweight

Front-tined 5 hp.

Rear-tined 8 hp.

tined tillers are great for turning up the soil in flowerbeds, especially if you're putting in lots of annuals," advises Lee Higginbotham of Advanced Mowers in Mountain Brook, Alabama. Prices for the various front-tined models range from about $450 up to about $700, depending on horsepower and manufacturer.

Lightweight. The latest generation of tillers, these small machines weigh in at 20 pounds or so. They are easy to tote around, making them ideal for the home gardener. And their lower cost (about $350) makes them attractive, too. These tillers are for the easiest jobs: weeding (as long as the weeds aren't up to your knees), scratching the soil surface of established flowerbeds prior to setting out seeds or small transplants, and dethatching small lawns. Depending on the model, lightweights have a whole host of attachments available, such as a lawn aerator, edger, and hedge trimmer (about $40 to $140, depending on the type you choose).

Which one is for you? Choosing the right tiller depends on the size of your garden and how you'll use the tiller. Leon Hamrick uses a self-propelled, rear-tined tiller to work in leaves and till the soil for his big vegetable garden in Mountain Brook. Over the years, it's helped transform rocky, red clay into rich soil. For his small in-town garden, Clay Nordan, managing editor of *Southern Living*, uses a lightweight tiller. "I've used the dethatching tines on a compacted lawn that a tree had fallen on, and they worked great," Clay says.

Buying? These things aren't cheap, so it's better to rent or borrow one to see how it works for you. If you plan to use a tiller only once or twice a year, you're better off renting one. Rear-tined tillers are generally more expensive than front-tined models but are easier to control. Also, many tillers have attachments for other yardwork, such as dethatching the lawn. Using a tiller for other jobs will make it easier to justify the expense. *Mark G. Stith*

PHOTOGRAPHS: TINA EVANS

Like the proverbial loaves and fishes, Japanese roof iris multiply miraculously. Five years ago,
Bob Sharman received a dozen plants. Now thousands bloom in his woodland garden.

His Iris Went Forth and Multiplied

"Be fruitful, and multiply." We're reasonably sure this biblical command wasn't aimed at plants. But some took the hint anyway. For proof, check out Bob Sharman's woodland garden in Birmingham. Thousands of Japanese roof iris bloom beneath tall shade trees, covering an area of several thousand square feet. All come from about a dozen plants Bob received from a friend a mere five years ago.

This particular iris (*Iris tectorum*) gets its name from the Japanese superstition of growing it atop thatched roofs to bring good luck. Each April and May, spikes of blue or white blossoms stand 10 to 12 inches tall amid fans of handsome light-green leaves. Roof iris propagates easily enough by division, but Bob says you'll get better and many more plants by gathering and sowing seed.

Bob lets spent flowers form seedpods, then waits till midsummer when the pods turn brown, a sign that the seed is mature. He opens the pods, gathers the seed, then sows them directly into his garden. "I scratch up an area of soil, plant the seeds about ¼ inch deep, and throw the soil back on top of them," he explains.

Spikes of blue or white blossoms stand 10 to 12 inches high amid fans of handsome light-green leaves.

Seedlings emerge in thick stands within two months. Both the blue- and white-flowering forms come true from seed, he notes, but the blue seems to set more seed. When the seedlings reach 2 to 3 inches tall, he separates and transplants them to empty spots in his garden, spacing them about a foot apart. To extend the bloom, he combines them with other plants, such as hellebores, narcissus, Siberian iris, columbine, and daylilies. The garden sparkles from February through June.

Bob says there's no need to coddle roof iris. He doesn't feed them—they get all the nutrients they need from existing soil enriched by years of fallen leaves rotting in place. Neither does he douse them with water or insecticide.

As much as Bob enjoys his iris, he doesn't want any more. "I can grow more each year than a half-dozen neighbors and I can use," he observes, chuckling with astonishment. If you'd like to suffer the same dire fate, we can supply you with a list of mail-order sources. Send a self-addressed, stamped, business-size envelope to Roof Iris, *Southern Living,* P.O. Box 830119, Birmingham, AL 35283.   *Steve Bender*

The Shape of Lawns To Come

The average lawn boasts no more shape than an amoeba. It either links a long chain of neighbors' lawns or it simply grows wherever something else doesn't.

Houston landscape architect David Foresman contends that a lawn should do much more. Treat it as an ornamental ground cover, he implores. Give it a shape, make it a major design element. That's what he did for the home you see here.

This new Regency-style house is what's called a "side-loader." You'll find the front door on the side, next to the parking. This frees the lawn from the need to harbor a front walk and steps. Instead, it becomes a sort of stage for the handsome home behind it. Foresman gave the lawn a symmetrical design, complementing the house's formal architecture. A short, brick wall combined with beds of Asian jasmine frame the lawn, further defining its shape.

Don't overlook the wide brick steps that allow easy access to the lawn. Four or five people could enter side by side. In a backyard, a lawn like this would be perfect for entertaining. But here, it serves as a level, easy-to-maintain playground for the owners' grandchildren.

This example raises some interesting questions. Will more lawns start to look like this? Or will they forever remain amorphous, green blobs? We can't say for sure. But if David Foresman has his way, this example could be the shape of lawns to come.

Steve Bender

Wide brick steps provide easy access to this elegant lawn, which serves as a level playground for the owners' grandchildren.

Beds of Asian jasmine combine with a symmetrical brick border to frame the lawn, emphasizing its shape.

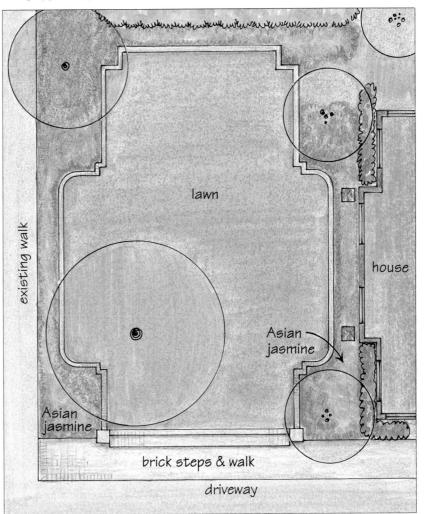

existing walk

lawn

house

Asian jasmine

Asian jasmine

brick steps & walk

driveway

Azaleas in Five Easy Steps

It seems only two kinds of gardeners exist in the South—those who have already planted azaleas and those who are about to. If the latter group includes you, you'll find success largely hinges on attending to five simple things.

#1—SHADE

Azaleas thrive in filtered light under tall shade trees. Protect them from baking afternoon sun. If you lack tall trees and want to plant azaleas next to your house, choose the cooler north and east sides over the south and west sides.

#2—WATER

Azaleas have shallow roots and suffer in prolonged droughts. Regular watering is essential during the summer. If your soil is sandy, you'll probably have to water twice a week during dry spells. For heavier soils, count on watering once a week. Water thoroughly—put the sprinkler out early in the morning, and leave it on for an hour or two.

#3—SOIL

Loose, well-drained, acid soil containing lots of organic matter is your goal. Here's how to provide it.

First, prior to planting, have your soil tested to determine its pH. A local nursery or your state's cooperative Extension service should be able to help you. The ideal pH for azaleas is between 5 and 6. The test results will specify how much sulfur or lime to add to bring the pH into the target range.

Next, use a garden fork or tiller to loosen the soil of your future azalea bed to a depth of at least 1 foot. This lone act dramatically improves soil drainage and aeration. To add the necessary organic matter, spread a layer of sphagnum peat moss (*not* "peat humus") over the soil, and till it in. Use about two 4-cubic-foot bales of sphagnum peat per 100 square feet of bed. Also till in any recommended sulfur or lime.

Sometimes your existing soil is so heavy or rocky that it isn't worth tilling. In this case, use timbers, brick, or stone to construct an 18-inch high raised bed atop the existing soil. Fill it with 18 inches of new soil consisting of 1 part composted pine bark, 1 part sphagnum peat moss, and 1 part coarse builder's sand.

#4—FERTILIZER

While your tiller's handy, seize the opportunity to work some azalea fertilizer into the soil. Cottonseed meal is a good choice, because it acidifies the soil, adds organic matter, attracts earthworms, and releases nutrients gradually. Till in 2 cups per plant.

If you prefer an inorganic, brand-name fertilizer, select one specially formulated for acid-loving plants. Look to see that its nitrogen-phosphorus-potassium ratio is approximately 2-1-1 (fertilizers labeled 10-5-5 or 12-6-6 are good choices). Make sure the fertilizer contains micronutrients, particularly iron, and that at least 33% of its nitrogen is slow release. Apply at the rate recommended on the bag.

#5—MULCH

Okay, you've prepared the soil, spaced your azaleas properly, planted them so that the tops of their root balls are even with the ground, and watered thoroughly. Now for the final step. Apply a 1- to 2-inch layer of pine straw or shredded bark mulch atop the azalea bed. Mulch inhibits weeds, adds organic matter, and helps keep the soil cool and moist. Just as important, it gives the bed a neat, finished look. *Steve Bender*

PHOTOGRAPH: VAN CHAPLIN

Use a garden fork or tiller to loosen the soil of the future azalea bed to a depth of 1 foot; then till in 8 cubic feet of sphagnum peat moss for every 100 square feet of bed.

Spot for A Swing

Some days have laziness in the air. Breathe it in and succumb to a drowsy spring breeze. Amble over to a creaky backyard swing; take a book if your conscience requires it.

An often overlooked spot for a swing is under the deck. Tucked away, a swing can convert wasted space into a quiet escape. Be sure to hang your swing from a well-braced joist (see sketch). The supporting posts should be no smaller than 4 x 4s for one-story decks. Taller decks require 6 x 6s or metal posts.

This homeowner paved the floor beneath the swing for easy maintenance, though you may choose to merely cover bare soil with a layer of mulch. Plywood siding was used to box in the area that houses the swing for a cozy effect.

Whatever finishing touches you choose to add, you won't regret the effort. A sleepy spring day is right around the corner.   *Jo Kellum*

Most homeowners only use the surface of their deck. Hanging a swing below makes the most of available space.

Hang your swing from a joist. Blocking between joists isn't strong enough to support additional weight.

BUILD YOUR OWN

To order plans, send a check for $3.50 (made out to *Southern Living*) and a self-addressed, stamped, business-size envelope to Swing Plans, *Southern Living*, P.O. Box 523, Birmingham, AL 35201. Please allow approximately four to six weeks for delivery.

If you can't find a swing you like, here's one you can build.

A Room Without Walls

BY JO KELLUM

PHOTOGRAPHY VAN CHAPLIN

The old cypress shutters, painted green by a long-forgotten someone and textured by time, were an unlikely inspiration to build a deck. But when the homeowner spotted them in a dusty junk shop, he knew they would be the perfect accent. Architect Wayne Hester worked with the homeowner to create a deck that would return the relics to their former glory.

But there was a catch: The deck had to be small. "I wanted storage space, access to the yard below, and a spot to sit outside," says the homeowner. "All this had to fit along an empty wall between the sunroom and the basement door." To meet these requirements and create a mood appropriate for the shutters, Hester lavished every inch of this small sideyard deck with detail.

WINDOWS OF IMAGINATION

A window is not made of panes of glass, but by what you see through it. Framing views from the deck created open-air windows; hanging the old shutters (which cost between $25 and $50) from the frames created windows of distinction and whimsy.

Builder Craig Simmons boxed in spaces for the frames between 4 x 6 posts. Oversized, the posts are turned so the larger face gives depth to the openings. Flat sills between posts are at elbow level, like real window ledges. The shutters operate for privacy.

(**Opposite page**) *Careful detailing maximizes the look of this 10- x 10-foot deck:* (**Top**) *Antique shutters frame views through open-air windows. Linseed oil preserves the weathered paint.* (**Left**) *Light fixtures recessed between 2 x 8 beams add unobtrusive deck lighting.*

The basement door opens onto a mulched work area. Storage for garden tools is hidden beneath the deck.

The posts also support an arbor. Hester designed it to be the same height as the sunroom ceiling. This gives the deck a charming intimacy and downplays the tall brick house. The overhead lumber is clear cedar, a soft wood suitable for decorative endcuts. Mounted on doubled 2 x 6 rafters, a ceiling fan helps shoo mosquitoes on hot summer evenings.

LIVING LARGE

The deck itself is only 10 feet square. To make it live larger, Simmons built a bench along the outer edge opposite the sunroom doors. The back of the bench is slanted for comfort, but custom 1 x 2 lattice disguises the sloping back from the yard below. The bench leaves the center

(Left) French doors lead from the sunroom to the deck. The arbor continues past the edge of the deck, making it seem larger than it is.

of the deck open; there's room for a removable cafe table and two chairs. The deck seats six to eight adults comfortably.

Just beyond the sunroom doors, steps leading to the yard are positioned for ease of traffic flow. The top step is enlarged to serve as a landing, a spot to pause and admire another shuttered vista. The deck and steps are built of pressure-treated pine for longevity.

ROOM TO SPARE

A storage area for garden tools is cleverly concealed in that often overlooked area beneath the deck. A sheet of corrugated plastic just below the floor of the deck keeps tools dry. The plastic slopes away from the house to shed water. Rakes and shovels slide under the plastic and are held in place by a simple wooden rack. Larger equipment sits on a bed of gravel.

Instead of trying to grow grass right up to the storage space, the homeowner opted for mulch. This created a small work area just outside the basement door.

The spot is hidden by a fence extending from the side of the deck. Vertical 1 x 6s banded with horizontal 1 x 4s give the fence a texture reminiscent of a rusticated stone wall. A matching hinged panel camouflages the storage area.

SOME SUN

Morning sun filters through the shutters until midday; hot afternoon sun is blocked from the west. Because the deck is built on the southeast side of the house, it's pleasant in winter, too.

"The house blocks the northwest wind, which makes the deck a wonderful winter sun trap," says the homeowner. "It's a room without walls that I enjoy year-round." ◇

May

Shade-loving perennials

CHECKLIST FOR MAY

ANNUALS

Set out summer annuals when the danger of frost is past. When buying bedding plants, be sure to look for ones that are *not* in bloom. These will get the best start. You can also sow seeds of zinnias, cosmos, and sunflowers directly into prepared beds.

BLACKBERRIES

Wait until the fruit has darkened completely before picking blackberries (they won't continue to ripen after they've been picked). Prune fruit-bearing canes down to the ground after harvest; then fertilize the plant with ¼ cup of 16-4-8 fertilizer.

CLIMBING ROSES

Prune climbing roses after they finish blooming. Take out old canes and weak, spindly growth. However, if your climbers are only a year or two old, hold off on the pruning until the plants can develop strong, healthy canes.

COLD DAMAGE

Don't be in a hurry to pull out plants damaged by last winter's cold. Wait another month. Even if the top appears dead, you may see signs of life returning from the soil surface. Even when killed to the ground, plants with established root systems grow quickly and often overtake newly planted ones.

CONTAINERS

Fill window boxes, planters, and hanging baskets with a mixture of upright and trailing plants. For example, combine caladiums and a miniature ivy in the shade. Use bedding dahlias and narrowleaf zinnia in the sun.

FERTILIZER

Remember to use a dilute solution of fertilizer at least once each week when watering outdoor containers.

Due to frequent watering, nutrients quickly wash out of the soil. Buy a liquid product formulated for this use. Apply as directed on the label.

FLOWERS

In Florida, plant hot-weather annuals now, including coleus, crossandra, hollyhock, impatiens, kalanchoe, and marigold. Pentas, Madagascar periwinkle, portulaca, verbena, blue daze, and zinnias are other good choices to add color to your yard this month.

FRENCH HYDRANGEAS

Pick blossoms in full color for fresh arrangements. Blue blossoms will fade slightly but will retain most of their hue if picked before they dry on the plant. If picked later, they will fade to lavender or beige.

HERBS

Traditionally these plants were grown near the kitchen door, and that is still the best place. If you don't have a sunny bed nearby, grow them in a pot. Easy-to-grow herbs include basil, thyme, oregano, chives, and parsley. In Florida, plant summer herbs now. Sage, marjoram, ginger, catnip, chives, summer savory, lemon verbena, rosemary, tarragon, mint, and oregano should survive the heat if shaded from afternoon sun.

JAPANESE BEETLES

These metallic-green beetles plague gardens in the Middle and Upper South, and they are moving into the Lower South. You may need to combine methods to control these pests. Use carbaryl on plants that are already infested. Apply milky spore to the lawn and garden soil where the beetle larvae feed on plant roots. If large numbers are

a problem, use traps. Beetle traps use an attractant to lure insects, so be sure to place traps at least 30 feet away from vulnerable plants, or you may unintentionally make matters worse.

LACEBUGS

The mottled leaves on azaleas, pyracantha, and cotoneaster could be a sign of lacebug damage. Lift a few of the leaves and check for black speckles and tiny, silvery-winged insects. Spray the plants with malathion; direct the spray to cover the underside of the leaves. Repeated applications may be necessary.

LAMB'S-EARS

Clip the flower spikes of lamb's-ears for use in fresh flower arrangements. These silvery-stalked, fuzzy-stemmed blooms provide an unusual look with other seasonal flowers. Clipping also takes away the ragged appearance the flowers give the otherwise even-textured ground cover.

LAWNS

Contrary to popular belief, leaving grass clippings on the lawn does not cause thatch. If you are in the market for a new mower this spring, consider a mulching mower. It's designed to cut clippings into small pieces and blow them into the lawn. One thing to remember: With a mulching mower, you need to mow often enough so that you're only removing one-third of the grass blade's height each time you mow your lawn at the correct height for your grass. If you can't mow that often, you should stick with a bagging type. In Texas, now's the time to establish warm-season lawns, such as St. Augustine, Bermuda, centipede, and buffalo grass.

Make sure the area has been tilled and raked smooth, regardless

BY STEVE BENDER
PHOTOGRAPHY VAN CHAPLIN

"Tell me," I said to the old Zen master seated on a pallet in a Buddhist shrine. "Why do Southerners love zinnias?"

"Ah, Grasshopper," the master replied, "your eyes are open, but they do not see. Does not the philosophy of Zen teach us to achieve enlightenment through meditation? And have you not spoken with many wise gardeners who know the rapture of moist, well-drained soil? Hear their words, see their faces. The answer," he said, touching first his forehead and then his chest, "lies both here and here."

The telephone rang. I awoke with a start. Wow—that's the last time I watch back-to-back reruns of "Kung Fu" and "Victory Garden." But you know, there just might be something to this Zen thing. Maybe if I meditate like the master said, the source of zinnias' popularity might be revealed.

OOOOOMMMmmmmm. Wait a minute, wait a minute—I've got it.

Revelation #1:
Zinnias Are Southern

Okay, so zinnias really originated in Mexico, their flowers started out lavender, and the plants were so scrag-

gly that Spanish conquistadors lovingly referred to them as *mal de ojos* ("eyesore"). Point is, ever since the improved, double-flowering types first appeared around 1856, they've been in our gardens. "They're nostalgic," observes zinnia fancier Harvilee Harbarger in Huntsville, Alabama. "They're something you remember from your childhood."

Revelation #2:
Zinnias Make Us Feel Good

No annuals outdo the big-flowered zinnias (*Zinnia elegans*) in terms of sheer eye-popping spectacle. Their warm, sunny colors chase away thoughts of overdue bills, school projects, and a family car with so many rust holes in it that birds fly through. From her home in Poplarville, Mississippi, Julia Anderson sums it up this way: "It's hard to have a bouquet of zinnias in your house or look at a row of them in your garden and feel unhappy." Amen.

Revelation #3:
Zinnias Are Simple To Grow

Unlike seeds of petunias, begonias, impatiens, and other flowers, seeds of zinnias are large and easy to sow. Planted in full sun when the outside air reaches 70 to 80 degrees, they come up quickly, usually within a week. Such immediate gratification makes zinnias good flowers for beginners. "They're great plants to start children out with," notes Julia. Grownups, too.

Many gardeners believe zinnias do better when sown directly into the garden. Each year around April 1, Harvilee mixes seeds of different colors together in a brown paper bag. Then she sprinkles them by hand into a pair of furrows 8 inches wide and 24 inches apart atop a raised bed. She barely covers the seed with soil. Julia, on the other hand, likes to set out transplants because mole crickets and beetle larvae often eat seedlings in her garden. She spaces her favorite tall-growing zinnias, called State Fair, 20 inches apart.

Zinnias aren't fussy but perform better in fertile soil. Harvilee tills shredded leaves into her beds each year. Julia enriches her soil with several different kinds of organic matter. In Chapel Hill, Texas, Carolyn Zimmermann—who, according to friends, grows zinnias taller than Shaquille O'Neal—works kitchen compost, wheat straw, and composted manure into the soil.

Any supplementary fertilizer should be relatively low in nitrogen and higher in phosphorus. Harvilee sprinkles 5-10-5 alongside her plants once in spring and again in summer. Julia prefers several feedings of slow-release, organic fertilizer. Carolyn doesn't fertilize at all. Take your pick.

Revelation #4:
The More You Cut Them, The More They Bloom

Just as children need discipline, zinnias need cutting. Otherwise, they'll go to seed, stop blooming, and die. Harvilee grows more zinnias than

she can use, so she opens her garden to supper club and sewing club friends. "Everyone plans their picnics around my zinnias," she says. "I do ask them, though, to cut a few dead ones while they're cutting all those good ones."

Revelation #5:
Zinnias Are Unpretentious

Don't worry about offending polite society with intemperate, uncultured displays. When it comes to zinnias, throw away the rule book. Plant a solid mass of one color if that suits you. Or mix all the colors together (just between you, me, and Billy Bob, they look better that way). Also, when searching for a container to hold cut zinnias, don't bury your nose in hoity-toity catalogs that sell $150 solid copper watering cans. Zinnias look good in almost any container. "You can put them in something fancy," declares Julia, "or you can put them in a Coke bottle."

Revelation #6:
Perfection Isn't Required

Even with the most meticulous care, zinnias grow a bit ragged by August, as mildew and other nasties corrupt the foliage. But everybody's plants look this way, which takes the pressure off. However, if you're determined to reduce disease, there are two good ways to do it. First, keep cutting those flowers. Thinning your plants improves air circulation and dries the foliage. Second, never wet the foliage while watering. Harvilee and Carolyn use soaker hoses to wet the soil. Julia likes drip irrigation.

Revelation #7:
You Can Even Save Seeds for Next Year

Every September, Carolyn cuts spent flowers of each color of zinnia she wants. She dries them in her attic on a piece of screen. Then she pulls the flowers apart and stores the seeds in zip-top, plastic bags. Such seed-saving pleases the skinflint in all of us. More importantly, it keeps heirloom varieties in circulation, ensuring that zinnias of the father will be visited upon the son.

"You see, Grasshopper," intoned the old master. "You knew the truth all the time. Now you must teach it to all of your faithful readers. They too must contemplate the Zen of zinnias."

All together now—OOOOOOO-OOOMMMMMMMmmmmmmm. ◇

Once the soil is properly prepared, be sure to space the plants the appropriate distance apart. Correct spacing ensures that the hedge will fill in after a few years.

Dig the hole at least 1½ times the size of the container to promote good growth.

When the planting is complete, add a soaker hose and a 4-inch layer of pine straw mulch.

HOLLIES FOR HEDGES

Holly	Height *	Spacing
Burford	12 to 15 ft.	3½ to 4 ft.
Dwarf Burford	6 to 8 ft.	2 to 3 ft.
Foster's No. 2	16 to 18 ft.	2 to 4 ft.
Greenleaf	14 to 16 ft.	3 to 5 ft.
Hetz	5 to 6 ft.	2 to 2½ ft.
Nellie R. Stevens	10 to 12 ft.	3 to 4 ft.
San Jose	8 to 10 ft.	3 ft.
Savannah	10 to 14 ft.	4 to 5 ft.
Willowleaf	5 to 6 ft.	2 to 3 ft.
Yaupon	10 to 12 ft.	3 to 4 ft.

*Height after 6 to 8 years, assuming 3-gallon-size plant installed

How-to for Holly Hedges

Most homeowners have, want, or need a hedge. If you are in the want or need group, following are a few guidelines to help make installing a hedge easier.

First, measure your space and determine the size of the hedge you need. With proper plant selection, you can grow just about any size without shearing it every time you turn around. For the hedge shown here, we used a 4- to 5-foot Willowleaf holly (see chart for other good selections).

Once location and plant type are decided, soil preparation is the key to making sure the plants grow well and evenly. If sod is present, remove it. Till the soil to at least 1½ times the depth of the plants' containers.

After the soil has been thoroughly tilled, amend it. If your soil is on the clay side, add enough sand and peat moss to raise the planting bed 2 to 4

inches. (If the area does not drain well, mound the soil at least 4 inches.) If your soil is on the sandy side, add peat moss or other organic matter to help it hold water. In either case, till again to mix in the amendments. Oftentimes, at this stage, it is okay to wait before planting the hedge. In fact, some people prefer to wait weeks to let the soil settle.

Once you are ready to plant, decide the spacing of the hollies; before digging the holes, mark each spot or place plants the desired distance apart. Dig the hole at least 1½ times the size of the container. Gently remove the plant from the pot. Make sure that you do not pull on the trunk because this can damage the root ball. Once the hole is dug and the plant is in place, add 1 tablespoon of Osmocote (20-10-5) to the bottom of the hole, and then fill it with soil. Make sure the soil line is level with

the previous soil line of the plant.

Water well, and pack the soil around the root ball. Because the bed is raised, you will need to water the plant again prior to mulching and throughout the season. One of the best ways is to install a soaker hose under the mulch. This allows water to slowly soak into the ground. It also is an efficient use of water and an easy way to keep these plants watered for years to come. Once the soaker hose is down, mulch heavily; at least 4 inches is best.

Now that you have finished, stand back and look at your handiwork. This is a good time to decide if any shoots look out of place and need pruning. With good maintenance practices, such as regular watering, fertilizing, and annual shaping to remove stray branches, your hedge should be an asset for many years.

John F

(Before) *The tiny (850 square feet) backyard of Wade and Debbie Martin's older home was a cozy space but too cluttered to be its best.*

(After) *A new brick terrace and raised, wooden deck make the same backyard look larger than life. A 6-foot-high fence adds security and style; the gate at left leads to a storage area. The air conditioners are hidden by the low brick wall topped with a pergola.*

A Terrace in Tight

What do you do with a basic, boxy, bland backyard? Owners Wade and Debbie Martin weren't sure, but they certainly wanted to enjoy theirs in an older neighborhood in Charlotte. That's why they contacted landscape architect Brian Zimmerman for some professional advice.

"You can do anything back there," Wade said, "Just so I don't have to mow it." Given pretty much a free hand to design a new look for the old yard, Brian allowed the site to dictate what would work. Three shade trees located near the back property line were essential to cooling off the back~~~ The tight quarters made ~~~nce a must. Oh yes, and

~~~ainstorming resulted in a ~~~ing area enclosed with a ~~~ fence that's cleverly ~~~ the trees. At the back

corner of the house is a small storage unit; a low brick wall and pergola extend along the back of the house from the storage area to the deck.

Now, that sounds fairly straightforward, but it's the little details that make all the difference. The fence, for example, has ¼-inch spaces between the vertical members to allow breezes in and still keep curious eyes out. The back edge of the raised deck is trimmed with a 6-inch-high curb rail to prevent things like serving carts from tumbling off into the shrubs. The decking lumber was set at an angle that parallels the zigzagged rear fence. Both the fence and pergola were painted gloss white to match the house and further the illusion of spaciousness.

The Martins are now free to relax either on the deck or the brick patio, which together provide lots of room

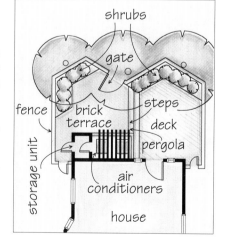

for outdoor entertaining. And they can do so without making sitting out a spectator sport. Neighbors may hear the murmur of pleasant conversation, or the sizzle of steaks on the grill, or an occasional bark from the Martins' bulldog, Digby. But they'll never hear growling from a lawnmower—or from Wade.

Mark G. Stith

A large terra-cotta bowl filled with a hardy water lily (Texas Dawn), water hyacinths, variegated sweet flag, and dwarf arrowhead perfectly accents a deck or patio.

Wet and Wonderful

■ Compromise was the inspiration for making this container water garden—actually, a couple of them. First compromise: I do love water gardens and envy those who have them. But I really couldn't see putting one in my sloping backyard.

■ Second compromise: I had seen several quite attractive container water garden kits, but they were too expensive. After calling around to experienced water gardeners and getting some advice, I decided to try putting one together. Here's what I learned in the process.

■ Buying your own pots and plants costs less than purchasing most kits. I used a 24-inch terra-cotta pot that worked fine.

■ It's better to go with a container that does not have a drainage hole. I sealed the hole in my pot with a waterproof concrete patch used for sealing mortar cracks in concrete or cinder block walls. It worked fine,

but another clay pot I patched the same way didn't work as well. Many nurseries that sell water garden plants also sell containers especially for water gardens. Some also have plastic liners to fit in oak half-barrels.

■ The inside of the pot was coated with a clear sealer of the type used to coat wooden decks. Would this be toxic to plants, fish, and snails? I just made sure the sealer had dried completely before adding any plants and critters. To my delight, neither fish nor foliage cried "foul!" I also used a clear masonry sealer product with another container—no problem there either. Mail-order garden plant suppliers also sell a black, rubber-based sealer for this purpose.

■ What plants are recommended? Hardy water lilies are best, according to Chuck Thomas of Aquatic Gardens in Birmingham. "They're smaller than tropical water lilies and will do quite well in a container," he says. Other good plants include parrot feather, water hyacinth, dwarf arrowhead, water clover, and sweet flag. Just don't overdo it: a composition of three or four, with the water lily as the centerpiece, is plenty. You may have to put a brick under the plant to set it at the correct height. Most hardy water lilies like to be about 3 inches deep.

■ The container was perched on my deck to get nearly full sun, and the plants and water were added. Topping it off with water occasionally and feeding the plants with a fertilizer tablet monthly was all the work required. I never had a problem with mosquitoes (there are special "doughnuts" you can buy to control them).

One delightful bonus was that the container became the local "watering hole" for birds, squirrels, and even our cocker spaniel. That could explain why the goldfish we bought stayed hidden under the lily pads (we eventually gave him to a good home).

■ What do you do in the winter? Terra-cotta doesn't take to constant freezing and thawing. So it's better to drain the pot and store it indoors. Hardy water lilies can stay outside as long as their roots aren't frozen, but you'd have to use a container that won't crack in the cold and is deep enough (in our area, about 18 inches) to never freeze solid.

Waterproof concrete mix serves as a patch for the drainage hole of the bowl.

Water sealer applied to the inside of the pot prevents water damage.

After the sealer dries thoroughly, the plants find a home.

Keeping the container in a protected area or covering it with canvas or thick plastic stretched over a couple of boards can help. You can store hardy (and tropical) water lilies indoors; just trim off their leaves and stems, and keep them in a cool area. The roots need to be moist constantly.

One thing is for certain: My container water garden may have started out as a compromise, but the results were grand. *Mark G. Stith*

Fertilizing the Right Way

Fertilizing your lawn is such an easy and rewarding garden chore. When you do it right, there's the pride in knowing that your efforts produced that lush green lawn the neighbors admire. And today's slow-release fertilizers can feed your lawn over an entire season, making lawn fertilizing a one-time affair. But there are some common mistakes people make when fertilizing their lawns. Here are some dos and don'ts:

Don't "feed the chickens." It's tempting, it's money-saving, but it's a big mistake to think you can spread fertilizer evenly by hand. That works fine for Old MacDonald tossing cracked corn to the hens and chicks, but won't do for your lawn. What you'll probably end up with are a bunch of deep-green patches where the handful hit the ground. Use a spreader (like the one shown in the picture) or a hose-end sprayer.

Be a better spreader. Let's say you've read the directions on the bag and have figured you'll need to put out two bags of fertilizer on your lawn. First, make sure your spreader opening is set to the right number. (This is usually recommended by brand name on the fertilizer bag. If it isn't, just go with a lower setting than you think you'll need.) It's best to apply half the fertilizer in parallel paths across the lawn, then the other half in paths that crisscross at a 90-degree angle. That way, you'll avoid the "American flag" look of dark-green strips of grass next to light ones.

Know your hose-end sprayer. Those plastic containers which fit on the end of your garden hose are good for getting a quick green-up before the in-laws come to visit. Some of the newer types come pre-mixed with fertilizer, so all you do is screw the container on the end of your hose and spray the lawn. Remember that liquid fertilizers feed the lawn all at once, so you'll probably need to reapply several times during the growing season to keep that beautiful green look.

Pace yourself. It's pretty alarming to see the hopper almost empty after you've only completed one strip of the lawn, or the hose-end sprayer with just a half inch of juice left—and

you've just done one corner of the yard. If possible, "test drive" your spreader on the driveway or sidewalk before going out on the lawn (rinse or sweep off the fertilizer afterwards). For a hose-end sprayer, give the lawn a quick once-over to see how fast the container empties. You can always go back and pour it on with a second pass.

Water, water. Water the lawn after applying granular fertilizer. Never apply granular fertilizer when your lawn is wet, such as in the early morning when the grass is covered with dew. That may sound contradictory, but watering the lawn washes the fertilizer granules down to the soil. If the lawn is already wet, fertilizer clings to the blades of grass. When the job is finished, be sure to wash out the hopper. Fertilizer is corrosive to any metal parts on your spreader and can build up deposits that can clog or ruin your feeder. Rinse out hose-end sprayers, too.

Now, sit back and watch the neighbors drive by and slow down to ogle your lush green lawn. *Mark G. Stith*

A drop spreader will help you get an even distribution of fertilizer on your lawn. Make sure the spreader opening is set properly before applying fertilizer.

Brazos penstemon is a native of Texas, Louisiana, and Arkansas. It tolerates a variety of growing conditions and makes a dependable showing in spring.

Although no relation to true foxglove (Digitalis sp.), wild foxglove thrives in Texas gardens and pastures.

From Nature To the Garden

Every garden flower began as a wildflower. Someone saw it, dug it up, and planted it outside his door. One gardener shared it with another until it reached a region where it did not grow wild, and the wildflower became a cultivated plant. Penstemon (PEN-sti-mun) is a good example.

Texans have several native species. Two of the best for the garden are wild foxglove (*Penstemon cobaea*) and Brazos penstemon (*P. tenuis*). Both of these are in full bloom this month at the Antique Rose Emporium in Brenham, Texas. Owner Mike Shoup observes that the Brazos penstemon is the easier one to grow. "I'd call it garden friendly, because too much water doesn't bother it. It ranges from areas with alkaline soil to those that are more acid."

Although its flowers are much smaller than those of wild foxglove, Brazos penstemon has more of them,

and each plant grows several flower stalks. The purple-pink flowers on branched stalks grow up to 2 feet tall. If cut back after the flowers fade, the plants may bloom a second time, but they will not be as full of flowers.

Although Brazos penstemon can be grown from seeds sown in winter, gardeners with established plants can transplant volunteer seedlings that appear in the garden or divide rosettes in early spring or late fall.

Wild foxglove can be found growing in hot, dry Texas pastures where bluebells grow. These areas are typically alkaline and well drained. Consequently, wild foxgloves perform best in sunny gardens with well-drained soil and no crowding from nearby plants. Gardeners can collect seeds in the fall, refrigerate them until January, and sow them outdoors. Plants are also available in some nurseries. They will not bloom the first spring,

but will remain rosettes of foliage, like leaf lettuce. They will then bloom the second spring, as well as the third, and possibly the fourth. Although perennial, plants are short-lived. It pays to let the seeds mature on the plant and to scatter them in the garden to produce new ones.

Borne on stems 18 to 24 inches tall, the flowers of wild foxglove vary in color from white to pink to purple, blooming like a big bouquet on each stem. Blooms last up to six weeks in the middle of spring.

Of the two Texas species, Brazos penstemon adapts better to Southeast gardens and naturally ranges into Arkansas and Louisiana. However, the Southeast is not without its preferred penstemon.

Ken Moore of the University of North Carolina Botanical Garden in Chapel Hill recommends *Penstemon smallii,* a native of rocky cliffs in the mountains of North Carolina, Tennessee, South Carolina, and Georgia. Its blooms resemble those of Brazos penstemon, except the flower stalks keep some of the leaves from the rosette as they grow taller. With multiple flower stalks, plants reach 2 to 2½ feet tall and 2 feet wide and the show lasts for about a month.

Like its Texas cousin, *Penstemon smallii* is short-lived, but will reseed, particularly in a gravelly soil. Although tolerant of up to a half-day of shade, it will rot if surrounded by moist, organic mulch. Keep the rosettes uncovered in winter; the burgundy winter foliage is worth seeing.

Linda C. Askey

This Pool Is A Natural

You've heard it before. "We want a pool; we just don't want it to *look* like a pool." You know—the white-bordered, blue-rectangle variety. Fun to swim in, sure. But let's face it, not much fun to look at.

That's just how San Antonio residents Gary and Janet Beahm felt about putting in a pool when their new home was being built. "We wanted a pool at our new house," recalls Janet, "but with more of a pond effect. Gary also wanted a fountain and a hot tub."

For help with such a tall order, the Beahms asked landscape architect Terry Lewis to devise a pool and outdoor entertainment area that met all their needs. "I really wanted to get as far away from a rectangular pool as possible," he recalls. The pool's final shape, which loosely resembles a dumbbell, is a pleasing departure from plain old pool geometry.

But just as important as the pool's shape are the materials used in its construction. "I usually don't use flagstone around pools when the house is brick, but I found some stones that were the exact colors of the house," Lewis says. In addition, large moss rocks are laid around the pool and in raised planting beds near the house. A series of three waterfalls spills down a simulated outcropping of boulders and into the pool.

The 10- x 20-foot cabana, located at the far corner of the pool, also avoids that added-on appearance. The cabana's brick columns and gray-concrete roof tiles blend with the house. "The cabana is the perfect place for entertaining and cooking out," notes Janet.

In fact, Lewis may have made the Beahms' pool look a little *too* much like a pond. "This spring, we had a pair of mallard ducks come visit," Janet says with a laugh. "They even crawled up in the rocks and made a nest." *Mark G. Stith*

(**Above**) *Large boulders, lush plantings, and soft-toned brick and flagstone make this pool and cabana look natural and inviting.*

(**Left**) *Huge moss rocks, collected from the surrounding area, were set among the flagstone, reinforcing the pond effect.*

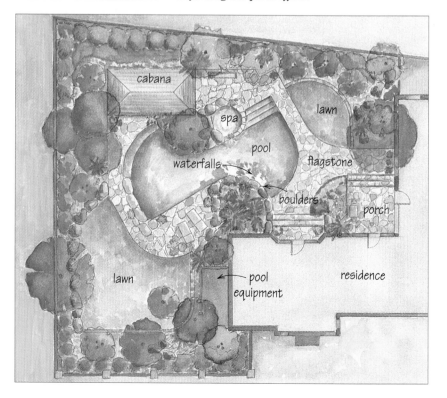

cabana

spa

lawn

pool

waterfalls

flagstone

boulders

porch

lawn

pool equipment

residence

(**Right**) *A narrow planting area and windowless walls made Confederate jasmine the perfect choice for dressing up this small deck. A trellis supports the vine.*

(**Above**) *Profuse flowers are best known for their fragrance. They are in bloom for six to eight weeks in late spring.*

Sweet-Smelling Confederate Jasmine

Confederate jasmine—now that's a Southern name! This woody vine twines around whatever is handy, making it an excellent choice to grow on trellises, arbors, fences, lightposts, and mailboxes. Each April and May, the vine is hung with tiny star-shaped blooms. The creamy petals are pretty, but the real attraction is the fragrance—a heady perfume that lingers through the muggy spring days of the Lower and Coastal South.

Confederate jasmine (*Trachelospermum jasminoides*) grows in a thick tangle, so trim renegade shoots in the spring and summer to keep the plant neat. It may also be grown as a ground cover, but upright shoots must be removed to keep the vine horizontal. (Asian jasmine—*Trachelospermum asiaticum*—lacks the trademark fragrance but stays compact, making it a better choice for ground cover.)

Confederate jasmine's glossy foliage stays green year-round, unless temperatures dip below freezing. Cold-damaged leaves will turn brown and cling to the stems, but the roots usually survive. Cut injured plants back to the ground in early spring to stimulate growth. In areas prone to cold weather, plant the vine in a protected area, such as a walled courtyard. Or plant in a container you can move inside. And be prepared for everyone to ask in the spring, "What smells so good?"   *Jo Kellum*

> ## CONFEDERATE JASMINE AT A GLANCE:
> **Foliage:** Evergreen
> **Blooms:** White, late spring
> **Soil:** No specific requirements
> **Light:** Sun to partial shade
> **Salt tolerant:** No
> **Range:** Lower and Coastal South

White Nancy lamium and white and pink forms of fringed bleeding heart combine handsomely in the shade.

This Richmond garden reveals how richly planted a shaded area can be.

Perennials For the Shade

Too often gardeners shun the shade. They bemoan the fact that nothing will grow there, and if it does, it doesn't have much color. Well, the shade border of Pooh and Bill Steele of Richmond challenges the naysayers, revealing a rich palette of colors.

The foliage of the Steeles' shade border ranges from silver to blue to gold. Most prominent is the metallic silver of White Nancy lamium. Its white flowers—along with the mottled silver foliage of strawberry geranium and Japanese painted fern—are perfect complements to its silver leaves.

The strawberry geranium produces a cloud of small white flowers that hovers among the pink of fringed bleeding heart. Although its foliage resembles a fern, fringed bleeding heart carries a profusion of pink or white flowers in spring, followed by a sprinkling of flowers throughout the summer and fall. The foliage is a delicate gray green that would be worthwhile in itself, but with its flowers, it's a champion.

Not to be overlooked are the bold leaves of Elegans and Frances Williams hostas. They are tall and visually demanding enough to command attention beyond the delicacies that grow before them. And around the trunk of a dogwood stand numerous ferns, many of which were collected from the woods on Pooh's grandmother's country home.

Grouped in green sweeps of a single kind, the perennials chosen for this shady border make a statement with their mass. The pattern of each variety is also distinctly different from the adjacent leaves. Thus, the perennials are distinguished by the color of their foliage and flowers and by their texture.

"We've never had a real plan; it sort of evolved," says Pooh. "When we go to the mountains, we bring things from Andre Viette's nursery. And we order from Wayside Gardens. As we see things, we buy them and put them in. And if we don't like the way they look, we move them."

After refining the design over several seasons, Pooh thinks this shade border is one of her nicest. But no garden is static, and her secret to keeping it going is to keep digging. "I am constantly digging up pieces and giving them to people," she says.

One reason the plants grow so vigorously is the care they receive. Each February Bill pitches a load of rotted manure onto the garden beds about 2 inches deep. This builds up organic matter in the soil, keeping it loose and moist while supplying nutrients to the plants. As the new spring growth emerges, he adds mulch around the plants. *Linda C. Askey*

PERENNIALS FOR SHADE
White Nancy lamium
  (*L. maculatum* White Nancy)
Fringed bleeding heart
  (*Dicentra eximia*)
Strawberry geranium
  (*Saxifraga stolonifera*)
Frances Williams hosta
  (*H. sieboldiana* Frances Williams)
Elegans hosta
  (*H. sieboldiana* Elegans)
Maidenhair fern
  (*Adiantum* sp.)
Japanese painted fern
  (*Athyrium nipponicum* Pictum)
Cinnamon fern
  (*Osmunda cinnamomea*)
Virginia bluebells
  (*Mertensia virginica*)

Don't Give Up On Roses

Sooner or later, most gardeners try their hand at growing roses. And sooner or later, most gardeners are sorry they didn't realize the amount of work involved.

That's because roses fall victim to a number of pests that ruin their appearance. But don't despair. Here are five of the most common pests, along with some easy, effective ways to control them.

1. Problem—Black spots on leaves. Leaves turn yellow, then drop. Plant loses vigor and blooms sparsely.

Pest—Black spot

Solution—Spray foliage every 7 to 10 days throughout growing season with Funginex or Daconil fungicide. Do not water with sprinklers. Rake up and destroy fallen leaves. Spray entire plant with lime-sulfur dormant spray in late winter. Apply 1 to 2 inches of fresh mulch atop rose bed each spring.

2. Problem—Yellow streaks or blotches on leaves. Leaves may curl. Flowerbuds may be malformed. Plants may become stunted.

Pest—Rose virus

Solution—Virus is transmitted during grafting or budding at the nursery. It rarely spreads from plant to plant in the home garden. There is no successful way to control this virus with chemicals. Remove and destroy an infected plant if it becomes too weak to bloom properly.

3. Problem—White or gray powdery coating on leaves, stems, and flowerbuds. Leaves curl and drop. New growth is stunted. Flowerbuds do not open.

Pest—Powdery mildew

Solution—Spray foliage with Funginex fungicide at first sign of mildew. Spray again at intervals of 7 to 10 days if mildew reappears. Rake up and destroy fallen leaves.

4. Problem—Devoured flowers. Holes chewed in flowerbuds. Foliage

Black spot

Rose virus

Powdery mildew

Japanese beetle

eaten until only leaf veins remain. Plant loses vigor.

Pest—Japanese beetle

Solution—Spray flowers and foliage with carbaryl once a week from June until September. It is best to spray during evening to avoid killing bees. Do not rely on beetle traps. They will not prevent damage to your plants.

5. Problem—Some flowerbuds expand, then fail to open. Petals of open blossoms develop brown streaks or edges. Young green leaves become distorted and speckled with yellow.

Pest—Thrips

Solution—Remove and destroy infested blooms and buds. Spray flowers, buds, and foliage with Orthene insecticide three times at intervals of 7 to 10 days.   *Steve Bender*

Thrips

Build a Trellis for a Garden Wall

This simple trellis attractively frames a vine against a wall. The basic plan for the trelliswork is a 12-inch open grid that may be easily doubled or tripled to suit the proportions of your wallspace.

At the home of Linda and Bob Bible in Pawleys Island, South Carolina, narrow trellises flank the entrance to a garden storage house. Opposite the storage house, a trellis built from the same basic plan (but three times as wide) fills a proportionately wider wallspace.

Landscape architect Robert Chesnut of Charleston says, "To keep the trellises from appearing too close to the house, we mounted them on brackets or pieces of wood that project at least 3 inches from the house. This placement creates interesting shadows, adds a feeling of depth, and gives room for vines to twine around the trelliswork." A low-voltage lighting fixture positioned below each trellis creates dramatic shadow effects at night.

You can construct the trellises of 1 x 2s or 1 x 3s made of redwood, cypress, or a No. 1 grade of pressure-treated pine. Use wood glue and galvanized nails or wood screws for joining the pieces of wood. Plan for the bottom of each trellis to rest directly on the ground.

When it's time to repaint the wall on which you've mounted the trellis, the brackets may be easily detached from the house, the vines kept intact, and the trellis laid on the ground during painting.   *Julia H. Thomason*

Planted in evergreen wisteria, a narrow trellis adds interest to wallspace beside the entrance to this garden storage house.

Blooms That Aren't Bashful

WALLFLOWER
AT A GLANCE

Light: Sun or partial shade
Soil: Loose, fertile, moist
Water: During dry spells
Pests: None serious
Propagation: Sow seeds in spring or late summer for blooms next year.

We all know a *human* wallflower isn't exactly the life of the party. But the plant version does anything but fade into the crowd. Siberian wallflower's golden-hued blooms are among the liveliest of the spring flowers. What's more, the fragrant blossoms keep on going after the spring bulbs and other cool-season characters have pooped out.

"Mine get about a foot tall and are absolutely a mass of gold, yellow, and orange flowers," says Ruth Mitchell of Griffin, Georgia. "They look great with tulips like Olympic Flame [yellow petals flamed with red] or even a white tulip." Wallflowers also look good with forget-me-nots, primroses, pansies, and blue phlox. Ruth says the effect is much like a ground cover, so wallflowers are a good choice for borders or in a windowbox or other container.

Siberian wallflower (*Erysimum allionii*; it goes by several scientific names) is a close cousin to the popular English wallflower (*Cheiranthus cheiri*) but performs better in the South. In Ruth's Lower South garden (about as far South as wallflower will grow), the flowers last until June. Middle and Upper South gardeners can expect sporadic blooming through the summer, especially on plants in sunny spots. And even though the plant is listed as a short-lived perennial, it reseeds freely, so once you've got it, you've got it.

To make sure she has plants in bloom next spring, Ruth will sow seeds in flats in late summer and set out the plants in late November. Or you can sow seeds in spring and set them out later, but flowers won't appear until next year. Space plants about 8 to 12 inches apart in partial shade or full sun. They'll do great on a hillside; avoid low, wet areas.

Glasnost Mixed, a new selection, has pastel-colored flowers of lemon, apricot, cream, tangerine, gold, and lilac. *Mark G. Stith*

Wallflower fires up the spring flower border with long-lasting, fragrant blooms that cover the compact plants.

*Of course they have a nice garden.
They own a nursery.*

Work Is Their Pleasure

BY LINDA C. ASKEY / PHOTOGRAPHY SYLVIA MARTIN

Only eight years ago David Lichtenfelt was an attorney. His wife, Deborah, worked for South Carolina Vocational Rehabilitation. But the call of childhood memories in the country turned their lives around.

They started Lichtenfelt Nurseries in Greenville, South Carolina. And then they planned a garden for their home. "People ask, 'How can you work with plants all day and want to go home and deal with them?'" says David. "But Deborah and I both enjoy gardening. During the long days of summer we go home and spend a couple of hours in the evening—until it's too dark to work out there. You know how it is with gardening; it doesn't seem like work if you enjoy it."

In addition to their home garden, they have display gardens at their nursery, where they offer seminars on Saturday mornings. "One of the seminars is a tour called Open House

(**Left**) *An arbor draped by wisteria provides a restful vantage point. An antique iron fence panel creates the illusion of a window into the garden beyond.*
(**Right**) *A stone terrace, dominated by a river birch, serves as both the entry and the crossroads of the garden.*

A rectangular garden of vegetables and herbs features a center walk lined with garlic chives that will bloom in late summer.

fire pit in the middle," says Peeples.

David and Deborah take advantage of their home garden to learn about the shade-loving plants that won't grow in their sunny gardens at the nursery. They also take cuttings and divisions from the garden to sell at the nursery. But most of all, their garden is a pleasure shared with each other, and with their customers. ◇

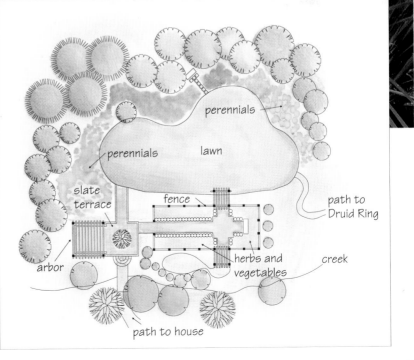

perennials

perennials   lawn

slate terrace

fence

path to Druid Ring

arbor

herbs and vegetables

creek

path to house

June

Freshly harvested vegetables

CHECKLIST FOR JUNE

ANNUALS
You still have time to set out summer bedding plants, even in the Lower South. Keep them watered until the roots grow into the surrounding soil. Plants in full sun will benefit from the temporary shade of pine needles sprinkled lightly over the transplants. Throughout the state of Florida, set out transplants of coleus, ornamental pepper, red salvia, marigolds, gomphrena, and portulaca. It's not too late to add impatiens if you plant them in the shade and water them frequently.

AZALEAS
Feed plants with an acid-forming fertilizer, such as 11-5-5; the same product can also be used on camellias and gardenias. Apply as directed on the label. If the leaves are yellow with green veins, apply iron chelate (Greenol), or treat the surrounding soil with aluminum sulfate.

BEDDING PLANTS
In Florida, cut back salvia and impatiens left over from last year for more blooms. Trim each plant about 6 to 8 inches shorter than the desired height, and feed with a water-soluble fertilizer, such as Peters, Miracle-Gro, or Pro-Sol. In Texas, to stimulate more blooms, remove faded flowers on marigolds, salvia, and other colorful annuals. With coleus and caladiums, however, it's the foliage you want. Pinch off their flowers to encourage lush, leafy plants.

CUTTING GARDEN
Roses, annuals, and perennials need a boost after the first round of flowering. Apply a cup of granular fertilizer (5-10-10) per square yard, or water every two weeks with a soluble fertilizer.

FLEA BEETLES
They hop like fleas but feed on vegetables and leaves. Apply carbaryl or rotenone at the first sign of damage; repeat treatment as needed. Remove debris from the garden after harvest to keep flea beetles from overwintering.

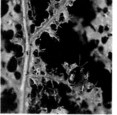

FLOWERING SHRUBS
Prune azaleas now in South Florida; trim azaleas in North and Central Florida by the end of the month. Trim gardenias lightly after blooming. To fill in gaps in the foliage, cut tips of shoots to encourage branching.

FLOWERS
Set out transplants of heat-tolerant flowering plants, including zinnias, salvia, cleome, and cosmos. This is also a good time to plant mums, asters, firebush, and fall salvia for colorful flowers in autumn.

HURRICANE PROTECTION
In Florida, remove dead or damaged limbs from large trees before hurricane season begins. Delay cutting healthy branches, if possible; pruning encourages new growth, which may be susceptible to high winds.

LAWN
Bermuda, St. Augustine, and Zoysia lawns are due for their second feeding. Apply a good quality granular fertilizer that contains at least 30% slow-release nitrogen. Read the label carefully for recommended application rates. For all lawns, apply granular or liquid fertilizer to all turf grasses except centipede (which does not do well with frequent fertilization). Use about 5 pounds of 16-4-8 or similar analysis fertilizer per 1,000 square feet of lawn. Distribute fertilizer with a drop or whirlybird spreader to avoid streaking and green patches.

PALMS
In Florida, you can add palms to your landscape now. Abundant rainfall and warm soil temperatures are ideal for encouraging root growth. To help protect the bud from sun scald, keep the palm fronds tied with twine.

PERENNIALS
For a splash of color in Florida, plant Gold Mound and Weeping Lavender lantana in full sun. Both types are low and spreading. In a container or in the ground, the blooms last all summer and will come back every year in Central and North Florida.

POTTED PLANTS
Feed container plants and hanging baskets every other time you water with a water-soluble fertilizer, such as Miracle-Gro or Pro-Sol. Container plants can dry out very quickly this time of year, so be on the lookout for wilted leaves as well as other signs of dry conditions.

ROOTSTOCK ROSE
An unfamiliar flower on grafted roses means that the rootstock is blooming instead of the grafted portion. Cut the rootstock branch back to the ground to prevent it from becoming dominant.

SHRUBS
Containerized evergreen and deciduous shrubs for accents or foundation plantings can be planted all summer; just keep them watered, and mulch after planting. Be sure to ask about suggested spacing requirements when planting masses of the same plant.

STAKING
Hollyhocks and other tall flowering plants need stakes to keep them from falling over after summer rainstorms. One stake often can support two stalks.

STRESS

Avoid fertilizing or spraying during extreme heat or drought. When plants are under stress, the leaves may be damaged. Water well the day before spraying, and apply pesticides only when temperatures do not exceed 90 degrees.

SUNFLOWERS

Brighten your Florida garden by replacing spent crops with patches of sunflowers. In about 75 days you can harvest seeds to save for winter bird food.

TOMATO ROT

If tomatoes develop circular brown spots on their lower side before ripening, they have blossom-end rot. Remove affected tomatoes and treat the others with a calcium spray, such as Stop-Rot. Keeping the soil evenly moist helps avoid this problem.

TREES AND SHRUBS

Remove any dead wood or weak branches on crepe myrtles so new growth will be vigorous and show good form. Cut back fast-growing shrubs, such as elaeagnus, privet, and photinia, as needed. Prune spring-flowering shrubs after their blooms have faded if they need to be reshaped or to have an errant branch removed. In Florida, prune stray branches from tree-form ligustrum to keep the canopies dense. Also remove suckers from ligustrum and crepe myrtle trunks.

VEGETABLES

You still have time in Texas to plant seed of okra, black-eyed peas, beans, peppers, and summer and winter squash now for a late-summer harvest. Side-dress vegetable rows with a 2-inch-wide strip of 10-10-10 all-purpose fertilizer. Space the fertilizer several inches from the stems; water after applying.

June Notes

TO DO:
- Fertilize warm-season grasses
- Prune spring-flowering trees and shrubs
- Remove faded blooms from annuals
- Apply post-emergence weed killer to lawn
- Mow your grass at the tallest recommended height for greater drought tolerance

TO PLANT:
- Container-grown trees and shrubs
- Heat-tolerant summer annuals
- Tomatoes for fall harvest
- Summer- and fall-blooming perennials

TO PURCHASE:
- Lawn fertilizer
- Post-emergence weed killer
- Transplants and seeds of summer annuals

TIP OF THE MONTH

Here's a good way to get rid of a large area of nutgrass. First, pull the larger plants; then water the area thoroughly. Next, soak entire sections of newspaper in water for an hour or two. Cover the nutgrass area with sections of wet newspaper, several pages thick. "Patchwork" the sections around desirable plants. Cover the entire area so that no sunlight penetrates. Finally, cover the newspaper with a couple of inches of your favorite mulch, and water again. You will enrich your soil as the newspaper disintegrates and solve your nutgrass problem.

J. B. Davis
Winter Haven, Florida

Annuals
That Handle the Heat

Do your flowers fizzle when the sun begins to sizzle?
These blooms bask in the glow of a summer day.

Here in the South, summer is served right out of the oven—nice and hot. Now imagine you're a plant, stewing in the heat. Add the challenge of being expected to look good for weeks and months on end, rooted to one spot. But actually, there are lots of annuals that thrive when the thermometer rises. We dropped in on a few hot spots across the South where the flowers were flourishing. Here's a look at what we found, including some praises from proud gardeners.

TEXAS TOAST

Like your garden well done? Take a look at Texas this time of year. Anything that can take this kind of weather deserves vigorous applause.

"We rely a lot on lantana and Mexican firebush," says Calvin Finch, county horticulturist in San Antonio. "Although they are technically tender perennials, we use them as annuals."

Other plants that get high marks are wax begonias, especially the Cocktail series, Madagascar periwinkle (annual vinca), and sun-loving selections of coleus, such as Burgundy Sun, New Orleans, Eclipse,

and Alabama. (Although many gardeners have problems with annual vinca, Calvin says that planting late—mid-May in his area, which means when the weather is good and warm in yours—reduces disease.)

In Dallas, garden designer Paul Fields of Lambert Gardens loves the look he gets by combining flowers and foliage, especially the soft pastel of pink verbena and Lance Horton

Verbena sends a river of pink flowers tumbling over the edge of this concrete planter. The matching pink caladiums are Lance Horton, a selection that tolerates sun.

caladiums. "Those caladiums are pretty tolerant of sun," he adds. "We have them planted in one landscape where they are shielded from afternoon sun, and that seems to help." Paul also uses perennials such as coreopsis Moonbeam, *Rudbeckia* (yellow coneflower), and purple and white coneflowers (*Echinacea purpurea* and *E. alba*, respectively) for annual color.

COOKIN' IN CAJUN LAND

John Harris, horticulturist for Longue Vue Gardens in New Orleans, likes impatiens for one simple reason. "They're the only plants that will flower for us this time of year in the shade," he says with a laugh.

John gets his impatiens from Steve Bellanger, co-owner of Acadian Nurseries in Hammond, Louisiana, a couple of swamps north of New Orleans. "Impatiens do very well down here," Steve agrees. "They're almost tender perennials, and will last

BY MARK G. STITH
PHOTOGRAPHY VAN CHAPLIN, SYLVIA MARTIN

This massed planting of impatiens looks as cool and refreshing as a pitcher of pink lemonade. Given good soil, some protection from afternoon sun, and ample water, impatiens really show off this time of year.

Narrowleaf zinnia bears masses of sunny flowers all summer long.

way into fall." Tops on his list are the Dazzler series, which are more compact than most selections and can tolerate a morning's worth of full sun. Flower colors run the gamut—red, apricot, white, salmon, and the like. He's also keen about the new Deco impatiens, which have a lush, dark-green (almost bronze) leaf and also come in a wide range of colors.

FLAME-BROILED IN FLORIDA

You might think that getting plants to *stop* growing—even annuals—would be the main problem for Florida gardeners. Well, it is, but the heat and humidity can also be bad news for plants.

Still, gardeners manage glorious results, like Susan Osteryoung in Tallahassee. "Melampodium does terrifically in the heat and humidity," she states. "It sometimes gets dry around here, but melampodium keeps blooming with those lovely, yellow flowers." Other annuals that Susan praises are Mexican heather ("It's called an annual, but it comes back even bigger and better if I cut it down to the ground in winter."), and gomphrena, also called globe amaranth.

In Orlando, landscape architect Frank Joseph Brooks gets a lot of mileage out of pentas (Egyptian star clusters). Although gardeners in the land of hard freezes must treat it as an annual, it's still a great plant for anywhere it gets hot. "They get huge down here—up to about 4 feet high," Frank notes. "The pink-flowered form gets the largest." (White- and red-flowered selections are also common.) The star-shaped flower clusters are preferred pit stops for bees, butterflies, and hummingbirds, too. The new selections of dwarf pentas, Pink Profusion and Lavender, offer the same petal-power on much smaller (about 2 feet or so tall) plants.

BAKING IN BAMA

Sandra Williams put some pretty flowers around her mailbox post in Birmingham. Being a good gardener (and a realistic one), she knew that whatever grew out there by the hot street would have to be tough.

That's why she chose narrowleaf zinnia (*Zinnia angustifolia* or *linearis*), which delivered clean white blooms to accompany the daily mail. "Believe me, they can withstand the heat," Sandra attests. "I planted them from 4-inch pots in May, and each one grew about 12 to 14 inches high and spread 18 to 24 inches. They stayed neat, didn't need to be cut back, had no problems with powdery mildew, and I *maybe* watered them four times all summer long."

Well, there you have it. Torrid testimonials from some of the hottest parts of the South. The moral of the story? If these plants can take the worst of summer, they should do just fine in your yard, by your mailbox, or in your planter. ◇

The purple puffballs of gomphrena glow in the heat.

SOME LIKE IT HOT
Here are 10 ovenproof annuals for the South. Unless noted, all do better in full sun.
Those marked with an asterisk are tender perennials used as annuals.

COMMON NAME	SCIENTIFIC NAME	SELECTIONS
Begonia	*Begonia* x *hybrida*	Whiskey, Gin, Vodka, Rum, and Brandy
Blue Daze	*Evolvulus nutillianus*	
Globe amaranth	*Gomphrena globosa*	Buddy
Impatiens	*Impatiens* x *hybrida*	especially Dazzler, Deco, and Shady Lady Improved series (shade/morning sun)
Lantana	*Lantana* sp.	Gold Mound, Lavender Weeping, Nana Compacta*
Melampodium	*Melampodium* x *hybrida*	Showstar or Medallion
Narrowleaf zinnia	*Zinnia angustifolia*	Classic White or Orange
Salvia	*Salvia* sp.	many species, look for Lady in Red, Victoria*
Spider flower	*Cleome* sp.	
Rose verbena	*Verbena canadensis*	pink, red, purple*

Retreat to The Front

Jane Guiles knew her cute little bungalow needed a little perking up. New paint? No problem. Removing those awful awnings? No big deal. But what about that tiny front yard? And the concrete sidewalk to the front door? She didn't know exactly what to do about them. However, she did know landscape architect—and good neighbor—Greg McDonnell of Garden Renaissance in Mobile could help her out.

BEFORE

AFTER

A new wooden walkway replaced the short concrete sidewalk; the walk expands to an intimate patio on the far side. Lush plantings create a sense of separation from the nearby street.

"Originally, I had wanted to use flagstone or brick to replace the sidewalk," Jane recalls, "But they were just too expensive." Loose stone or gravel were much cheaper, but she ruled those out as being too difficult to maintain.

That's when Greg suggested building the walkway out of pressure-treated wood—essentially, a boardwalk. And not just a walkway, but expanding it to include an intimate patio (about 10 x 12 feet) off to the side. "Wood was a nice choice," Jane says. "I have two decks in the backyard, so the walkway and patio really fit in."

A gracefully curved hedge of boxwood, massed azaleas, a canopy of small trees, and a huge oak make the patio feel more like an enclosed, intimate space. Ground covers, including mondo grass and ajuga, and seasonal annuals complete the special retreat.

From early summer on, bold swaths of White Queen caladiums and Super Elfin mixed impatiens flank the walkway and patio. "I set them out in April, and they look good all the way until January," Jane says. "Sometimes, I'll just get tired of looking at them and replace them in December with pansies and dianthus (pinks) or ornamental cabbage," she adds.

The overall effect is a setting that looks nice enough to show off to the neighbors, and is comfortable enough to be a great place to relax in front of the house. *Mark G. Stith*

PHOTOGRAPHS: SYLVIA MARTIN

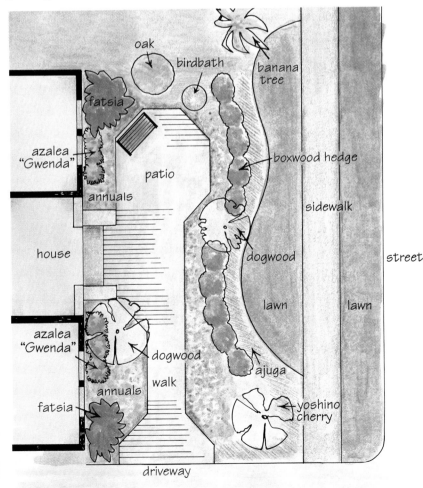

Yes, You Can Grow Tomatoes

Over the years *Southern Living* and its sister magazine *Progressive Farmer* have published hundreds of articles on growing tomatoes. Rules have been laid down, and carefully planned directions have been offered for prize-winning tomatoes.

But what about those of us who want a good-flavored tomato but not the grand prize for the biggest and best at the county fair? And what about those of us who will be planting a crop of tomatoes now, when most of the plants available locally are often tall and lanky?

While many a good gardener plants tomatoes as soon as the danger of frost is past, the real trick for a long tomato crop is staggered plantings. If you have already planted your first set of tomato plants, now is the time to plant for midsummer harvest. Then around the Fourth of July you can plant more for fall harvest.

If you're planting now, you can have great-tasting tomatoes without slavishly adhering to the old strict rules. Rules such as the following.

RULE ONE:

Look for the letters VFNT (meaning it's disease resistant) after the tomato's name on the plant tag. While that's still important, this time of year such things as healthy plant color, a good root system, and absence of insects, such as whiteflies, are even more important.

RULE TWO:

You have to have a rich organic soil with just the right pH. While it's true that tomatoes *do* love rich soil full of organic matter, you can produce a fine crop of tomatoes in most backyards across the South, unless your backyard is a rock cliff or a swamp.

To grow excellent tomatoes, dig a good-size hole, at least a foot wide and a foot deep. Mix the soil from the hole with as much organic matter (compost or peat) as you have available, making sure you remove any clods or lumps of old soil from the planting soil. Now you're ready to add a nice healthy tomato plant.

RULE THREE:

We've told you—plant your transplants deeply, leaving the bottom leaves about 2 inches above the ground. But all you really have to do is plant the tomatoes as deep as your prepared spot will allow. Because transplants this time of year tend to be tall, just do the best you can; don't worry if they aren't deep enough.

It's a good idea to stake the tomatoes to help prevent rot. But just a good mulch like pine straw for the plant to sprawl on also works. Even if you have staked your tomatoes, mulch is a good idea.

RULE FOUR:

This is the one rule you should follow, whether you are going for prize-winners or just table-pleasers.

The most important steps for success are fertilizing and watering.

Once the plants begin growing, you can fertilize in a couple of different ways. Prior to fruit set, apply ¼ cup of 10-10-10 or similar analysis fertilizer around each plant and work into the soil. Or use a liquid fertilizer every two to three weeks, mixed according to label directions. Once fruit is set, repeat the granular fertilization application or increase the frequency of liquid fertilization to about every 10 days. Keep the soil moisture even, moist but not constantly wet; this helps prevent fruit crack. As long as you water enough to keep the plants from wilting, you will have a fine crop. *John Floyd*

Stagger plantings for tomatoes all summer and into fall.

Growing several inches high, fringed campion becomes a mat of blooms in late spring.

Fringed Campion— Back From the Brink

The lavender-pink petals are fringed on the end.

At a time when so much of what we hear about the environment is depressing, it's nice to learn about an endangered plant whose story has a happy ending. Fringed campion (*Silene polypetala*), once on the verge of extinction, is now making a spirited comeback thanks to the intervention of concerned horticulturists.

A member of the carnation family, fringed campion is pretty much restricted in the wild to hardwood forests in five counties in Middle and South Georgia. There it ekes out an existence on hillsides and slopes of steep ravines. The isolation of individual colonies is thought to have contributed to the species' declining numbers, as such populations often lose genetic diversity, making them prone to environmental stress.

The Natural Heritage Inventory of the Georgia Department of Natural Resources recognized just how rare fringed campion had become. It ap-

proached various people with the idea of saving the plant by discovering how to propagate and grow it. One of these individuals was Michael Dirr, professor of horticulture at the University of Georgia in Athens. Michael found that the plant could be easily propagated by division, as well as by a process known as tissue culture. After producing sufficient numbers of the plant, he and others distributed them to commercial growers, who are beginning to offer it to the public.

Just about every gardener who comes upon fringed campion in full bloom instantly falls in love with it. Lavender-pink blossoms, up to 1½ inches across, smother the foliage for weeks in May and June. In the garden, the plant behaves a lot like carpet bugleweed (*Ajuga reptans*). The prostrate, herbaceous evergreen spreads by runners so that one or two plants soon become a patch. Fringed campion makes a serviceable ground cover and is a likely candidate for a rock garden. You can also grow it in a wildflower garden, naturalized

area, or herbaceous border.

Although fringed campion tolerates poor soil, it certainly doesn't prefer it. Rather, it seems to enjoy a moisture-retentive, acid, well-drained soil that contains a good bit of organic matter. The high shade of tall pines or hardwoods is desirable, too. Regular fertilizing isn't required nor is regular watering once the plant is established. Diseases and insects are seldom a problem. Seedheads turn yellow soon after the flowers fade, so you may want to trim them off for aesthetic purposes. To get more plants, simply snip a runner to detach a "daughter" plant from the "mother."

Fringed campion is winter hardy throughout the South. It should grow well in all areas, except perhaps South Florida.   *Steve Bender*

Because fringed campion is endangered, it cannot be shipped across state lines. Contact your local nursery or garden center to find sources in your state.   ◇

This split-rail fence separates the garden from green pasture. The Williamses built it to keep cattle from devouring Dorothy's handiwork.

Peace of the Country

"Wyatt and I were married in 1937 and have lived here ever since," says Dorothy Williams. "Can you imagine such a thing?" A moment's glance at their serene, simple garden in the gentle countryside near Orange, Virginia, supplies me with the answer. Yes, Dorothy, I can.

"We never meant to live here," Dorothy confesses. "We thought we had secured an apartment in town, but the people never moved out. So we came here on our honeymoon and moved into what had been a tenant house." The structure, which offered little more at the time than a fresh coat of paint, sat on property owned by Wyatt's family. Years of refurbishing made the house a comfortable

home. But Dorothy also wanted to improve the outside, and she longed to grow wildflowers and shrubs underneath a grove of stately hardwoods out front.

Fortunately, she and Wyatt were fast friends with one of Virginia's most accomplished landscape architects, Charles Gillette, who lived in Richmond, about an hour away. "Whenever Charles was out working this way, he'd call up and want to know if he could come to lunch," recalls Dorothy. During these lunchtime discussions, he laid the groundwork for the garden. Years later, Ralph Griswold, another prominent landscape architect from Richmond, helped refine the design.

Today, a placid pond fed by a well stands as the garden's centerpiece. From the house, you descend a slope and arrive at water's edge using steps and paths blanketed with woodchip mulch. Dorothy chose the mulch because of its natural look and easy maintenance. "You don't notice when the birds mess it up," she explains. "You couldn't *give* me bricks to use under those trees."

Past president of the Garden Club of Virginia, Dorothy nurtures a wide variety of plants in the sunken garden around her pond and gazebo. Wildflowers fascinate her. She feels quite sentimental about a patch of twinleaf (*Jeffersonia diphylla*) presented to her many years ago by a friend.

Viewed from the house's second-floor balcony, the pond and garden nestle beneath the cool shade of hardwoods.

"Collecting plants that your friends give you is the fun of a garden," she proclaims. Virginia bluebells (*Mertensia virginica*) that pop up near the pond in April stir another fond memory. "In spring, my father and I used to go horseback riding near Blacksburg and *Mertensia* was all over everywhere."

Until recently, the Williamses raised Angus cattle on the pastures beyond the garden. A split-rail fence stopped the animals from grazing the garden, but didn't prevent them from making their presence known. "Cattle are so curious," Dorothy notes. "We used to be in such a temper because we'd take company down to the garden and the cattle would all hang their heads over the fence and

make a mess." Dorothy and Wyatt eventually solved the problem by installing an electric fence.

The garden sees frequent and enthusiastic visits from tour groups, garden clubs, friends, and the like. Dorothy understands their delight. "It's such a tiny garden and so unimportant, yet it seems to speak to people because it *is* small," she observes. "It's not grand or fancied up. When my city friends who give themselves airs ask where we live, I always say, 'We live in a tiny house in the middle of a large pasture.'

GARDEN AND HOUSE ARE ONE

"The key to the whole thing," she continues, "is that the garden and

house are one. We've opened up the house so you can see out into the garden. My typewriter, for instance, sits on a table right inside a window in my office upstairs. I can look out into the garden and see the hellebores blooming; tiny, little cyclamen; and things like that. It's just a constant pleasure."

Dorothy and Wyatt's two children live far away—a daughter near Mobile and a son in Houston. So they've placed their roughly 400 acres in the Virginia Outdoor Conservancy to maintain it in perpetuity as open, undeveloped land. Dorothy sums up her family's devotion to the land this way: "It's the peacefulness of it we love." Thanks to their forethought, the peace will continue. *Steve Bender*

A sweeping curve of wall separates lawn from ground cover in this Florida landscape.

Curving Across The Landscape

Raised planting beds don't have to follow straight lines. Instead of laying timbers lengthwise, landscape designer Michael Perry used upright 6 x 6 posts to terrace a sloping yard in Winter Park, Florida. The low retaining wall curves its way through the landscape.

Because each pressure-treated post would be buried halfway for stability, Michael bought lumber twice as high as the proposed wall height. After deciding on the wall's shape, Michael dug a curved trench as deep as the wall's height to accommodate the posts. (If you have clay soils, a few inches of gravel in the bottom of the trench will help keep water away from the end of the post.)

Each post was leveled both vertically and horizontally. Michael stapled tar paper on the back side of the wall to prevent soil from eroding through the spaces between posts. The posts were braced with overlapping steel reinforcing bars. Sunken in the bed, a few concrete blocks were anchored to the bar with ⅛-inch wire to keep the wall from leaning forward. Soil was then added to fill the trench and raised bed.

Unlike typical angular wooden retaining walls, this eye-catching wall complements natural shapes and curved planting beds.

Jo Kellum

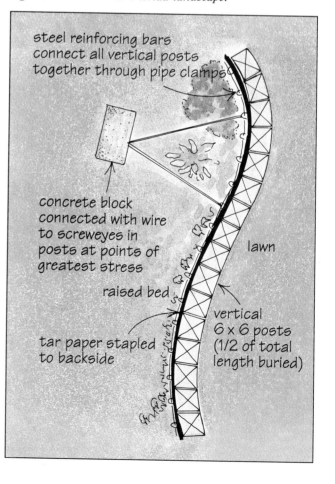

steel reinforcing bars connect all vertical posts together through pipe clamps

concrete block connected with wire to screweyes in posts at points of greatest stress

lawn

raised bed

tar paper stapled to backside

vertical 6 x 6 posts (1/2 of total length buried)

After. *Replacing boxwoods with crepe myrtles provides needed screening while still allowing views of the house.*

Big Changes, Not Big Bucks

Homeowners often think that redoing the front yard requires the wealth of Fort Knox. But as this example demonstrates, you can make big improvements without owning the bank.

This is the home of Dick and Doris Dickinson of Tuscaloosa, Alabama. Family and friends liked to sit and talk on their front porch, which looks out on a narrow, quiet street. But a poor planting design hindered the necessary sense of intimacy and welcome. Barton's Nursery supplied the answer.

Barton's began by removing a pair of massive old boxwoods flanking the front door. The shrubs called too much attention to the steeply pitched roof and high gable above the entry. They also visually overpowered the porch. Replacing them with crepe myrtles solved both problems. Now you focus on the front door, not the gable. And while the crepe myrtles provide needed separation between the porch and yard, you can see between their trunks to the house behind them.

Next in line for a redo—the tiny front lawn. Before, the lawn fell off sharply to the right beside the porch, which led your eye around the corner to a side yard. Barton's brought in soil to make the corner level, then wrapped the lawn and porch with evergreen shrubs and ground cover. The result? Your eye stops at the corner. The plantings foster the feeling of enclosure and intimacy the area formerly lacked. Plus, the lawn now sports an attractive curved shape.

The final touch involved surfacing the plain concrete walk with handsome tile pavers that match those of the porch. Like other improvements to the yard, this was a simple and not very expensive change. But what a difference it made.   *Steve Bender*

Evergreen shrubs and ground cover border the lawn and porch for an intimate feeling.

Before. *Boxwoods overemphasized the high gable and detracted from the porch.*

Gaura Takes Summer in Stride

A gardener's first efforts in painting a floral picture are usually bold strokes: the broad swaths of color delivered by big blooms. But as the garden and gardener mature together, subtleties give the greatest satisfaction. That's when gaura, a native perennial, is apt to find its way into the garden.

Although gaura (*Gaura lindheimeri*) grows wild in the prairies and pinelands of Texas and Louisiana, it is perfectly adapted to gardens throughout the South, even the coldest ex-

GAURA AT A GLANCE
Light: Full sun to partial shade
Moisture: Tolerates drought but not standing water
Soil: Well drained
Propagation: Seedlings; blooms within one year
Pests: Occasional leaf spot—no harm to the plant
Size: Stems 18 inches to 5 feet tall; flowers 1 inch across
Color: Pink buds, white flowers

tremes of the Upper South. When gaura is planted in a flower border, its long, reddish stems bear delicate pink buds that open into white flowers from early summer until frost. They hover above and between more dense clumps of flowers, creating a mass of fine blooms that makes the otherwise unobtrusive gaura really stand out.

In the South, cold hardiness is not always an issue; heat tolerance is. By virtue of its native habitat, gaura withstands the extremes of summer with apparent ease. Individual flowers may shrivel by noon in the midsummer sun, but fresh blooms unfurl each morning from late May or June until frost.

This continuous bloom results in long stems that reach lengths of 3 to 5 feet with the passing summer days. Its long stems are an advantage in flower borders because they stand above the deepening masses of daylilies, black-eyed Susans, and purple coneflowers.

Some gardeners prefer to control the ultimate height with timely pruning. Allen Bush of Holbrook Farm and Nursery in Fletcher, North Carolina, explains, "The first flush of bloom lasts about a month. Then in July, I cut it back to approximately 18 inches." The result is a second bloom that is shorter and thicker than the first.

This taprooted perennial propogates by seedlings that spring up around the plant, so it seldom needs to be divided. When Bush cuts back his gaura, he always leaves one plant unpruned so it will reseed. You should transplant seedlings while they are young, using care not to sever the carrotlike root. These young plants will grow to a flowering size after just one year.

Plant gaura in full sun to partial shade where the soil is well-drained. In fact, sandy soil is preferred over a rich organic soil where gaura outgrows its ability to stand up straight. Because it is deep-rooted, gaura tolerates dry summers better than most perennials.　　　*Linda C. Askey*

At the Holbrook Farm and Nursery, in Fletcher, North Carolina, gaura makes a strong statement in a mixed border.　PHOTOGRAPHS: VAN CHAPLIN

(INSET) *The delicate, mothlike flowers and pink buds show off all summer long atop wiry stems.*

Kinder Killers

Back in the sixties, life in the garden was elementary. When you found a bug chomping your tomato plants, you simply drowned it in a wave of lethal insecticide, and that was that. You didn't worry about poisoning the soil or creating mutated ants the size of school buses.

Today, we fret about the heavy-handed use of broad-spectrum pesticides because we know the dangers. Thanks to widespread concern about the misuse of chemicals, gardeners can now choose from a variety of products that won't harm people, pets, or the environment.

Bt briquettes (also called "mosquito dunks"). People love water in the garden, whether it's in a lily pond, reflecting pool, or birdbath. Trouble is, mosquitoes breed in standing water, then land on your arm and drink their fill. The answer—small doughnut-shaped briquettes containing *Bacillus thuringiensis israeliensis* (Bt), a bacterial insecticide that kills mosquito larvae, but won't harm people, plants, or animals. Each briquette treats 100 square feet of water and lasts 30 days. Just float it on the surface.

Yellow sticky traps. For some strange reason, aphids, whiteflies, and other small insects find the color yellow irresistible. So they readily land on these plastic strips coated with adhesive and get stuck for life. Simply replace the inexpensive strip when insect bodies completely cover it. Besides killing insects, yellow sticky traps tell you which bugs are currently in your garden, so you can head off a major infestation.

Diatomaceous earth. This whitish powder consists of the fossilized skeletons of microscopic aquatic plants, called diatoms. When slugs, aphids, and other soft-bodied pests contact the powder, it scours their skin and absorbs their oily, outer coating. As a result, their insides ooze out. Diatomaceous earth remains effective as long as it's present. If a heavy rain washes it away, you'll have to reapply it.

Steve Bender

Garden and home centers often carry these products. For mail-order sources, send a self-addressed, stamped, business-size envelope to Kinder Killers, P.O. Box 830119, Birmingham, AL 35283. ◇

Mosquitoes breeding in your pond? One Bt briquette will kill larvae in 100 square feet of water for 30 days. And it won't harm fish, people, or plants.

(Above) *When aphids, whiteflies, and other small insects land on a yellow sticky trap, they're stuck for life.* **(Above, left)** *Slugs chomping your seedlings? Spread diatomaceous earth around them, and watch the slugs melt away.*

Beautiful Bounty

The plot of Dallas dirt tended by Kay Shirley isn't your garden variety vegetable garden. Flourishing in small islands surrounded by neat garden paths, the vegetables are nearly too pretty to eat.

A birdbath, centered in a bed of herbs, poses against a backdrop of okra. The leafy tops of root crops—turnips, beets, radishes—fill beds to bursting. A sharp green smell wafts from the corner, where tomatoes spill from their cages.

The unruly profusion of foliage bisected by the straight, tidy paths is reminiscent of an English cottage

garden. Growing among the vegetables, a patch of zinnias adds a bright surprise. Antique roses swarm over a rustic trellis just past the cucumbers and continue their way down a fence top. A miniature orchid grows between the fence and a public sidewalk—gardening space that many homeowners overlook. Figs, apples, peaches, and Japanese persimmons erupt everywhere. "I have to share my peaches with passersby, but they don't know what the Japanese persimmons are," Kay laughs.

The neat paths crisscross through the garden. "I wanted small beds that I could reach from all sides," says Kay. "You don't get as dirty that way." Paved with dry-laid brick mixed with various colors of Pennsylvania stone, the paths give the garden an Alice in Wonderland charm. Bordering the beds, simple curbs made of bricks turned on end and buried halfway in sand enable Kay to mound the beds slightly as she adds compost, improving drainage.

Starting with good soil is half the battle; Kay removed about a foot of original dirt from each bed and replaced it with compost before the first planting. She works fresh compost from her perpetual pile into the planting beds each winter.

One of Kay's gardening secrets is to use compost for mulch, as well. "I add a layer of coarse compost about 2 inches thick; as a result, I really don't have any weeds," she says. The compost also helps keep the soil from getting too warm

during summer months. A self-taught organic gardener, Kay averages about two hours a week in the garden. After preparing the soil in the winter and planting in the spring, weekly chores include harvesting, watering, and fertilizing. The results: A garden that is as beautiful as it is bountiful.

Jo Kellum

SECRETS OF KAY'S SUCCESS

■ Instead of planting in rows, mark off small areas for each crop. Sprinkle seeds on the soil, and rake in. Thin sprouts to avoid overcrowding.

■ Beneficial bugs eat destructive insects. Kay releases the aphid-eating ladybugs and scatters lacewing eggs periodically across planting beds to destroy soft-bodied insects. Tiny stingless trichogramma wasps help control cutworms and moths. Lizards also live in her garden and dine on pests.

■ Plant nasturtiums to enjoy in the garden and with meals. Their petals add bright color and a lemony taste to salads.

■ Plant winter crops, such as arugula, spinach, and lettuce, to help break down new compost and eliminate erosion.

■ Fertilize plants weekly with a mixture of seaweed, molasses, and fish emulsion. It's smelly, but the plants love it. Similar mixtures are available at organic garden centers as well as through mail-order suppliers.

■ By the time winter crops die out, the summer crops are already in place, and it's too late to start new ones. In the gaps left from removing spent vegetables, plant patches of summer flowers to brighten the garden and keep weeds from filling in.

(Above) *Kay Shirley's potting shelf is just the right height for sorting a day's harvest.*
(Left) *In a small space between the okra and zinnias, a tiny herb garden encircles a birdbath. Basil, rosemary, oregano, cilantro, thyme, and lemon thyme thrive here.*

Flowers & Family

How can you grow beautiful gardens and juggle two careers without going absolutely nuts? The answer will astound you.

BY STEVE BENDER / PHOTOGRAPHY VAN CHAPLIN

Meet the Curetons, quite possibly the only family left in America that puts seed packets in their children's Christmas stockings. (From left) Delilah, Vicki, Alex, Nicholas.

Y ou're about to meet a family who has lost all perspective—a family who readily admits "we're slaves to our garden." When they're not weeding about plants, they're reading about plants. The kids even receive seed packets in their Christmas stockings. Clearly, things have gotten out of hand.

Be that as it may, Alex and Vicki Cureton offer no apologies. The way they see it, their family works together pursuing a style of life they love. And what could be better than that?

The mail says the Curetons live in Tallahassee, but don't look for their home and garden there. That's just a postmark. Instead, drive northeast toward Miccosukee, into the very tip of Leon County, Florida, just a hair from the Georgia line. This is old plantation country, where massive live oaks spread their moss-laden rafters over lonely, two-lane, graveled roads. Every mile you go takes you back another decade in time.

Twenty years ago, Alex and Vicki took possession of their land, a wedding present from her family. The gift didn't include a house, so they built themselves a cottage, drawing plans for it on a piece of notebook paper. Offspring of handyman fathers, they did all the work themselves, except for some carpentry and wiring. Their self-reliance would pay big dividends when they later began to fashion a garden.

The only sunny spot in their 10 acres was a tract of horse pasture on which Alex cultivated vegetables. It might have stayed that way had Vicki not attended a slide show about perennials at Callaway Gardens in Pine Mountain, Georgia, six years ago. As slide after slide of beautiful flowers appeared on the screen, she experienced a horticultural epiphany. "I was so inspired," she recalls, "I said to Alex, 'We've got to have a sunny garden. We've got to start plowing.'"

Plowing came harder than truth to a politician, thanks to classic red clay soil. But their determined, 20-year effort to improve it by regularly adding every kind of organic matter they could obtain—compost, pine bark, barnyard manure—has paid off. Successful gardens, they learned, don't happen overnight. "You have to have patience," Vicki says. "So much patience."

Despite the hard work, Alex and Vicki laid out the new borders with the same optimism, improvisation, and adventurous spirit with which they had raised their cottage. "We never had a formal plan," she reveals. "What we'd do is get our beers and walk and talk and say, 'Well, let's do this here and let's do that over there.'"

As they collaborated, they discovered that each partner's talent complemented the other's. "Alex's strength is defining space and establishing bed lines," she notes. "My thing is filling in the spaces. He likes structure and organization. I like clutter and spontaneity."

Today, the garden epitomizes the ideal of the country cottage garden—an exuberant collage of annuals, perennials, herbs, old roses, and small trees tied together by paths of mown meadow grass. Petunias, verbena, phlox, salvia, larkspur, poppies, zinnias, butterfly bush, and iris each lend distinctive flavor to a hearty broth of bloom that simmers in every season.

Like many flower gardens, this one changes from year to year and from week to week. Alex and Vicki constantly experiment with new plants and new colors, testing which flowers will "do," and mixing different flowers together. They start many flowers from seed. Floral combinations

Whenever a fair wind blows, you'll find Vicki in the garden snipping blossoms and herbs for flower arrangements.

EASY FLOWERS FROM SEED

- Bachelor's buttons
- Globe amaranth
  (*Gomphrena*)
- Larkspur
- Poppies
- Spider flower
  (*Cleome*)
- Zinnias

Fog lifts from the Florida countryside at dawn, revealing elaborate borders and the Curetons' summerhouse. What better place to stroll and sip your morning coffee?

range from the audaciously bold—scarlet geraniums and yellow sedum—to the subdued—blue spiderwort and Queen Anne's lace.

Where do they get their ideas? "So many people don't realize the resources all around them," comments Vicki. "I like to look for color combinations in fabrics, in a piece of china, or in a single flower, like a pansy." She's also a fan of the late, famed British garden designer Gertrude Jekyll and devours every book about her she can find.

An effective garden needs a focus. Here, it's the combination toolroom, storage shed, office, and pavilion Alex and Vicki call the "summerhouse." A screened-in room, cooled by a ceiling fan, occupies half the structure. The family uses this for relaxing, entertaining friends, and evading sudden rainstorms. Behind it sits an office, where Alex and Vicki regularly lock horns with a personal computer in a valiant attempt to organize their two thriving businesses. He runs a lawn and landscaping service; she grows and arranges cut flowers and herbs for weddings, parties, and other events.

Right about now, you're probably thinking one of two things—a day in Tallahassee lasts 36 hours or Alex and Vicki are really androids from the 23rd century. I mean, how else could they shepherd a family, operate two businesses, and still maintain immaculate flower borders that cry every hour for attention? The answer is—please be seated, as the following information may be too graphic for sensitive readers—*the kids help out.* Honest, they do.

Nicholas, 13, and Delilah, 8, represent that rare breed of youngster who still performs daily chores. Their duties include weeding, fertilizing, mowing, and hauling plant debris to the compost pile. Key to their cooperation, their mother points out, is praising their efforts and explaining that shared labor is part of being a family.

Someday, their parents hope, Nicholas and Delilah will inherit this land and continue a tradition of country gardening that spans four generations on both sides of the family. More than flowers are at stake—an entire way of life is under the gun.

"We live in one of the last rural areas of Leon County," says Vicki. "And the developers are really pushing hard on us." If the kids won't agree to keep the property intact, the elder Curetons have one final trick up their sleeves. "We'll be buried here," she says with a chuckle, "so our children can't sell it." ◇

Delilah helps keep the garden in shape by grooming plants and weeding.

VICKI'S FAVORITE PLANT COMBINATIONS
- Orange California poppies and blue bachelor's buttons
- Pink Drummond phlox and red petunias
- Indigo Spires salvia and pink garden phlox
- Pink old roses and lamb's-ears
- Rosemary and Crimson Pygmy barberry
- Green leaf lettuce, pinks, and sweet alyssum

July

Backyard garden with Oriental flair

CHECKLIST FOR JULY

ANNUALS
Apply fertilizer to annuals and perennials now. Add about ¼ cup of 16-4-8 fertilizer per 10 square feet of annual and perennial beds. Avoid getting granules on the foliage, and wash fertilizer in after application. In Florida, plant blue daze, purslane, zinnia, marigold, melampodium, and portulaca for bright color that can take the summer heat. In Texas, ageratum, marigolds, cockscomb, portulaca, Madagascar periwinkle (annual vinca), copper plant, and Joseph's coat can still be added to flower beds for colorful displays.

BULBS
Plant caladiums now and they will have plenty of time to grow before cool weather. Work compost and slow-release bulb fertilizer into the soil. Remember that they need a well-drained site.

CENTIPEDE LAWNS
Yellowing centipede lawns probably need liquid ferrous sulfate to restore a dark green color. Apply at a rate of 2 ounces per 3 to 5 gallons of water to cover 1,000 square feet of lawn.

CITRUS PROBLEMS
In Florida, greasy spot disease often appears on citrus leaves in wet weather. Spray affected areas with copper fungicide and remove fallen leaves to keep the disease from spreading.

DAYLILIES
If thick with foliage but thin on flowers, daylilies need dividing. Dig up individual clumps, and use a sharp knife or spade to separate the roots into hand-size pieces. Replant in a sunny area, spacing them about 18 to 24 inches apart.

FALL PERENNIALS
Mexican mint marigold, bush sage, and asters should be set out now for the fall garden. Chrysanthemums should be available soon; shear back established mums for fuller plants.

FLOWERING SHRUBS
In Florida, remove (at the point of origin) overgrown stems from azaleas and camellias only when necessary. Avoid heavy pruning, which will remove next year's flower buds.

FLOWERS
In Texas, cut the faded flower stalks of cannas for continued blooms. Remove spent blooms on marigolds to stimulate more flowers; pinch back tips of coleus to produce more compact, showier plants.

HEDGES
Continue to shape formal hedges when new growth reaches 6 to 12 inches long. For a dense screen of foliage, keep the base of your hedge wider than the top.

HERBICIDES
To prevent drift onto surrounding plants, use a wick applicator that applies the chemical like a wet sponge on a long stick. You can also use a plastic cup and an old paintbrush for small jobs.

HERBS
Don't be afraid to cut sprigs of your favorite herbs for use in the kitchen. Regular cutting encourages new growth.

HYDRANGEAS
To dry flowers for winter arrangements, cut when the flowers have aged slightly, as indicated by a change in color. French hydrangeas will fade slightly, while oakleaf hydrangeas will get a tinge of pink. Cut  the flower stalks as long as you need them, and strip off any leaves. Hang the stalks upside down in a cool, dry place.

LAWNS
Renovate bare areas of warm-season lawns by sowing seeds or laying sod of same or similar grass. This is a good month in both Florida and Texas to establish new sod. Water daily for the first week; then water only when there has been no rain for three days or when blades begin to curl. Water in the morning to keep lawns moist during the hottest part of the day and dry at night.

PALMS
In Florida, yellow fronds are a symptom of manganese deficiency, caused by heavy summer rains. Spread granules of 12-4-8 fertilizer containing manganese (check the label) at a rate of 1 to 2 pounds in a circle around the trunk.

PEACHES

When fruit rots just as it begins to ripen, the problem is a disease called brown rot. Control it by spraying ripening fruit with garden sulfur or captan fungicide as directed on the label.

POWDERY MILDEW

This grayish-white coating on the foliage and flowers of crepe myrtles is a common problem. Spray affected trees when the problem first appears to prevent it from spreading. Apply Funginex or benomyl according to directions.

POTS

Containers dry out quickly this time of the year. Be sure to water your plants until water runs out of the bottom. If the soil is so dry that it has pulled away from the sides of the pot, use a pencil to poke holes in the soil, and water several times so it's thoroughly moist.

ROSES

Continue cutting blossoms on roses to encourage more flowers. Prune the stem down to the second set of five leaflets.

SHRUBS

Apply ½ tablespoon of 16-4-8 or similar fertilizer per foot of plant height to established shrubs. Apply evenly around the edge of the plant. Be sure no fertilizer touches the stem, and water thoroughly after application. You don't need to pull back the mulch when fertilizing.

VEGETABLES

Replant beans, squash, corn, and cucumbers now for a continual harvest into late summer. Set out more tomato plants for fall. If you plan to grow your own transplants of collards, cabbage, and other fall vegetables, now is a good time to sow seeds for planting in the garden next month. In Florida, plant heat-loving vegetables throughout the state. Set out calabaza, okra, pumpkins, and Southern peas. Start seeds of eggplant, peppers, and tomatoes to have transplants available late next month. In Texas, sow or set out plants for a late crop of summer vegetables, including tomatoes, peppers, okra, and beans. Add one cup of 12-4-8 per 100 square feet of soil before planting fall vegetables. Use a tiller or garden fork to work the fertilizer in 6 to 8 inches deep. Enrich poor soils by tilling in an inch or two of compost or aged manure.

July Notes

TO DO:
- For a second flush of blooms, snip off the tips of flowering stems of crepe myrtle after they've faded
- Cut herbs often to keep them growing
- Keep tomatoes watered during drought to prevent the onset of blossom-end rot

TO PLANT:
- Pots of flowering annuals
- Summer vegetables as others are harvested

TO PURCHASE:
- Rain gauge to measure amount of water received by lawn and garden each week

_____

_____

_____

_____

_____

_____

_____

_____

TIP OF THE MONTH

Sometimes high humidity causes granulated plant food to harden in its container. If you place a piece of bread in the container, replace the lid, and leave the container closed for a day or two, the hardened plant food will again become granular.

Mary Frances Owens
Louisville, Kentucky

Use pieces of sphagnum sheet moss to create a natural liner for a wire basket. Begin by covering the lower half only.

After adding potting soil, insert companion plants into the sides of the basket to provide contrasting texture and color.

Finish lining the basket with moss. Then set the impatiens off-center, leaving room to insert other companion plants on one side.

an inch or two of potting soil into the bottom of the basket, she raised the plant (as shown) so it would not be growing any deeper in the new basket than it was in the old.

"When you are planting on the sides, you need to do it as you build the basket," Ellen says. "Sticking small plants through the moss into a finished basket is hard to do. It's much easier to do it in layers." She selected the variegated forms of creeping fig and miniature ivy. Once in place, she added more moss to completely cover the sides of the wire frame.

After removing the wire hanger from the plastic pot, she tapped the pot on its side to dislodge the impatiens. By setting the plant into the wire basket so that it was off-center, she left one side open for companion plants on the soil surface.

Ellen filled the empty spaces with additional potting soil, and began to tuck in more companion plants. She used sweet alyssum and asparagus fern to fill in the top of the basket.

Once she had planted the basket, Ellen used U-shaped pieces of florist wire to pin long stems of creeping fig and ivy to the moss where they will take root.

A good watering settled the soil around the roots of the new plants. Drainage will never be a problem because excess water drips through the moss.   ◇

TIPS FOR DISPLAYING YOUR BASKET

■ Use wall brackets or S-shaped extenders to lower your basket to eye level. At this height, the plant will get more light because it is not too close to the structure from which it is hung.

■ If you don't want to piece together the sphagnum sheet moss, you can buy liners for your wire basket.
■ Spray shiny hardware with black paint to give it a hand-wrought look that will not detract from the flowers.
■ To make a basket that looks like a sphere of flowers, set the same kind of plant into the sides of your basket as you put in the top. Eventually they will grow to cover the moss and wire. With the aid of a little trimming, it will begin to look like a ball of flowers and foliage suspended by a chain.
■ Because you will have to water your basket daily as it matures, nutrients will wash out of the soil. Feed it weekly with liquid fertilizer as directed on the label.

OTHER BASKET COMBINATIONS

Tropicana Rose	Angel Wing begonia
Madagascar periwinkle	Blue Daze evolvulus
Dusty Miller	Variegated Vinca minor
Blue Wonder Scaevola	. . .
White verbena	Red geranium
. . .	(Tango or Kim)
Ornamental or chili	Lemon Drop marigold
pepper	Purple verbena
Yellow lantana	Tropic Snow *Zinnia*
Lady in Red *Salvia*	*linearis*
coccinea	. . .
Golden Orange *Zinnia*	Prostrate rosemary
linearis	Silver-edged thyme
. . .	Bergarten sage

Constructed entirely of pressure-treated pine, our pergola project provides a good introduction to outdoor construction techniques. Detailed step-by-step plans are available by mail; see details below.

Gateway to The Garden

Building this garden structure was easy. The hard part was figuring out what to call it. Resembling a shade arbor and functioning as a trellis for climbing vines, our latest project stands at this garden's threshold.

We dug through architectural history books and came up with "pergola," which is a pair of colonnades supporting an open roof of cross beams. But no matter what you call it, our project adds a classic touch to any garden.

Overall dimensions are only 56 x 36 inches, measured to the outside of the posts. Height, measured to the bottom of the cross beam, is 86 inches.

Construction is simple and straightforward. We selected pressure-treated Southern pine for economy and long life. Four 6 x 6

posts support a 2 x 6 beam. For a cleaner look, the beams fit into notches in the tops of the posts. Rafters support a lattice "roof" of 2 x 2s. We copied the decorative rafter ends of the house and repeated them on the pergola for a custom look.

The pressure-treated pine was pressure washed, bleached, and given a light-gray stain to cover the green look of treated lumber.

Detailed plans, including a complete materials list and concise step-by-step instructions, are available by writing to: Pergola Plan, *Southern Living*, P.O. Box 523, Birmingham, AL 35201. Enclose a check or money order for $3.50 made out to *Southern Living*. Please include a self-addressed, stamped, business-size envelope. Allow at least four weeks for delivery. *Louis Joyner*

Black-eyed Susans Can't Be Beat

Black-eyed Susan is the perfect plant for people with brown thumbs. Growing in sun or shade in all kinds of soil, it needs no pampering. This isn't to say that accomplished gardeners don't value it as well. They find this perennial to be a summer stalwart, providing mixed borders and naturalized areas with months of golden blossoms during hot weather.

The true black-eyed Susan (*Rudbeckia hirta*) is actually a half-hardy perennial, which means that the plant may come back for several years, but don't bet on it. In most cases, this native acts like a biennial, growing leaves the first year, flowering the second, then dying and scattering seed. The seed quickly germinates, so black-eyed Susans in the wild often colonize fields, unmowed banks, and roadsides.

Bright-yellow flowers, 2 to 3 inches across, appear atop 3-foot plants from July until mid-September. Each wild flower form has a black cone or "eye" in its center, giving the plant its name. However, a selection called Irish Eyes bears large, yellow blossoms with clear, green eyes.

People often refer to a second species, *R. fulgida,* as black-eyed Susan, but the correct name is orange

Black-eyed Susans are among the South's brightest flowers. Some species reseed, while others spread by stolons to form clumps.

coneflower. It's easy to confuse the two species, for they look very much alike. But there are important differences. For one thing, orange coneflower is fully perennial. For another, it doesn't multiply aggressively by seed, but spreads by stolons to form large clumps.

A particular selection of orange

coneflower, Goldsturm, has become one of the South's most popular perennials. Shorter and denser than black-eyed Susan, it grows just 24 inches tall and has handsome, dark-green foliage.

You can use both Rudbeckias in perennial borders, mixed borders, cutting gardens, naturalized areas, and the foreground of foundation plantings. Because of the penetrating color of their flowers, plant them in groups and drifting masses, rather than singly here and there. Otherwise, you'll get a polka-dot effect.

Both black-eyed Susan and Goldsturm coneflower are sinfully simple to grow. They prefer moist, fertile soil but tolerate dry, poorer soils as well. They do ask that the soil be well drained, however. Full sun produces bushier plants and more blooms, but light shade doesn't cause problems. Neither do insects or diseases. Goldsturm never needs staking; black-eyed Susan is a little looser, so you may need to wrap a wire or string around its perimeter to hold the stems upright. To get more plants, divide Goldsturm every third or fourth spring; black-eyed Susan reseeds itself, so just keep an eye out for seedlings.   *Steve Bender*

Trimming a basket with dried flowers lets you easily create a long-lasting arrangement. Fill the basket with small clay pots, and add potpourri for a touch of fragrance.

Edged in Flowers

This attractive arrangement has an appealing garden look that's yours in just a few easy steps. Gather your materials from the list and you are ready to begin. Here's how.

■ Pour a small amount of paint onto a paper plate or other disposable surface. (To duplicate the terra-cotta color of the clay pots, we mixed red oxide paint with a small amount of burnt umber.) Dampen a sponge with water, and dab it into the paint; then sponge the paint onto the basket. Apply several light coats to both the interior and exterior.

■ Snap off the flower stems to about 6 inches in length. Glue the flowers to the basket, overlapping the stems and arranging them close to the rim. (*Don't* touch the glue while it's hot.) Use a metal spoon to press the flower stems to the basket until the glue cools slightly.

Fill the basket with stacks of small clay pots turned at angles; then add potpourri and more dried flowers. Complete your arrangement by tying a few strands of raffia around the basket handle.   *Julia H. Thomason*

MATERIALS LIST
Light-colored,
unfinished basket
Acrylic paint
Sponge
Dried flowers
Hot-glue gun
Clay pots in different sizes
Potpourri
Raffia

Purchase an unfinished basket in a light color. Use a damp sponge to apply light coats of acrylic paint.

Break the dried flower stems to approximately 6 inches in length. Use a glue gun to attach the stems to the rim of the basket.

A simple wood bridge spans the pool and leads to the pavilion. The 12- x 12-foot structure was set in the corner of the garden to maximize space.

Touches of the Orient

For Riley Owens, a trip to the Orient is as close as his Greenville, South Carolina, backyard.

But that hasn't always been the case. "It was a square grass place before," says Riley. Working with landscape architect J. Dabney Peeples of Easley, South Carolina, Riley has transformed his "square of grass" into a Japanese garden.

The area for the new garden mea-sured about 50 feet square. Existing holly hedges defined the sides. A large asphalt parking area stood be-tween the house and the garden.

To make the most of the available space, Dabney located a pavilion in the far corner, so it would seem farther away. This allowed views from the pavilion to be across the diagonal of the garden, making that seem larger.

The pavilion is a simple structure, measuring 12 feet square. The floor sits about 22 inches above ground level and is made of 5/4- x 6-inch decking. Four 4 x 4 columns sup-port doubled 2 x 8 beams, which in turn support 2 x 8 joists. The ends of the beams and joists are cut in a decorative pattern. A low-pitched V-crimp metal roof tops the structure.

To give some substance to the pavilion, the landscape architect wrapped cut lengths of smokewood vine around the posts and the beams. The twisted, gnarled vines bring a rich texture to the simple outbuilding. "Otherwise, it would look like a little shed sitting out here," adds Dabney.

For a more roomlike feel, Greenville interior designer Jim Clamp added simple tieback draperies to the pavilion. He used painter's drop cloths from a home-center store, hung from plastic conduit mounted to the inside face of the beams. The draperies can be tied back for the open look shown in the photograph, or closed for privacy or protection from wind, sun, or rain.

Riley added a small pond in the center of the garden, bordered with rock. A recirculating pump, hidden on the edge of the garden, provides a steady trickle of water over a decorative rock.

A simple plank bridge extends over a narrow portion of the pond and joins a low boardwalk that leads to the garden gate. Because the boardwalk runs at an angle from the gate to the pavilion, it helps make the garden seem even larger than it really is.

To separate the new garden from the parking area, Dabney designed a fence and gate with Japanese detailing. The 6-foot-high fence is supported by 4 x 4 cedar posts, set 4 feet on center. Horizontal rails, also from 4 x 4s, form an open area at the top of the fence. Half-inch-diameter lengths of bamboo, set on a diagonal, fashion a decorative grillwork. Soft copper wire binds the bamboo strips together. The rest of the fence is of cedar 1 x 6s.

Within the compact garden, Dabney used a wide assortment of plants, including such Oriental selections as Yoshino cherry, greenleaf Japanese maple, cleyera, sasanqua camellia, and mondo grass. These are combined with other plants to give a wide range of leaf sizes and shades.

Although Riley is color blind, these contrasts of textures and shades of green provide a visual interest he can enjoy. For seasonal color, Dabney used plants with bright yellow flowers, such as Goldsturm rudbeckia, coreopsis, and Stella d'Oro daylily, for maximum contrast. Even the bark of trees, such as the river birches that stand outside the fence, were chosen for maximum texture.

And, Riley adds, "They brought in two tons of mushroom compost, so everything we stick in the ground grows."

Louis Joyner

Smokewood vine wraps around the structure of the pavilion to give both detail and substance.

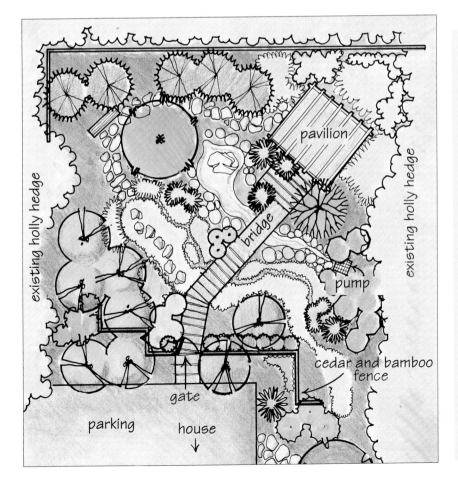

ORIENTAL EXPRESSIONS

Here are some tips for adding an Oriental garden.

■ Establish a sense of enclosure with high fences or evergreens.

■ Vary foliage textures and shapes; for example plant hostas with ferns.

■ Except with structures, avoid right angles in the design; pathways and plant beds should be gracefully curved.

■ Go with an unbalanced plan; don't match a plant in one corner with its mirror image in another.

■ Oriental gardens depict the world in miniature, with water, boulders, and plants representing oceans, mountains, and forests.

■ Create a series of views within the garden, such as a mass of ferns next to the water's edge.

■ Avoid the "man-made" look; use natural materials, such as bamboo, native stone, and wood. Let them weather; age imparts a distinction to Oriental gardens.

the lawn rangers

Why waste time reading or cooking when you could be cutting the grass? As these Southerners have discovered, where there's lawn, there's life.

Every neighborhood has one. You know who it is. It may even be you. I'm talking about the attorney who glimpses Nirvana every time he straddles a riding mower; the schoolteacher whose pleasure receptors fire whenever she hears the word "dethatch"; and the accountant who solemnly advises his son, "Be ready at first light, boy. Tomorrow we overseed."

You've met these people—dyed-in-the-wool, mow-in-the-dark, lime-till-I-scream lawn fanatics. Invisible in the workplace, such creatures invariably reveal themselves at home, betrayed by peculiar impulses. They'll roar their mowers under your bedroom window at dawn on Saturday. They'll use T-squares when edging to ensure 90-degree angles. They'll nearly pop a cranial artery at the sight of a hated dandelion.

Two summers ago, we asked our readers to nominate their favorite lawn fanatics. A prime requirement was that

BY STEVE BENDER
PHOTOGRAPHY VAN CHAPLIN, GARY CLARK

George Robinson of St. Louis is the Noah of lawn equipment. He has at least two of everything.

nominees had to do the work themselves—no lawn services allowed. Hundreds of you responded, for which we're deeply grateful. And while we couldn't visit everyone, the following people we did encounter typify the breed. They think grass. They dream grass. We just hope they don't eat grass.

PERFECT—AND THEN SOME

He owns four lawnmowers. Three spreaders. A leaf blower. A lawn sweeper. A power dethatcher. A backpack sprayer. An aerator. A string trimmer. A traveling sprinkler. And an emergency sod intensive care unit. His name is George Robinson. He lives in St. Louis, Missouri. And if you want him to show you the finest lawn you've ever seen, well, he'll show you.

Just how committed is he to his lawn? Consider this. One of his close friends is George Toma, groundskeeper for baseball's Kansas City Royals and famed throughout the sporting world as the "Guru of Grass." It's Toma who gets natural grass fields in tip-top shape for the NFL playoffs and Super Bowl. Two years ago, our Mr. Robinson flew south to Florida to visit the Royals in spring training. Was he interested in that hot new prospect at shortstop? Nope—he just wanted to talk turfgrass with Toma.

Some talk. Toma and International Seeds, Inc., of Halsey, Oregon, collaborated on a special seed mixture for George that produces a thick, green carpet year-round. This magic mix consists of (we'll pause here briefly while you locate a pencil and paper) 65% Ph.D. perennial ryegrass for summer color and durability; 25% Longfellow Chewings fescue and Cindy creeping red fescue for shade tolerance; plus 10% Sabre rough bluegrass (*Poa trivialis*) for vivid green winter color and persistence in wet spots.

"The whole idea was to find an alternative to warm-season grasses, which are so popular here in St. Louis," explains George. "My lawn takes our summer heat, humidity, and drought, thrives in the shade of huge sweet gums, and stays green all winter. It's the envy of the neighborhood."

> George sometimes offers daughter Katie a $5 bill for every weed she can find. (He still has the $5.)

But as any member of the Royals can tell you, it's easier to get to the top than to stay there. Challengers always want their shot at the champ. Keeping his title as the Top Gun of Turf means George Robinson can never rest. He works on his lawn every day. And when he goes to bed at night, the last thing he sees before he shuts his eyes is the latest news printed in his turf management magazine.

It's a jolly holiday when George overseeds and fertilizes. He does so on Labor Day, Thanksgiving, and Christmas. He employs a slow-release 20-5-5 formulation for the first two feedings, then switches to lower nitrogen for the third. In addition, he applies 2 pounds of potash per 1000 square feet every month throughout the growing season. "Potash gives the lawn muscle—good heat and drought resistance," he notes.

However, even George's lawn develops brown spots. No problem—he simply strolls to his 10- x 10-foot turf nursery in the backyard, removes sections of lush, green sod, and plugs them into the lawn. Or just to prove he can do it, he'll "pre-germinate" grass seed by soaking it in water. He then mixes the pre-germinated seed with compost and sand and spreads it on bare spots. By doing this, he gets cool-season grass seed to sprout in hot weather.

To George, mowing is both a science and an art. He owns four mowers—two rotaries, one riding, and one reel. How come? "My rotary has cutting heights of 1 inch, 1½ inches, 2 inches, 2½ inches, and 3 inches," he says. "But I have another that cuts at 1¼, 1¾, 2¼, 2¾, and 3¼ inches. So I can cut in increments of a quarter-inch." He needs such precision to cut his lawn at 1¾ inches until July, when he switches to 2½ inches for the rest of the summer. Cutting

Tommy Roberts, his wife Margaret, and their daughter, Paige

higher in summer puts less stress on the grass, he points out.

As for his other two mowers, George's riding model is far too oafish to provide a proper cut. So it just tows garden equipment. The reel mower, on the other hand, is George's paintbrush. "I use it on special occasions to create patterns in the grass, like the checkerboard look of Candlestick Park in San Francisco," he says.

Given George's quest for the perfect turf, you might think his lawn contains so many chemicals it could qualify as a future Superfund site. Not so. "I'm a firm believer in environmental controls," he asserts. "I use slow-release fertilizer to keep nitrates out of the groundwater. I adjust pesticide use to target only specific pests. I bag clippings and put them in the compost. I even ask my daughter, Katie, to spot-weed." Ever the generous father, George sometimes offers Katie a $5 bill for every weed she is able to find. (He still has the $5.)

In large part, George credits his lawn success to the inspirational words of his mentor, the venerable Toma. "Toma's favorite saying is, 'And then some,'" George explains. "And that really applies to good grass. See, if someone puts in 6 hours of work on a Saturday and I put in 6½, and we have the same size yards, I'm gonna have the better yard. It's because I did the usual, 'And then some.'"

MOWN ON THE FOURTH OF JULY

It begins as a distant, muffled groan. But with every passing second, the sound builds and builds, channeling down between the trees, headed, you know, you fear, right for you. It's louder now, angry, a mysterious thunder, closer, closer, ever closer. Then—what's that?—you spot it at last, bearing down upon you from beneath a covered bridge. Is it a herd of stampeding buffalo? An advancing column of German tanks? No—it's just the unique way a neighborhood in East Tennessee celebrates the Fourth of July.

Every Fourth, the men and women of Mill Run (near Chattanooga) hop aboard riding mowers festooned with flags and bunting and parade around the neighborhood. Rearbaggers, mulching mowers, lawn tractors, side dischargers—these

> "My husband and I have four children," Margaret says. "Well, three kids and the lawn."

gaudy chariots of patriotic turfdom claim the open road.

Sporting a green cap at the head of the parade is Tommy Roberts. Tommy became a lawn fanatic a few years ago out of sheer self-defense. When he and his wife, Margaret, bought their new house, the surrounding half-acre was nothing but hard red clay. They planted grass seed the first spring and it sprouted reasonably well. "But about mid-July, my whole lawn disappeared," he recalls. "It was so hot and dry, there was no way to keep the clay moist." So he put down topsoil mixed with compost and installed a sprinkler system. Two years later, his Rebel II tall fescue lawn stands so thick and green a lawnmower company filmed a commercial on it.

Ask Tommy for his secret to great grass and he really can't offer one, other than using Rebel II and watering regularly. He operates by gut instinct, rather than established science, and constantly experiments. "I just like playing with the lawn," he explains. "I like to throw seed out there, throw the fertilizer to it, and get the grass as dark green as I possibly can." Sometimes, though, his

> ## Dennis attributes the lawn's appearance to a single principle — *cut it often; cut it high.*

instincts betray him, like the time in July he spread fresh chicken manure on his grass and nearly burned it up. "That stuff was so hot, you could still see the feathers in it," he remembers. "Boy, I won't ever do that again."

These days the apple of Tommy's eye is his prized 18-horsepower riding mower. During the mowing season, you'll find him scooting across the lawn every Wednesday and Saturday. And since his model comes with headlights, he can even mow at night. He trades up for a new mower about every four years, whenever some new feature grabs his attention. "The next time I trade, I'm going for one with a hydrostatic shift," he declares. That'll allow him to go forward or backward without shifting gears.

Tommy views his time atop the mower as a respite from the cares of everyday life. "I'm so busy in the summer with work and the kids," he says. "For that one hour, I can get away, think things out, and feel I'm in another world." Paige, his 3-year-old daughter, looks forward to riding like Dad. Another lawn ranger in the making? Well, considering her very first word was "memow" (translation:

"lawnmower"), it's a pretty good bet.

To Tommy, that green stuff outside the front door is like a member of the family. Margaret acknowledges the truth. "My husband and I have four children," she says. "Well, three kids and the lawn."

CRAWFISH UNDER GRASS

Think you have problems with chinch bugs, mole crickets, white grubs, and other lawn vermin? Then visit the home of Dennis and Jill Kirkonis near Houston and see how stress-free your life really is. Wimpy insects don't worry Dennis and Jill. They have to battle subterranean crawfish.

Crawfish under grass? Sounds like nouvelle Creole cuisine to me, but the situation nearly drives the Kirkonises bonkers. Their yard sits at the bottom of a hill. Every time it rains hard, the water table rises, forcing underground crawfish to construct 6-inch-high mud mounds across the lawn so they can breathe.

Despite the marauding mud bugs, Dennis and Jill manage the prettiest St. Augustine lawn in Cleveland, Texas. They figure they spend six to eight hours working on their half-acre every summer weekend. Jill does the mowing, while Dennis handles the edging.

Dennis attributes the lawn's appearance to a single principle—*cut it often; cut it high*. "My theory is, if you don't let your grass get too long or cut too much at one time, you won't send it into shock," he states. "We try to cut it every four to five days and set the lawnmower just as high as we can, between three and four inches. If you cut St. Augustine too short, the sun down here will bake the ground. Keeping the grass high shades it." All of which means the lawn stays greener in summer, needs less water, and chokes out the weeds.

Tall grass once posed a problem for Jill, however. It made it hard to push the mower. Her salvation arrived in the form of a brand new mower equipped with inflatable rear tires that look like they fell off a little kid's bike. Now she rolls over 4-inch grass and crawfish mounds with no more effort than it takes the average person to complain about taxes.

The Kirkonises enjoy lawn work because it's a hobby they can pursue together. "Weekends find us with mowers and trowels, fertilizer and ant powder, refrigerator mugs and portable telephone, and grins on our faces," declares Jill.

That is, of course, unless it rains and the crawfish rise again.

ONE MAN, ONE LAWN, AND TWO DOGS

No man is an island, but Jim Nugent lives on one—Kent Island in Maryland's Chesapeake Bay. He moved to Kent six years ago to escape the hurly-burly of fast-growing Baltimore, Washington, D.C., and Annapolis. Out here, nothing breaks the morning silence but the chirp of a cardinal, the hoot of an owl, and the din from Jim's riding mower.

Spending 12 hours a week on the 1½-acre lawn means Jim often cuts it twice a week accompanied by his dogs, Megan and Jenny. "Fortunately, we have woods on one side. And my neighbor on the other side only lives there in summer," he notes. "I can fire up my mower at six in the morning, and the only person I bother is my wife."

The Nugents' verdant carpet had the humblest of beginnings. "It was a wooded, poison ivy-filled lot when we built the house in 1988," Jim recalls. After carefully clearing the site, he tilled four huge tractor-trailer loads of composted sewage sludge into the soil to add organic matter. Then he planted a mixture of Rebel and Falcon tall fescue.

Once out of every three cuts, Jim uses his cherished riding mower. He likes it because it turns on a dime, mows a 60-inch swath, and "cuts as fast going backward as it does going forward." But it doesn't bag clippings. Therefore, Jim switches to his standard mower for the following two cuts. He cuts the grass high, 3½ inches. "But because it's so thick and cut so evenly, it fools people into thinking I cut it low," he observes.

To take the guesswork out of fertilizing and liming, Jim has his soil tested every year by the cooperative Extension service. "If they tell me I don't need fertilizer or lime, I don't put it down," he says. He also consults his county agent for advice on disease and insect problems.

Maintaining a perfect lawn is like caring for a baby, but Jim has no regrets. "I like people to come by and talk to me about it," he remarks. "They all say, 'Man, could you come over and get my lawn looking good?' It's a big ego trip. I love it." ◇

Watchdogs Megan and Jenny keep an eye out for weeds, as Jim Nugent patrols his lawn.

> "I can fire up my mower at six in the morning, and the only person I bother is my wife."

August

Late-blooming roses

CHECKLIST FOR AUGUST

ANNUALS

Add marigolds, kalanchoe, coleus, or salvia now to freshen your Florida flower beds. Four-inch or larger pots give a quick display. In Texas, set out 4-inch or larger pots of marigolds, firebush, coleus, or salvia to liven up flower beds that have faded during summer. They'll give color until frost.

BULBS

In Florida, plant agapanthus, African iris, and amaryllis bulbs for color that returns yearly. Other bulbs to plant now include society garlic and rain lilies. In Texas, fall crocus, colchicum, and spider lilies can be added to the garden now for fall blooms. Mass plantings (at least 50) of smaller bulbs make a more effective display.

CHINCH BUGS

For problems in Florida and Texas, spray affected areas and slightly beyond with Diazinon or Dursban insecticides. Browned-out areas of St. Augustine lawns are a typical sign that your yard has an infestation of these small, black insects.

COLCHICUMS

Available this month at garden centers, these late-summer bulbs look like over-size crocuses. Plant immediately; if you delay, they will bloom in the bag. But once in your garden, they will come back year after year.

CONTAINER PLANTS

Because of heat and limited soil in a container, water plants in pots often. Frequent watering washes nutrients out of the soil, so feed them often with liquid 20-20-20 mixed according to label directions. If you used a slow-release fertilizer in spring, you will still need to liquid feed these plants because the fertilizer may be depleted by now.

CREPE MYRTLES

For a second flush of blooms this fall, trim each stem after flowering finishes. Cut stems no thicker than a pencil directly below the lowest developing seedpod. Expect fresh blooms in four to six weeks. In Texas, remove faded blooms to encourage more flowering. Your second crop may be smaller, but they will provide a good show. If faded blooms are not removed, they will form seedpods and not flower again.

FLOWERS

Cutting fresh or faded annual and perennial flowers will prevent seed production and will encourage more blooms. That's good news for flower arrangers. The more you cut, the more flowers you get.

GERANIUMS

In Texas, take cuttings 3 or 4 inches long and begin rooting. Remove the leaves from the lower third of the stem; set the stems in a container or tray of sand, vermiculite, or perlite. Water; then enclose the container in a clear plastic bag. When plants have rooted (about two to three weeks), remove the plastic and treat the geraniums as houseplants until setting them outdoors next spring.

HERBS

In Florida, plant herbs now to harvest this winter. Sow seeds of basil, chives, and dill. Start transplants of mint, oregano, and sweet marjoram.

IMPATIENS

To encourage new sprouts at the base, cut back leggy plants, leaving several inches of stem. Use soluble  20-20-20 fertilizer at the rate recommended on the label to hasten new growth.

LAWNS

Warm-season lawns of Bermuda, St. Augustine, or Zoysia need a late-summer feeding of a low-nitrogen fertilizer, such as 8-8-25. This will help your grass survive any extreme winter temperatures and also encourage early greening in spring. Apply fertilizer according to the label recommendations.

LETTUCE

Sow lettuce seeds in the Middle and Upper South now for fall salads. Plant fast-maturing selections, such as Black Seeded Simpson, Salad Bowl, Oakleaf, or Red Sails. These do not grow into a tight head, so you can harvest them a leaf at a time.

MARIGOLDS

It's still too early to set out pansies, so go to garden centers for pots of marigolds to replenish flower beds. They'll provide plenty of color until frost.

PALMS

In Florida, remove dead or discolored fronds that threaten power lines or scrape rooftops. Dead fronds cling to many varieties of palms, such as Mexican Washingtonias, but do the plant itself no harm. Do not remove green fronds, which are needed to manufacture food.

PEARS

Harvest pears a week or two before the fruit is fully ripened. Store in a cool, dry place to allow the fruit to ripen without developing stone cells (these will give the pears a gritty texture).

PERENNIALS

Daylilies can be divided now in the state of Florida. Once flowering is finished, divide big clumps; replant immediately. Prune at least 50% of the foliage from those divisions.

POWDERY MILDEW

Prevent this disease from affecting new growth by spraying with a fungicide, such as benomyl, Funginex, or Bayleton. It generally appears as a white, powdery coating on the leaves of zinnias, phlox, crepe myrtles, dahlias, roses, or other plants.

ROSES

To get your hybrid tea roses ready for their fall flowering, prune now.

SCAB

In Florida, hot, humid weather often encourages the growth of scab in poinsettias. Prune declining limbs that have brown spots or bumps on leaves and stems. Apply fresh mulch to keep spores of this damaging organism from spreading.

SEEDS

Use individual envelopes to collect seeds from mature pods of spider flowers, poppies, rose campion, purple coneflowers, and other flowers. Store in a cool, dry place during winter; then sow indoors in early spring for transplanting into the garden after frost.

SPIDER MITES

Hot, dry days are prime times for these almost microscopic creatures. They feed on the underside of leaves of azaleas, roses, marigolds, foxgloves, and many others. Look for faded, yellowed, stippled leaves. Spray with insecticidal soap or kelthane to control them. Even a strong blast with the hose will help.

TWIG BEETLES

Dying tips of branches on dogwoods may indicate the presence of twig beetles. Prune and destroy damaged twigs. These pests bore into twigs and establish a fungus in the stems as food for larvae; pruning is the most effective control.

VEGETABLES

Plant watermelons by the tenth of the month in Central Florida. Plant sweet corn, cucumbers, and summer squash by mid-month in South and Central Florida. Wait and add eggplant, onion, and broccoli in late August throughout the state. In Texas, sow seeds of leaf lettuce, spinach, and other fall vegetables in the upper two-thirds of the state. Make sure the soil stays moist until the seed comes up. Plant early-maturing selections of tomatoes from Austin southward and along the coast.

WATERING

On hot Texas days, water-efficient drip irrigation systems or soaker hoses work well for flower or shrub beds and vegetable gardens. A timer can make watering even less of a chore. Check newly planted trees and shrubs for wilting, water deeply, and mulch to conserve moisture.

WEEDS

Save yourself a lot of work next year by pulling weeds before they set seeds. Just make sure to get the roots when you pull.

August Notes

TO DO:

■ Deadhead marigolds, petunias, scarlet sage, zinnias, verbena, snapdragons, ageratum, and spider flower to prolong blooming
■ Put out a hummingbird feeder
■ Prune shrub roses to remove errant branches and direct new growth; do not prune climbers at this time
■ Root cuttings of favorite annuals and tender perennials that you would like to shelter through the winter
■ Preserve garden flowers by hanging them upside down to air dry
■ Harvest garlic that was planted in the spring
■ Start seeds of perennials for fall planting

TO PLANT:

■ Cool-weather vegetables for fall
■ Fall-blooming crocuses, colchicums, and spider lilies

TO PURCHASE:

■ Cabbage, broccoli, brussels sprouts, collards, and kale transplants
■ Hummingbird feeder
■ Fall-blooming bulbs
■ Seeds of fall-blooming perennials

_____

_____

_____

_____

TIP OF THE MONTH

To keep garden supplies handy, I put an old mailbox on a post in the garden. In it, I keep a trowel, plant markers and pen, twine, garden gloves, hand pruners, bags, and a small notebook.

Mrs. Jack Archer
Summerville, South Carolina

A
Garden
For
Butterflies

*Authentic in detail and timeless in appeal,
the new plantings at Biltmore House and
Gardens have attracted the attention of
butterflies and visitors alike.*

BY LINDA C. ASKEY
PHOTOGRAPHY VAN CHAPLIN

Lochinch Butterfly Bush

Cherry-pink zinnias and orange narrowleaf zinnias attract butterflies, while ornamental grasses and yellow mums are added to fill out the fall border.

Gardens change with time, as do the interests of gardeners. Such is the case with the Butterfly Garden at Biltmore Estate in Asheville, North Carolina. Where landscape architect Frederick Law Olmsted originally specified a simple swath of turf, grows a garden rich in color and fluttering with life.

Landscape curator Bill Alexander explains, "The use of the estate today is entirely different than it was in the 1890s. It is no longer a gentleman's private estate; it is now visited by three-quarters of a million people a year. So we want to offer the best of what Olmsted planned for the estate, but with consideration for today's needs. We want to provide an opportunity to learn, and what better way than with a butterfly garden."

Three years ago landscaping supervisor Suzanne Habel

Stately late bloomers anchor the back of the border. They include golden narrowleaf sunflower, lavender tartarian aster, yellow Autumn Sun rudbeckia, and the red-flowered pineapple sage.

and crew leader Ellen Blair attended a garden symposium at Callaway Gardens, where a conservatory and garden for butterflies have stirred interest across the South. They took home a healthy measure of enthusiasm and proposed a new garden for the Biltmore Estate.

"The only design that we have for the walled garden, which was labeled a preliminary design, called for a fruit and vegetable garden," recalls Bill. "But in a note on the plan to Mr. Olmsted, Mr. Vanderbilt said, 'I want a garden of ornament, rather than utility.' "

So Suzanne and Ellen started work on a location in front of the conservatory, an area that would not only be a gathering spot for visitors, but one that would also be hospitable to butterflies—full of sunshine and protected from wind.

The butterfly garden takes the place of the herb garden, which is now confined to the side nearest the conservatory. Behind it is a display of summer and fall perennials that would rival any flower border, but with an extra measure of appeal—butterflies.

In addition to gourmet butterfly flowers, they have added birdbaths, known locally as butterfly baths. In each is a sponge to provide a moist perch, just like butterflies have when they gather at a mud puddle.

Host plants, such as butterfly weed and parsley, offer places for butterflies to lay their eggs. Suzanne remembers the first time she and Ellen saw the caterpillars: "They were just munching out. Our first reaction was to panic and say, 'Oh no, they are eating up our butterfly weed; we are going to have to spray.' Then we looked at each other and laughed, because they were doing exactly what we wanted them to do."

Although the monarch caterpillars devour the butterfly weed, it comes back, just like it does in nature. Suzanne and Ellen want visitors to learn that half-eaten plants are as much a part of butterfly gardening as the flowers. But they have also learned to plant other host plants near the back of the borders where they are not as evident. After all, a butterfly garden is for people, too.

Several books about butterfly gardening have been published recently, including *Butterfly Gardening for the South* by Geyata Ajilvsgi (Taylor Publishing Company, Dallas, Texas; $34.95). Callaway Gardens offers an activity book called *Discover Butterflies!* ($7.95) and *Butterflies* video ($19.99). The activity book and the video can be ordered together for $24.95 plus $3.50 shipping by calling 1-800-282-8181. ◇

BUTTERFLY FAVORITES
Annuals
Hybrid zinnia
Narrowleaf zinnia
Pineapple sage
Cosmos
Single marigold
Verbena
Pentas
Mexican sunflower (Tithonia)

Perennials
New England asters
Butterfly weed
Joe-pye weed
Swamp sunflower
Purple coneflower
Autumn Sun rudbeckia
Garden phlox

Shrubs
Abelia
Butterfly bush
Blue Mist Caryopteris

PHOTOGRAPHS: VAN CHAPLIN

Bordered by lush plantings, this handsome brick landing frames a view of the house and welcomes visitors.

New Walk Is a Step Up

Bill and Pearl Duke's original walk was a disaster. Consisting of little more than pieces of slate dropped atop the ground, it ran parallel to the house between the front door and parking. Not only was footing treacherous, Bill and Pearl couldn't see company coming. And visitors were denied a flattering view of the handsome Richmond home.

Landscape architect Preston Dalrymple designed the solution. Now when you park your car, a solid-brick landing welcomes you. It's 20 feet wide, so a single parked car can't block the way. Lush plantings of variegated Japanese pachysandra and leatherleaf mahonia border the landing, framing an attractive view of the house. Together, the plants and landing indicate that you've arrived at someplace special.

Once on the angled walk, you ascend a total of eight steps to get to the front steps. Here's where Preston made a crucial, as well as correct, decision. He could have placed all of the steps in the walk together and fashioned a more direct route to the door. Instead, he used a series of broad landings to separate the steps into twos. Two steps up and a landing; two steps up and a landing; and so on. As a result, the approach seems less steep and tiring, even though you walk slightly farther.

To sum up, this walk accomplishes three things every good walk should. It says welcome. It takes visitors safely and comfortably to the front door. And it shows off the house to its best advantage. *Steve Bender*

Silver Edge Japanese pachysandra sparkles at curbside beneath the deep-green leaves of leatherleaf mahonia.

With the walk separated into a series of two steps followed by a landing, the ascent to the door seems less steep and tiring.

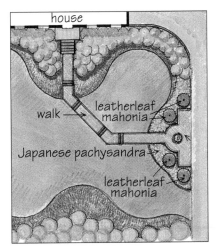

house

walk →   leatherleaf mahonia

Japanese pachysandra →

leatherleaf mahonia

base. If the plant is a vigorous one like Queen Elizabeth, you may need to reduce its height. Always cut above an outward-facing growth bud so the new growth does not become a tangled mess in the middle.

Remember that cutting roses is a form of pruning. When you cut a bloom, the leaves closest to the flower have only three leaflets. Go below these to a leaf with five leaflets; one that faces the outside of the plant is the best place to cut.

Fertilize roses monthly all season long. According to Paul, the amount you apply depends on the size of the plant, varying "anywhere from a tablespoon to a small handful or more." In the Lower South, he recommends feeding until September and then one more time lightly in October. If you live in the Middle or Upper South, you would make your last application in September.

Spraying should be ongoing from the beginning of the season to the end. As long as the foliage is green, continue weekly applications through fall. For Paul, that means the season lasts into November. He advises that although powdery mildew is a small problem in summer, roses are particularly susceptible to both powdery and downy mildew in the fall. Funginex will help to control both. Be sure that the spray has had time to dry before a rain washes it away.

Watering is essential, especially if autumn is dry or your soil is sandy. Paul applies 1½ to 2 inches of water each week. Although he prefers to irrigate beneath the plants, his garden is not set up for it. He waters with overhead sprinklers. Because of his regular applications of fungicides, leaf diseases have not been a problem.

Linda C. Askey

When it comes to growing roses, autumn is even better than spring. The flowers are usually the highlight of the entire season.

Roses Get Ready for Fall

In the last days of winter you pruned, fertilized, and sprayed to get your hybrid tea roses ready for spring. Now it's time to prepare for fall, their second season. As the nights cool down, roses grow larger.

"Our best blooms come in October," says Paul Hjort of Thomasville, Georgia. As owner of Thomasville

Nurseries, Inc., and judge and keeper of an All America Rose Selection display garden, he should know. To get those October blooms, Paul begins in August. Here's how he does it.

Pruning in late summer removes dead and unproductive shoots, opening bushes up to light. This encourages new canes to sprout from the

Now is the time to prune, feed, spray, and water your roses so they will be the best they can be.

After: A new, gray-stucco exterior, second-story porch, larger windows, French doors along the porch, and paired columns create a totally updated look. The low wall in front matches the exterior of the house and helps define a pull-in space for guest parking off the street. The owners now access the house from an alley.

A Sensation of a Transformation

They're common oversights. Just about everybody makes them. People want to make their front yard more pleasing, but they often forget that they've got a house sitting out there, too. And when they want to spiff up the front of the house, they tend to look right over the bushes and such.

But not Ben and Teresa Mc-Caleb. They knew that whatever was done to their San Antonio home and landscape had to form a pleasing, compatible, and comfortable unit. That's why they worked with both an architect, Rick Archer of Overland Partners, Inc., and a landscape architect, Terry Lewis, to come up with a total makeover from the street to the front steps.

Teresa had a good background for such a task, too. "I used to redo houses as a business and had extensively remodeled other houses I had lived in," she says. Even so, she still felt the need to seek help from Rick and Terry. "For example, I knew I wanted a porch, but Rick came up with the idea for a two-story porch," she recalls.

It was apparent to everyone that

Before: Composition siding and a single-story overhang gave the house a dated look. Overgrown shrubs and a misshapen shade tree obscured the front. The narrow driveway almost grazed the side of the house and took up valuable space in the front and side yards.

the driveway on the side would have to go. Fortunately, there was an alley in back that could provide access for the McCalebs to come and go. Tearing up the driveway solved one problem, but it created another.

"Removing it gave us that extra 12 feet on the side and in the front for more yard and garden space, but left the problem of how to handle parking in the front," Rick says. The final solution was a pull-in parking area that

paralleled the street. There was an even stronger incentive for off-street parking because parking on the street is illegal in the McCaleb's neighborhood during certain hours.

The low, stucco walls, capped with D'Hanis tile that matches the brick walkway and parking pad, make the front parking area "belong" to the house. "I like to repeat material used for the house, so the landscape looks like it matches the residence," adds Terry. "Also, they have such a small yard in front, the wall really helps define that space." Taking out the old shade tree in front, and replacing other plants with drought-tolerant alternatives, such as yaupon (*Ilex vomitoria*) and Texas mountain laurel (*Sophora secundiflora*), ensures that the new landscape will thrive in the dry San Antonio climate.

Unlike many "designed-by-committee" efforts, all the parts of the McCaleb's residential redo blend beautifully. "I think that's why this project was so successful," Rick says. "Teresa, Terry, and I collaborated to come up with a total plan that worked." *Mark G. Stith*

Sharing Plants With Catherine

Like any other gardener, Catherine Sims loves to tell you about her flowers. If you'd like some seed from this spider flower, just ask. Or she'll ask you.

Shun the scale when you visit Catherine Sims's garden in Homewood, Alabama. Because sure as the sun sets in the west, you'll weigh a lot more leaving than when you arrived. Catherine, you see, belongs to that venerable community of Southern gardeners who feel honor-bound to share plants that someone else once shared with them. You can't admire any of her garden treasures without hearing her say, "Oh, would you like a piece?"

I first strolled through her garden two years ago and found it a tangle of horticultural delight. Spider flowers, cosmos, peacock ferns, and old roses marauded throughout the yard, claiming every inch of ground not trodden bare by shoes. Only a few beauties had originated at a garden center. "I haven't bought many plants," explains Catherine. "Most came from friends, relatives, and ancestors."

Her white spice pink, which smells of cloves and vanilla, is one of them. "It came from a family named Kaiser in Gardendale, Alabama," she recalls. "They made their living selling chickens. We got eggs from them for many years and got to be friends. When they gave up their place, they invited me to come out and get anything I wanted. That's where I got the spice pink."

Catherine bestowed a piece of it upon me last summer. Despite an extended drought, this heirloom flower took hold immediately. This spring, it bloomed profusely, perfuming my entire garden.

Another passalong plant came from her mother. It goes by the curious appellation of turk's cap (*Malvaviscus arboreus Drummondii*). Also known as turk's turban and Scotsman's purse, this shrubby perennial gets its name from remarkable blooms that never fully open. Each bright-red, 1½-inch blossom consists of five petals twisted like a pinwheel around a protruding

column of stamens. This configuration doesn't bother hummingbirds or butterflies, which use long tongues to sip the nectar. But it frustrates the devil out of ill-equipped bumblebees, which finally plunder the flowers by tearing them open.

Several qualities, as Catherine showed me, set turk's cap apart. First, this Mexican native blooms at an unusual time, beginning in late summer and continuing well into fall. Second, it's one of the few perennials that bloom well in shade. Third, small, apple-like fruits change from white to red as they ripen. Finally, it grows in any well-drained soil and is easily propagated by seed, cuttings, or division.

PHOTOGRAPHS: VAN CHAPLIN, TINA EVANS

Favorites of butterflies and hummingbirds, the bright-red blooms of turk's cap consist of petals twisted tightly around protruding stamens.

For proof of this last point, just look around Catherine's yard. Myriad pots of seedlings and rooted cuttings litter the ground beneath her shade trees. Like many growers of passalong plants, she's an avid propagator. Trouble is, she always roots many more plants than she can care for. "I've just about rooted myself out of house and home," she admits. So every spring, she holds a plant sale to raise money for gardening supplies. "The best part of it all is meeting so many nice people," she notes.

Of course, you don't always have to pay. Just show up in her garden and admire something. She'll give you a piece of this, that, and maybe two or three other things. That's how I came by my turk's cap. That's also how I obtained some of her bright-red Flanders poppies (*Papaver rhoeas*). She received her seeds from a friend, Will Brown, who raked his hands through poppy fields as he fled the Germans during World War I. When he returned home, his mother found the seeds in his pockets and sowed them. Today, Catherine happily gives away the descendants of Will's poppies. Just ask.

But whatever you do, don't protest that you'd really like to come back and pick your plants up later. "The best time to accept a plant," Catherine asserts, "is when it's offered."

Steve Bender

We can't supply sources for the spice pink; we don't know its correct name. But we can for the others. Send a self-addressed, stamped, business-size envelope to Turk's Cap, *Southern Living*, P.O. Box 830119, Birmingham, AL 35283.

A cart laden with summer's tomatoes, okra, eggplants, and herbs is a delicious sight in Jefferson's garden at Monticello.

Summer Harvest Tips

Summer's vegetables and herbs can be both a bounty and a burden when they all mature at once. Here's how to deal with your harvest.

Biggest is not always best. When it comes to summer squash, beans, cucumbers, okra, and eggplant, harvest when they are tender—before the seeds mature and the outside grows tough and bitter. Pick every couple of days. When these vegetables are allowed to mature, the plants stop producing. So if you are going on a trip, ask a friend to harvest and enjoy them.

Let others mature. Winter squash (acorn and butternut) and pumpkins should be left on their vines until the skin is too hard to be punctured with your fingernail. At that time, cut them, leaving several inches of stem. Allow them to cure in a warm and ventilated place, such as a porch, for one to two weeks. Then store them in an air-conditioned room or a cool, dry basement.

Use damaged vegetables immediately. Sometimes tomatoes will crack after a heavy rain, or birds will peck ripe produce. Pick and prepare right away.

Keep harvested vegetables in the shade. If you pick a basket of tomatoes, a basket of beans, or a basket of squash, put it beneath a nearby tree or in the shadow of your wheelbarrow until you can take it to the kitchen.

Handle vegetables carefully. If cut, vegetables will be open to bacteria and fungi that can cause rot. Even bruises will make them spoil much more quickly.

HARVEST KNOW-HOW

Green beans: Pick before the pods get lumpy.

Swiss chard: Use outer leaves when 4 to 10 inches long.

Corn: Harvest when silks turn brown and dry. To test, puncture a kernel; juice should be milky.

Cucumbers: Length depends upon selection. Don't let them turn yellow.

Eggplant: Cut while young and glossy.

Okra: Cut when 3 to 5 inches long.

Southern peas: Harvest when pods change color, but before peas dry.

Summer squash: Get them while they are small.

Sweet peppers: Pick when a usable size or let them turn color.

Hot peppers: Let them turn red if you intend to dry them.

Tomatoes: Pick after turning red, but while area near the stem is still green. Never store below 50 degrees.

Pools
For Problem Places

Swim

through your

dreams,

even if your

yard is

grounded in

reality.

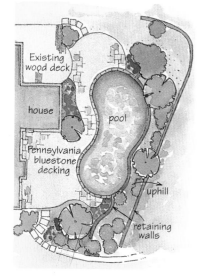

Splashing into a cool underwater world on a scorching afternoon is a true pleasure of summer. Dreaming of building a swimming pool all your own? A large, level backyard is no longer required. Small yards, sloping yards—just about any yard—can accommodate delightful pools.

TIGHT SITE

A wooded hillside rising behind this Bethesda, Maryland, home afforded lots of privacy, but left little room for a pool. The slope loomed close to the house, despite terraces created by a pair of stone retaining walls.

The homeowners turned to Jim Sines of Garden Gate Landscaping to turn their yard's limitations into a watery asset. Jim left the upper retaining wall in place, but rebuilt the lower one. "The solution was to push the slope back to fit the pool in," he says.

Reinforced concrete gives structural integrity, and a stone veneer makes the wall attractive. Mortar between the stone and wall holds the stone in place, but no mortar is visible in the wall's face. This trick gives it the look of dry stacked stone.

Jim designed the pool to complement its setting. Generous curves carve into the hillside; a dark-gray pigment in the pool's finish mimics the quiet waters of a pond. The tinting is dark enough to mirror trees on the surface, yet light enough to show the bottom.

BY JO KELLUM
PHOTOGRAPHY VAN CHAPLIN,
SYLVIA MARTIN

Curving like a woodland pond, this Maryland pool hugs the hillside.

September

Garden asters and ornamental grass

CHECKLIST FOR SEPTEMBER

ALLAMANDA

In Florida, yellowing leaves with dark green veins indicate a manganese deficiency. Spray the leaves with a foliar fertilizer containing this element, such as Sunniland Palm Spray, to correct the problem.

BELL PEPPERS

When harvesting green peppers, leave a few on the plant. With time, peppers will change color and develop more vitamin C.

BOUGAINVILLEA

In Florida, remove overgrown branches by the middle of the month. Later pruning may delay blooming.

BULBS

Buy now for the best selection. Remember to buy enough to have a real impact. A lot of one kind may be more effective than six of this and six of that. Keep them in the vegetable bin of your refrigerator for at least another month before planting.

CAMELLIAS

In Florida, fertilize camellias for the last time this year. Later feedings may encourage new growth, which is susceptible to freeze damage. Apply an acid-forming fertilizer that lists azaleas and camellias on the label.

CARROTS

Plant carrots now in North Florida, but wait until next month to plant them elsewhere in the state. Choose a selection that thrives in your soil type. Short carrots, such as Short 'n Sweet, grow well in heavy clay soils. Longer carrots, such as Imperator and Nantes, are well suited for sandy soils.

COVER CROPS

Enrich empty vegetable beds by sowing seeds of annual rye, crimson clover, or vetch now. They will get established before cold weather and grow during the winter months. A month before you want to plant, turn them under to provide organic matter to the soil. Farm supply stores are good seed sources.

FALL WEBWORMS

Look for grayish-white webs covering the leaves of pecan, persimmon, mulberry, and walnut trees. Remove them as soon as possible using long-handled pruners.

FIRE ANTS

Treat existing mounds with Diazinon, Dursban, or Orthene insecticides, applied according to label directions, or pesticide formulations specific for fire ants. Baits may also be effective.

GARDEN SOIL

Get your Texas garden or flower bed ready for planting later this fall or early spring by adding organic matter and turning it under. Work in 4 to 6 inches of compost, pine bark, peat, aged cow manure, or other organic matter as deeply as possible into existing soil.

HEDGES

Give your sheared hedges one last clip. They still have time to grow a bit and harden off before growth stops for the winter.

HERBS

Sow seeds of the biennial herbs coriander (cilantro) and chervil for a supply of flavorful foliage in winter and early spring. These plants have roots like a carrot, so they don't transplant well. Sow directly into good garden soil where you want them to grow.

HOUSEPLANTS

Spray plants with insecticidal soap or SunSpray Ultra-Fine Oil before bringing them back indoors for winter. This will reduce the number of pests, such as mealybugs, scale, spider mites, or whiteflies, you bring indoors. Gardeners in Central Florida and warmer areas of Texas should be prepared to move tender tropicals inside when a cold snap threatens.

LAWNS

In the Middle and Upper South it's time to fertilize bluegrass, fescue, and cool-season blends. Choose a good quality lawn fertilizer, such as 30-3-8 or 22-4-14, that contains a portion of its nitrogen in a slow-release form. Feed St. Augustine lawns now in North and Central Florida. South Florida gardeners should wait until next month before fertilizing. Apply 10-5-10 granular fertilizer with micronutrients to the lawn before watering. In Texas, feed cool-season grasses with 16-4-8 or similar fertilizer. Apply about 5 pounds of fertilizer per 1,000 square feet of lawn. Use a whirlybird or drop spreader to distribute granular fertilizer evenly.

LETTUCE

In Texas, sow seeds in loose, rich soil; just scatter the seeds, and lightly rake them in. Keep the soil moist and thin seedlings to 6 to 8 inches apart for leaf lettuce, 12 inches for head lettuce. Leaf-type lettuce selections to try include Buttercrunch, Bibb, and Capitan (green-leaved); Red Sails, Vulcan, and Ruby (red-leaved).

MUMS

For instant effect in Texas, set out blooming garden mums now. Concentrate masses of the same color in prominent areas to create a dramatic effect.

NASTURTIUMS

In Florida, try this cool-weather annual if you have sandy soil. Sow seeds directly in the garden or window boxes late this month. Darkness is required for germination, so cover seeds with a few inches of soil. For maximum blooms, don't fertilize or overwater the plants.

ORNAMENTALS

Now is an ideal time for planting container-grown trees and shrubs. Dig the hole at least twice as wide and as deep as the root mass; be sure to water thoroughly after planting, and apply a 2-inch layer of mulch. Water frequently until plant becomes established.

PERENNIALS

Dig and divide crowded perennials, such as cannas, crinum lilies, iris, dianthus, violets, purple coneflowers, and Louisiana and prairie phlox. Replant as soon as possible into good garden soil; water generously after planting.

POINSETTIAS

Don't prune poinsettias after the first of the month in Florida. Wait until after the plants produce brightly colored bracts for holiday decorating.

ROSES

Fertilize roses with 5-10-10 or a similar granular fertilizer. For large established shrubs and climbers, apply ½ cup per plant. Reduce applications for smaller or younger plants. Scratch the granules into the soil at the base of the plant, and water thoroughly. This is the last feeding for the Middle and Upper South. For a late flush of blooms, fertilize roses in North Florida with 5-10-10 or a specialty rose fertilizer (use the amount suggested on the label). Gardeners in the rest of the state should wait until next month to fertilize roses.

TENDER FAVORITES

Take cuttings of tender salvias, brugmansias, coleus, and other summer plants to root and overwinter indoors.

VEGETABLES

Don't stop now. Fall is the best time to grow lettuce, spinach, mustard, radishes, collards, turnips, and kale. Sow seeds directly into the garden. The cool weather to come will give leafy greens a sweeter flavor. In Florida, plant vegetables at staggered intervals to ensure a steady harvest throughout the fall. Successive planting is particularly advantageous for vegetables that have short peak periods, such as broccoli, bush bean, and kohlrabi. Staggered plantings also extend the harvest time for radishes, which mature quickly.

WATER

Don't be deceived by cooler temperatures—this month can be very dry. Continue watering regularly, and remember that it is better to water thoroughly once a week than sparingly every day.

WILDFLOWERS

In Texas, sow seeds of wildflowers in weed-free, lightly tilled soil for blooms next year. Bluebonnets, Indian paintbrush (East Texas), cutleaf daisy, Indian blanket, Mexican hat, blue-eyed grass, and lemon mint are just a few choices. One source of wildflower seeds is WildSeed, Inc., P.O. Box 308, Eagle Lake, TX 77434. Catalog is free.

September Notes

TO DO:
- Fertilize cool-season lawns
- Replace tired bedding plants with ornamental vegetables
- Replenish mulch in azalea and camellia beds

TO PLANT:
- Pansies
- Cool-weather annuals and vegetables
- Ground covers, such as big blue liriope, mondo, English ivy, periwinkle, pachysandra, and ajuga
- Lettuce

TO PURCHASE:
- Spring bulbs
- Lawn fertilizer
- Lettuce seeds
- Ornamental kale or cabbage

TIP OF THE MONTH

Here's a tip for organizing and storing caladium bulbs over the winter. I place smaller bulbs in the individual compartments of cardboard egg cartons (the ones that hold 18 eggs). I write the name and color of the caladiums on the carton. For larger bulbs, I use old shoeboxes and place hay between the bulbs.

Paul Wade
Mesquite, Texas

Take a Cue From NATURE

Late-summer heat giving your garden the blahs?
Wake it up with the first colors of fall—purple and gold.

Sometimes nature simply outshines the garden. Even while trees still boast rich greens and midday shimmers with heat, autumn is approaching and the roadsides come alive, dappled with purple and gold. Meanwhile gardens fade to a uniform green. Or brown. Take a cue from the South's native perennials—fill the void in your garden with autumn's other color scheme.

Let nature show you how—just drive through the countryside in your area. The wildflowers you'll see from the car are sun loving and drought tolerant, and are ideal for your garden, too. (Remember to take along a wildflower field guide.) Flat-topped clusters of purple ironweed, 10-foot-tall Joe Pye weed, and blue-purple New England asters are nature's premonition of fall. And along the South's byways, waves of goldenrod bow to the gust of wind as your car passes by.

So translate nature's fall colors into the language of garden plants. That field of goldenrod inspires a wispy mound of Fireworks goldenrod in the garden. New En-

Garden asters and ornamental grass echo Southern roadsides adorned with wild asters and broomsedge.

gland asters that complement goldenrod in nature do the same in the border. But here—unlike in a roadside jumble—you can stake stems so they don't flop on their neighbors.

Or try carrying the wild examples a little further. For example, Autumn Joy sedum has no relation to Joe Pye weed, but the dusty mauve flowers resemble one another, except for their scale. Even the dwarf form of Joe Pye weed grows 5 to 6 feet tall in the back of the flower border. Planting Autumn Joy sedum in the foreground sets up an echo of both color and form that gives the garden continuity.

Whether in color or form, you can select flowers and foliage that echo their likenesses from the wild to your garden and back again. And wherever those echoes occur, they form a connection to the beauty of the Southern countryside. Native and exotic alike, these are survivors—plants that endure the summer to color the garden as the season slips into autumn.

Turn to page 194 for our best bets for bringing nature into the garden.

BY LINDA C. ASKEY / PHOTOGRAPHY VAN CHAPLIN, SYLVIA MARTIN

The trees are still green, but the late-summer and early-fall border at Georgia's Callaway Gardens features purple spikes of Mexican bush sage, a late planting of pale-pink cosmos, pink pentas, and a border of Mexican heather with yellow lantana in the foreground.

These Plants Blend Summer Into Fall

Gardeners treasure flowers and foliage that fill the late-summer void. Plant the perennials later this fall for a head start next year. Set out annuals after frost next spring.

Common Name / Botanical Name	Lifecycle	Light	Height x Width	Region	Hints
Gold to yellow:					
Bur marigold *Bidens polylepis*	Annual	☼	3' x 3'	All South	Collect a few seeds on roadside plants. Will reseed in the garden.
Maximilian sunflower *Helianthus maximiliani*	Perennial	☼	9' x 2½'	All South	Cut back by half in June to reduce size.
Giant pale yellow sunflower *Helianthus giganteus*	Perennial	☼	9' x 5'	All South	Cut back by half in June to reduce size.
Yellow lantana *Lantana camara*	Annual	☼	1' x 3'	All South	Grows as a perennial in the Coastal South.
Gold moneywort *Lysimachia nummularia aurea*	Perennial	☼ ◑	1" x 1½'	Upper, Middle, and Lower South	Offers good foliage color year-round.
Fireworks goldenrod *Solidago rugosa* Fireworks	Perennial	☼	4' x 4'	All South	Fireworks will not sucker like many goldenrods.
Purple to pink:					
New England aster *Aster novae-angliae*	Perennial	☼	3' x 4'	All South	Staking is needed for this form.
Dwarf New England aster *Aster novae-angliae* Purple Dome	Perennial	☼	1½' x 3'	All South	No staking is required.
Raydon's Favorite aster *Aster oblongifolius angustatus*	Perennial	☼	3' x 2'	All South	Offers aromatic foliage and blue-purple flowers.
Dwarf Tartarian aster *Aster tartaricus* Jindai	Perennial	☼	4' x 2'	Upper, Middle, and Lower South	Flower color is more blue than violet.
Pink turtlehead *Chelone lyonii*	Perennial	☼ ◑	3' x 3'	All South	This perennial adapts to wet areas.
Mexican heather *Cuphea hyssopifolia*	Annual	☼	1' x 1½'	All South	Blooms all summer. Hardy in the Coastal South.
Ageratum *Eupatorium coelestinum*	Perennial	☼ ◑	2' x 4'	All South	Will spread underground and reseed. Control by pulling out extra portions and cutting back before seeds mature.
Dwarf Joe Pye weed *Eupatorium fistulosum*	Perennial	☼ ◑	6' x 4'	Upper, Middle, and Lower South	Dwarf forms from perennial nurseries reach 6 feet tall rather than 10.
Mexican bush sage *Salvia leucantha*	Perennial	☼	3' x 3'	Lower and Coastal South	Can be grown as an annual in the Middle and Upper South.
Autumn Joy sedum *Sedum* x *spectabile* Autumn Joy	Perennial	☼	2' x 2'	All South	Showy all season as a mound of gray-green foliage. It blooms mauve pink and fades to rusty brown in late autumn.

☼ = sun   ◑ = part shade

Street Wise

The pleasures of living in well-kept, older neighborhoods are many. Sidewalks, tree-lined streets, charming houses with front porches—you know the setting. But the typically narrow city lots and postage-stamp front yards leave little room for landscaping. What can you do with a yard that's not much bigger than a typical sofa?

Well, just take a look at this appealing "streetscape" designed by landscape architect René Fransen for the front yard of Robert and Ann Soniat's shotgun cottage-style home in New Orleans. It's not only pretty, but it's pretty smart, too. Here's why.

Looks. That's the first impression you get from the street: The neat, clean, and uncluttered appearance of the house, plants, and pavement. The house already looked picture-perfect when René was called in to help "fix" the front yard. For the sidewalk, brick pavers set in a herringbone pattern match the classy exterior of the home much better than the plain old concrete walk. Neat rows of boxwoods line two of the new shrub beds, which are all curbed with bricks laid on end. Mass plantings add emphasis without engulfing the house or hiding the porch's ornamental iron railing.

Logic. Everything—from street to steps—has its place and purpose, but a couple of twists made this project a bit of a challenge. For one, there were originally two sets of front steps leading up to the porch, but only one front door. René took out the steps on the left side of the porch, and highlighted the entrance on the right. "We redid the front steps," says René, "and topped them with flagstone." Another problem involved parking. The Soniats have to parallel park on the street and had always been forced to step from car to yard—or what there was of it. "We just got tired of stepping out into the mud," Ann recalls. "I love flagstone, and René came up with the idea of using flagstone along the street." Set flush with the brick walkway, the flagstone pavers ensure much less of a mess from car door to front door.

Landscaping. There's an interesting and appropriate mix of plants here. Let's take it from the street, where a trio of tree-form ligustrum form a shady, evergreen canopy for the sidewalk. Mexican heather, a low-growing shrubby perennial with purple flowers, makes a perfect ground cover under the ligustrum. In the new shrub beds, boxwoods frame mass plantings of pink-flowering dwarf azaleas (Sir Robert), butterfly iris, and gardenias. The loosely formed branches of Showa no sakae dwarf sasanqua camellias complement rather than cover up the iron railing of the porch.

Like many beautifully restored homes, the Soniats' classic cottage is a sight worth slowing down for. And thanks to some street-smart design, their front yard is bound to get a closer look, too. *Mark G. Stith*

Tree-form ligustrums in raised brick planters form a pleasant streetscape in an older neighborhood in New Orleans. Flagstone pavers meet the brick walkway, providing a pleasant landing for guests and homeowners, who must park on the street.

(Below) *Brick-edged shrub beds complement the neat appearance of the flagstone squares and brick pavers, which were dry-laid on a concrete base. Note how the brick border recedes into the walkway as it slopes toward the house.*

(Above, left) *Flagstone steps and herringbone-patterned brick pavers offer a clean and ordered look. Using low or slow-growing plants ensures that the plants won't hide the porch or its decorative iron railing.*

Peggy Osborne's bougainvilleas are at their best in fall, decorating her terrace with weeks of spectacular blooms.

Make Bougainvillea Bloom

"Why won't my bougainvillea bloom?" may not rank as one of life's great mysteries. But it's a question that concerns a lot of our readers. To find the secret to bounteous bougainvillea blossoms, we consulted Peggy Osborne, who's been growing this plant for 15 years on her Birmingham terrace. Her success lies in the following program of year-round care.

Autumn—At Peggy's house, fall is bougainvillea's showiest time. The plants bloom for weeks and weeks. But come November, it's time to take the plants indoors for winter. Peggy moves them into a dark, cool basement, even if they are still blooming.

Winter—Bougainvilleas need little care during these cold months. Peggy doesn't feed them and lets them go dry, watering only every three to four weeks. As a result, her plants lose most, if not all, of their leaves. "They look like sticks when I finally move them out of the basement," she admits. Though the bougainvilleas appear dead, they're only dormant and will quickly revive when warm weather returns.

Spring—After the danger of frost has passed, Peggy takes her plants outside to a sunny, south-facing terrace. She cuts off any weak, spindly growth left from the year before. Each plant then gets 2 tablespoons of Osmocote 14-14-14 slow-release fertilizer. Bougainvilleas bloom best when potbound, so Peggy leaves them in the same 14-inch clay pots in which they've always grown. She increases the frequency of watering to three times per week, letting the plants go a little dry between waterings. Blooms appear in this season, too, though they're not as plentiful as in fall.

Summer—Bougainvilleas need steady nutrition, so Peggy fertilizes with liquid 20-20-20 plant food every three to four weeks. From time to time, she trims off unwanted growth. The most important thing at this time of year is seeing that the plants soak up plenty of sun. They respond with flushes of blooms off and on throughout the summer. *Steve Bender*

Plant a Legacy Tree

It takes foresight and a generous heart to leave behind a legacy of magnificent trees. Chances are, the tree you plant today won't achieve maturity in your lifetime. But it will during your children's lives and their children's, too. And when they admire it, they'll remember you.

To establish your family's emotional ties to a legacy tree, plant it in commemoration of a family member or special event. It might mark someone's birth, graduation, wedding, or death. It might also remind you of a special holiday season.

Here are some things to consider before planting a living legacy.

Choose a long-lived tree. There's no point in planting a tree for 100 years hence that will die of old age in 30 years.

Plant the tree in an area that's likely to remain fairly undisturbed. This will reduce the probability that in the future someone will cut down your tree to make way for a driveway, swimming pool, room addition, or widened road.

Select a clean, pest-free tree with strong wood. Don't saddle your descendants with one that constantly showers the ground with gummy sap, gooey fruits, caterpillars, and shattered limbs.

Consider whether there's any particular attribute you'd like your legacy tree to possess. For example, live oak, white oak, and American beech display massive trunks and awesome silhouettes. Sugar maple, red maple, ginkgo, black gum, and white ash develop glorious fall color. And shagbark hickory, Chinese elm, beech, white oak, red cedar, and crepe myrtle offer handsome and interesting bark year-round.

The legacy trees listed at right will stand you in good stead with future generations. The abbreviations indicate regions of the South to which they're adapted.　　*Steve Bender*

Sugar maples, such as these planted along Rolandvue Avenue in Baltimore, make good choices for trees which will bring not only you but also future generations great pleasure. They live a long time, need little maintenance, develop outstanding fall color, and grow more beautiful with age.

MATURE HEIGHT

American beech–US, MS, LS 60'-80'
Atlas cedar–US, MS 40'-60'
Bald cypress–AS 50'-80'
Basswood–US, MS, LS 60'-80'
Black gum–AS 40'-60'
Canadian hemlock–US, MS 40'-70'
Chinese elm–AS 40'-50'
Colorado blue spruce–US, MS 30'-50'
Crepe myrtle–AS 15'-30'
Dawn redwood–US, MS, LS, CS 70'-100'
Ginkgo (male only)–AS 50'-80'

Hickory–US, MS, LS, CS 60'-80'
Live oak–LS, CS,TS 40'-80'
Norway maple–US, MS, LS 40'-60'
Norway spruce–US, MS 40'-80'
Pin oak–AS 60'-80'
Red cedar–AS 40'-50'
Red maple–AS 40'-60'
Red oak–AS 60'-80'
Shumard oak–AS 50'-80'
Sugar maple–US, MS, LS 50'-80'
White ash–AS 60'-100'
White oak–AS 60'-100'
Willow oak–AS 60'-80'

Key: US = Upper South; MS = Middle South; LS = Lower South;
CS = Coastal South; TS = Tropical South; AS = All South

Sweet Autumn Blooms

In the fall when the flowers of other plants are just faded memories, sweet autumn clematis is living up to its name. A lacy pinafore of creamy blossoms cascades over a skirt of plain green leaves each August and September.

"It looks like someone threw a handwoven quilt over the fence when sweet autumn clematis blooms," says Shaun Martin, who lectures on vines at Harry P. Leu Gardens in Orlando. "And it's wonderfully fragrant—you can smell it from 40 feet away."

Although its common name is easy enough to remember, this vine has more aliases than a bank robber. The Asian sweet autumn clematis can go by *Clematis ternifolia* or *C. maximowicziana, C. dioscoreifolia,* or *C. paniculata.* The native vine, virgin's bower, is *C. virginiana.* So when searching for it, just stick to asking for sweet autumn clematis.

Sweet autumn clematis disappears during the winter months across most of the South. To give the vine a fresh start the following spring, you can cut it back after blooming ceases. Or, you can leave it alone and let the old vine die off when cold weather arrives. In climates where freezes are rare, *Clematis maximowicziana* is the best choice.

Once you've got sweet autumn clematis, it's there to stay, though it's not as aggressive as Japanese honeysuckle. Able to withstand insects, diseases, and pruning shears, this thornless vine's only fault may be that it's too easy to grow. Seedlings regularly appear beneath the mother vine, spreading its reach.

Be sure to give sweet autumn lots of room; most selections can grow 20 to 30 feet in a year. "It's an excellent cover for a chainlink fence or the side of an unattractive building," says Sue Watkins of Tallahassee Nursery. "I also like it on a trellis or growing in a ditch as ground cover." Unlike ivy, this delightful fall bloomer climbs by twining tendrils that will not damage wood supports.   *Jo Kellum*

PHOTOGRAPH: SYLVIA MARTIN

Sweet autumn clematis is a loyal, sweet-smelling vine. It thrives on a diet of neglect and will forgive you if you cut it to the ground.

SWEET AUTUMN CLEMATIS AT A GLANCE

Foliage: Deciduous except in the Lower South
Blooms: White, early fall
Soil: No specific requirements
Light: Blooms best in full sun

Range: Throughout the South
Species: *C. paniculata, C. dioscoreifolia, C. virginiana, C. maximowicziana*

Edging the walkway, flowing around the boxwoods, and creeping partially up the front walls of this home, ivy transforms simple brick into an inviting entrance.

Gaining an Edge or Two

Funny what a little attention to details can do. Those extra touches can make a yard a garden, a house a home, or—in this case—a brick walkway a neat and inviting entrance. What's the trick here? It's elegantly simple. A brick-edged planting bed on both sides of the walkway of this Charlotte home gives the entry added presence and dimension. Instead of a flat strip of brick, the walkway becomes part of the landscape, not an interruption of it.

The brick-bordered planting bed starts out wide to accommodate a pair of English boxwoods at the driveway, narrows to approximately 12 inches along the sidewalk, then flares out again near the house. Along the walk, the beds are filled with English ivy, which flows into the shrub beds in front of the house and partially up the walls. The total effect results in a planned, manicured appearance that matches the clean lines of the two-story brick Colonial house.

The well-behaved look of this ivy border begs an obvious question: So how often do you have to prune this stuff back to keep it looking neat? Every 30 minutes? "Oh, no," says owner-gardener Robert Ragan. "I have to clip it back about once a month when it's actively growing, which is for about six months." Rob-

ert uses either hedge shears or hand pruners to do the job, and prefers their clean cut to timesaving nylon-string trimmers, which do the job quicker but leave a rougher edge.

The inspiration for this brick border came from the ivy itself, which was growing out of the shrub beds and into the lawn. "The ivy was spreading, so I came up with the idea of confining it with some bricks," Robert says. "A local landscape designer, Carole Joyner, and I were redoing the walkway and putting in an irrigation system, so it just seemed to make sense to make those brick borders." Smart move, Robert. Very smart.   *Mark G. Stith*

Patching Grass Is Easy

It's inevitable. No matter how finely honed your grass-growing skills, sooner or later a dead spot sullies your lawn. Don't throw a tantrum—a small dead spot is easy to patch. And this month is a good time.

Sod isn't cheap—a strip about 1 foot by 3 feet runs a dollar or two, depending on the grass type. But because you're patching only a small area, the whole job shouldn't cost much. And patching is definitely quicker than seeding. Your first job is to locate a reliable source of high-quality, certified sod. "Certified" means it's guaranteed to be free of pests and noxious weeds. Check with local garden centers, nurseries, and sod farms.

STEP 1:

- **Inspect** sod carefully before you buy. Choose the individual strips yourself, so you can pick exactly the sod you want.
- **Look** for firm, sturdy pieces that don't pull apart when lifted. They should be moist, not dry, and green, not brown or yellow.
- **Select** thin strips, no more than an inch thick. Strips with a thick layer of soil on the bottom take much longer for their roots to "knit" into the surrounding lawn.
- **Match** the sod to the type in your lawn. Patching Zoysia into Bermuda or St. Augustine into centipede will turn your lawn into a checkerboard.

STEP 2:

- **Store** your new sod in a lightly shaded spot and keep it moist until you're able to use it. Don't pile strips on top of each other.
- **Cut** and remove the dead sod with a sod cutter or sharp spade.
- **Loosen** the newly exposed soil, with a garden fork, to a depth of at least 8 inches. Loose, well-aerated soil is key to producing healthy grass.
- **Work** some organic matter, such as compost, into the soil at this time, if you wish.
- **Rake** the soil to level it.

Select firm, green strips no more than an inch thick. Strips with a thick layer of soil on the bottom take longer to knit into the surrounding lawn.

After removing the dead grass, use a garden fork to loosen the soil to a depth of at least 8 inches.

Place the strips atop the soil, making the joints between them as tight as possible.

PHOTOGRAPHS: SYLVIA MARTIN

STEP 3:

- **Place** the sod strips atop the soil.
- **Make** the joints between the sod strips as tight as possible.
- **Fill** the joints with some fine sand to help the strips knit together.
- **Tamp** the new sod lightly with your foot.
- **Water** thoroughly now and every day for the next two weeks. ◇

Plants grow right up to the edge of the pool. Instead of a paved terrace, a boardwalk leads from the pool to a seating area shaded by an arbor.

Natural by Design

Building a naturalistic pool is kind of like coloring your hair. It has to be done carefully or it ends up looking *un*natural.

This Dallas pool succeeds in imitating nature. Tucked into a landscape of predominantly native plants, a spa spills over a stone weir to the pool below. The water shimmers like a discovered woodland pond.

The pool's coloring contributes to its natural look. Instead of having a typical white finish that would make the water look aqua blue, the sides and bottom are finished with green marble dust plaster. "We like to mix a touch of black dye in the plaster to create a lagoon look," says garden designer Paul Fields of Lambert Gardens.

The spa is larger than typical; at about 15 x 15 feet, it's nearly the same size as the pool. Positioned above the pool, the spa is close to an outdoor fireplace. This arrangement extends the swimming season through most of the winter.

Both the pool and the spa are surrounded by Oklahoma stone. Because waterline tile would have given the pool a manmade appearance, Paul substituted ledge stone around the inside edge. The ledgestone extends just below the water's surface, hiding the concrete.

The stones perched along the water's edge are actual boulders, instead of 2-inch-thick stones commonly used for coping. "We planned where the boulders would go and

Irregular-shaped steps look like underwater stones.

widened the bond beam to 18 inches at those spots," says Paul. "The wider ledge made it possible to support the weight of the boulders and mortar them in place." Piers beneath large, cantilevered boulders support the waterfall.

The carefully planned touches make this pool more than just a place to swim. With French doors lining the back of the house, the pool also provides a stunning natural view.

Jo Kellum

Layers of greenery clothe this intimate, walled courtyard just off the master bath.

Private RETREATS

BY JO KELLUM
PHOTOGRAPHY VAN CHAPLIN,
SYLVIA MARTIN

Indulge yourself in seclusion. The addition of walls, seating, and a few personal touches converts these small spots into three garden getaways just a few steps from the indoors.

Children easily find leafy hide-aways, secret spots beneath interwoven branches of old overgrown shrubs. Squirreling away adventure books to fuel daydreams and cookies to spoil dinners, they retreat to worlds all their own.

But size conspires with dignity to keep grown-ups out from under the shrubbery. And so we must plan our own private sanctuaries, garden places capturing that bygone inner peace.

CURTAIN OF GREEN

There are no drapes on the glass-paned doors of this master bath. In-stead, a curtain of greenery encloses a private courtyard just beyond the French doors.

Fig vine (*Ficus pumila*) coats the wall's surface with dense foliage that remains green throughout the mild winters of the Gulf Coast. Muscular coils of wisteria flex their way around a wire trellis bolted into the top of the wall. The vine drips with clusters of purple blossoms each spring. A water-fall of river birches growing behind the wall ensures total privacy.

Inside the courtyard, glossy-leaved sasanqua camellias add another layer of green. They begin unfurling waxy blooms in November and then bloom again in early March. A foreground of potted annuals contributes a

changing palette of seasonal color.

There's just enough of a slate terrace to position one chair for sitting and another for foot-propping. The cooling sounds of a trickling fountain soothe the mind and bathe the soul.

EXPANDED HORIZON

The doors of this breakfast room open onto a view of the royal gardens at the Tuileries in Paris. The breathtaking vista seems to stretch for miles, though the actual spot is just 4 feet wide. A trompe l'oeil painting of the historic garden—painted in acrylics on marine-grade plywood and protected with a clear sealer—adds the illusion of depth to the tiny space. "Ideally, the French doors would look out at a garden, but there's not room for one," says the homeowner. "So the painting *is* the garden."

The quiet sitting area makes the most of the narrow space between the house and property line. A set of brick steps originally connected the French doors to the sloping lot below. Now, a deck is level with the floor inside.

The same posts that hold the deck also support a fence and arbor. The 6-foot fence offers instant privacy; the arbor filters the hot afternoon sun. Quick-growing yellow jessamine (Carolina) sprawls across the rafters.

A cafe table and chairs posed before the painting provide the perfect setting for morning air and coffee.

THE GARDEN WITHIN

What a difference a wall makes. Drivers pass by this wall, unaware of the cozy hideaway on the other side. Magnolias planted along the wall's outside face give additional privacy to the garden within.

Sliced from an end section of the yard, the small sitting area is a room of its own. Hexagonal concrete pavers create a tidy terrace two steps above the main garden level. Four pilasters, as tall as the wall, separate the niche from the rest of the garden. An iron gate gives the spot a touch of mystery without completely concealing it from view.

It doesn't take a staff of gardeners to maintain this landscape vista. A trompe l'oeil painting makes the 4-foot-wide space seem to stretch into the horizon.

ARTIST: JON ANDERTON

YOUR OWN RETREAT

It doesn't take a lot of room—just a little imagination—to create a cozy hideaway.

■ Although a hike through the woods to a remote spot sounds inviting, you'll enjoy your retreat much more if it's close enough for a quick cup of coffee.

■ Walls and fences are the easiest way to add seclusion. If that's beyond your budget, consider adding evergreen shrubs, a vine-covered trellis, or small, fast-growing trees. We suggest the following plants. Shrubs: lusterleaf holly, Nellie R. Stevens holly, and Japanese cleyera. Vines: trumpet honeysuckle, yellow jessamine (Carolina), and Armand clematis. Small trees: crepe myrtle, Foster's holly, and wax myrtle.

■ If there isn't a place to sit, you probably won't visit your getaway often. Comfort, not elegance, is the main requirement of outdoor seating. If you have an old bench or lawn chair you rarely use, add waterproof cushions for a quick fix.

■ You're creating a favorite place, so fill it with personal touches: a feeding station for wild birds, a wind chime to play its song in the breeze, or a fragrant blooming plant in a treasured container.

Symmetrical plantings and elegant furnishings contribute a formal air to this quiet spot.

LANDSCAPE ARCHITECT: NORMAN JOHNSON

October

Paperwhite narcissus, pansies, and ornamental cabbage

CHECKLIST FOR OCTOBER

ANNUALS
In Florida, set out transplants of snapdragons, calendula, begonias, and pansies now. North Florida gardeners can also set out asters, delphinium, and violas. In South Florida, plant impatiens, ageratum, marigold, and salvia in annual beds. Gardeners in the Keys can plant zinnias, torenia, and portulaca. In Texas, feed pansies, snapdragons, stock, and other annuals with Miracle Gro, ProSol, or similar water-soluble fertilizer every two to three weeks. Keep plants watered during dry spells, and replenish mulch as needed.

BUTTERFLY PLANTS
Butterflies and hummingbirds are frequent visitors to the fall garden. Encourage them to visit your patio or deck by setting out assorted hanging baskets and other containers filled with blooming firebush, petunias, salvias, pentas, and bougainvillea.

CALADIUMS
These bulbs will rot if left in the garden during winter. To save them, dig them up, wash away soil, and let dry. Brush away dead foliage, dust the bulbs with sulfur, and store them in mesh bags. Note that the bulbs usually decrease in size from one year to the next.

CATERPILLARS
These chewing pests often feed at night on oleander and bougainvillea leaves. Spray or dust plants with Dipel or Thuricide to control. Always spray before 10 a.m. to avoid applying chemicals at temperatures above 85 degrees, which may be harmful to foliage.

HERBS
It's time to plant chervil and cilantro (coriander) for flavorful foliage through winter and spring. Cilantro likes a sunny spot, but chervil appreciates some shade. Loosen the soil, and work in plenty of compost; then sow seeds directly. In Florida, sage, lavender, and French tarragon will thrive until the heat and humidity return. Rosemary, Greek oregano, laurel, and mint will live for several years. In South Florida, include basil and dill in your garden.

HOUSEPLANTS
If your plants have spent the summer outdoors and no longer fit into your home, take cuttings or divide them. Then give the big plants away.

LAWNS
Patch any bare or thin areas of cool-season lawns this month. Rake to remove any debris; then spread seeds (the same kind as your lawn) at the full rate where lawns are bare, or at half rate where the turf is thin. The recommended rate for tall fescue, for example, is 5 to 10 pounds per 1,000 square feet. In Florida, overseed to enjoy a lush green lawn all winter. Mow to an inch tall, and rake with a steel rake. Use a fertilizer spreader to distribute annual ryegrass seeds at a rate of about 5 pounds per 1,000 square feet. Work the seeds in by dragging the back of the rake across the surface. Water daily; mow when grass is 3 inches tall. In the state of Texas, from Dallas southward, give warm-season grasses a final application of fertilizer to improve their cold resistance and spring green up. Apply 7 pounds of 15-5-10 fertilizer per 1,000 square feet of lawn. In the Panhandle area, fertilize fescue types early in the month with a light application of 16-4-8.

MEALYBUGS
Speckled, yellowing foliage on palms may indicate mealybugs. Look for white fuzzy dots on the underside of fronds. Use Cygon or Orthene at a rate of 2 teaspoons per gallon of water poured on the base of the plant. The palm's roots will absorb the treatment.

PERENNIALS
Plant perennials now in the Middle and Lower South. The soil rarely freezes, so the roots grow all winter, producing a vigorous plant next spring. Gardeners in the Upper South should wait until spring because freezing soil can push new plants out of the ground, exposing them to the elements. After frost browns the tops of ferns, hostas, black-eyed Susans, and such, you can cut them back to the ground, or leave the seedheads for the birds, and let the dried plants add shape and texture to your winter garden. Now is an okay time to dig up and divide overcrowded clumps of daylilies, Shasta daisies, iris, and other perennials. Replant as soon as possible in well-prepared beds; water thoroughly and mulch.

RADISHES
This vegetable offers quick return, growing to a good salad size three weeks after sowing—which makes it perfect for a late planting. Children will enjoy pulling the red orbs from the soil.

ROSES
If you want another plant of your favorite rose (other than a patented rose), simply bend a long, flexible branch down so that it can touch the soil. Scratch the bark where it touches, cover with an inch of soil, and put a brick on it. It will root by spring. Then cut the young plant free from its mother plant and move it to a new location.

STRAWBERRIES
This is the best time to plant. Buy only certified, disease-free plants (ask the vendor before you buy), and set them so the crown is even with the surrounding soil. Apply 2 inches of mulch after the first frost to insulate plants and keep berries clean next spring. Now is planting time in North and Central Florida also, but wait until next month to begin

planting in South Florida. Prepare beds by adding 3 cups of 6-6-6 per 50 square feet of planted area. Space transplants 12 to 18 inches apart in mounded rows. Texas growers can now set out plants south of San Antonio. Space them 12 inches apart in double rows centered in wide beds enriched with organic matter. Pull up any runners that sprout away from the main plant. Gardeners in Houston, San Antonio, and northward should wait until spring to set out plants.

TREES AND SHRUBS
Limit pruning to cutting out dead or diseased limbs or light pruning of an errant sprout or two. Severe pruning encourages the plant to sprout new shoots that may not mature before the first frost. Delay cutting plants back until late winter.

VEGETABLES
In Florida, set out onions, shallots, and cabbage, and seed spinach, lettuce, and radishes. In Central Florida, plant kohlrabi, collards, and celery as well. Gardeners in South Florida can also plant tomatoes, peppers, potatoes, snap beans, and lima beans. Texas gardeners can set out transplants of lettuce, spinach, turnip greens, and radishes. Also plant herbs, including parsley, chives, thyme, garlic, and cilantro. In the southern half of the state, plant Texas 1015 onions now for harvest in May.

WATER LILIES
Give tropical water lilies shelter this winter. If you have a home greenhouse, set the pots inside in a washtub. Otherwise, break off small

tubers (potatolike roots) before frost nips your garden, wash away clinging soil, and let them dry. Then place dormant tubers in a plastic bag filled with water, and store it in a cool, dark place. Change the water whenever it becomes cloudy.

WEEDS
If cool-season weeds, such as henbit, clover, and chickweed, have sprouted up in lawns, apply a broadleaf weed killer, such as Weed-B-Gon, to eradicate them before they get out of hand. Be sure to follow label directions; spray on a calm day to minimize the herbicide drifting onto other plants.

WOODY ORNAMENTALS
In Central and South Florida, feed trees and shrubs with 13-3-13 fertilizer applied around the base of the plants. Start about a foot away from tree trunks and 4 inches from shrub stems, and extend a foot beyond the outermost branches. Hose the foliage and water the soil thoroughly after application.

TIP OF THE MONTH

My African violets refused to bloom, even though they were potted in special African violet soil and fed with African violet fertilizer. Then a friend told me her secret. Each time she empties a plastic milk jug, she pours a little water into the unrinsed jug and uses this to water her violets. So I tried it. Now my problem is finding enough room for the luxuriant, blooming plants I have!

Mrs. William W. Moore
Comer, Georgia

EVERGREENS *in* CONTAINERS

BY MARK G. STITH
PHOTOGRAPHY VAN CHAPLIN,
SYLVIA MARTIN

*If you think big potted plants are only for indoors,
consider these durable and delightful
ways to use them outdoors, too.*

Evergreen shrubs are without question the most versatile and frequently used plants in the landscape. So it's a little surprising that you don't see them in containers more often. But setting a boxwood, holly, or other evergreen in a pot or planter raises them to even higher levels of distinction.

We asked a few experienced folks around the South for their best tips on this fresh idea.

Placement: "Front door first!" emphatically states Louisville garden designer Mary Webb. "That's my favorite place—set a pair of pots on either side, or if the door isn't centered, then one good plant.

"My second favorite place, believe it or not, is by the garage door," Mary adds. "Why not make that entrance a little more enticing? And then, obviously, the third choice would be out on the terrace."

Plants: Choosing the right evergreen for a container is a matter of personal taste and the plant's requirements (see the chart on page 214 for a list of recommended plants). No less important is the plant's ultimate size and shape.

That's a big concern in warmer parts of the South, such as Florida, according to Eleanor Foerste, an

Huge, handlike fronds of saw palmetto reach out over the flop-eared foliage of foxgloves. Trailing ivy and dainty johnny-jump-ups complete the look.

agent with the Osceola Extension service in Kissimmee. "A lot of the palms just get too big to be practical for containers," Eleanor says. In addition, the warm and humid climate encourages insects and diseases.

But Eleanor does recommend certain palms, such as windmill palm and European fan palm. "Although the European fan palm can get as tall as 25 feet, it grows very slowly," she says, "so it would do well in a container in a partially shaded area." Broadleaf evergreens she suggests trying include common camellias and Japanese fatsias.

In Texas, Scott Brooks, senior gardener for the Japanese Garden at the Fort Worth Botanic Garden, has grown lots of evergreen, outdoor plants in containers. "In fact, with the kind of soil and weather conditions we have out here, I've found that it's actually easier to grow plants in containers than out in the garden," Scott says with a laugh. Scott likes Mugo and Austrian pines, upright and spreading junipers, bamboos, and native Texas plants, such as yaupon, yucca, Texas sage, and red cedar.

While climate can be limiting, it can also be liberating. Atlanta's mild climate allows Jeremy Smearman, of Planters Nursery and Garden Services, the

(Left) *A potted, tree-form Debutante camellia, generously underplanted with ivy, pansies, and lettuce, provides a contrast of foliage and flowers against the brickwork and potting shed.*

luxury of choosing from a broad range of plants. "I love to use everything from American boxwoods to waxleaf privet," he says.

Care: A potted plant is in a limited growing area and more or less depends on you for survival. "For pots in full sun, use a heavier soil mix so it won't dry out as quickly," Jeremy advises. Adding water-absorbing gels to potting soil can help keep them from drying out, but don't exceed the manufacturer's recommendations.

Good drainage is critical, regardless of the pot. Make sure your container has drainage holes. Placing a few large pieces of gravel or broken pottery over the holes also keeps the soil from clogging the openings.

Fertilizing a container-grown plant is essential, but again you have to be careful not to overdo it. Remember, if you've got a plant next to the house, be sure to rotate it every month to keep it growing evenly. Otherwise, you'll end up with a lopsided plant that you'll either have to prune back or replace.

Containers: Keep several things in mind when choosing a container: what it's made of, whether it's the right size, and whether or not it has a drainage hole. "I would really rather have a lead container than anything," admits Mary Webb, "But I also like wooden planters, as long as they're painted a dark color. The neat thing about wooden planters is that you can slip a plant in a plastic pot inside them."

Terra-cotta is a classic choice, as is concrete. But terra-cotta sometimes cracks during hard freezes, especially if the pot is waterlogged. Gardeners in colder areas of the South would be better off moving terra-cotta pots indoors or to a protected location, such as a porch.

New generations of colored concrete containers, lightweight plastic and foam clay pots, and fiberglass composite materials are worth considering, from the standpoint of price, durability, and appearance. Of course, there's the good old, whiskey-type oak half barrels. Just make sure that rustic look matches the surroundings. And don't be limited to what's out there on the market. Containers found and fabricated, from wheelbarrows to washtubs, can add a distinctive look, especially in old-fashioned gardens. ◇

(**Left**)*English ivy and creeping fig trained on wire forms can assume interesting shapes and patterns.* (**Right**) *A spreading cotoneaster pruned to a standard form makes a colorful sentinel beside this front door. Planting the base with ivy helps balance the otherwise top-heavy tangle of berries and foliage.*

TOP 10 EVERGREENS FOR CONTAINERS

PLANT	TYPICAL HEIGHT/ WIDTH*	FOLIAGE TEXTURE	REGION	LIGHT
Yew (*Taxus*—many selections)	Upright : 10'/4'; Rounded : 4'/3';	Needlelike	US, MS, LS (top half)	S/PS
Junipers (*Juniperus*—many selections)	Upright : 10'/4'; Spreading : 1'/6'	Needlelike	Varies widely with selection	S
Boxwood (*Buxus*—many selections)	American: 3'/3'; Korean: 2.5'/2.5'	Fine	American: US, MS, LS, CS; Korean: US, MS, LS, CS	S/PS
Arborvitae (*Thuja*—many selections)	Upright : 10'/4'; Rounded : 5'/5'	Needlelike	US, MS, LS	S/PS
Texas sage (*Leucophyllum frutescens*)	4'/4'	Fine	LS, CS, TS	S
Dwarf Alberta spruce (*Picea glauca Conica*)	6'/3'	Needlelike	US, MS, LS (top half)	S/PS
Common camellia (*Camellia japonica*)	7'/4'	Coarse	MS, LS, CS	PS
Palms (many species), Pygmy Date Palm (*Phoenix* sp.)	12'-15'/7'	Coarse	LS (some selections), CS, TS	S/PS
Hollies (*Ilex*— many selections)	10'-12'/7'	Fine to medium	Varies with selection	S/PS
Cherry laurel (*Prunus laurocerasus*)	8'/5'	Medium	US, MS, LS	S/PS

S=sun, PS=partial sun, SH=shade / US=Upper South, MS=Middle South, LS=Lower South, CS=Coastal South, TS=Tropical South

*Size is often affected by container size and pruning.

The pond's outer edge matches the curve of the wall, visually tying architecture and garden together.

A Different Sort of Fishpond

"Now that's a first," I said to myself, as I toured a garden in suburban Baltimore. "I've never seen a fishpond like that one." What caught my eye was a narrow body of water sitting smack up against the house.

The garden's designer, landscape architect Carol Macht of Anshen & Allen, explained that this feature came about in response to a room recently added to the back of the house. The room's unusual, curving facade needed to be visually tied to the garden. When the homeowner expressed interest in some sort of pond, Carol addressed both concerns in a single step.

You can discern the visual tie-in by closely examining the outer edge of the pond. See how its arc precisely echoes the arc of the wall? "Repeating the curve helps make the pool part of the architecture and part of the garden," explains Carol. Notice, too, how the wall extends several inches over the water. This gives the illusion that the wall is floating—another interesting way that architec-

Staggered stepping-stones lack visible support and appear to float. A black fiberglass liner gives the illusion of depth.

ture and garden cooperate.

Now observe the stepping-stones, which lead across the water. Like the wall, they seem to float. One reason

for this is that they're staggered, instead of arranged in lines. They're also larger than the concrete pedestals on which they rest, so you can't see any support. At night, camouflaged lighting beneath the stones enhances the floating effect. Just as important, it prevents missteps.

But even if you stumbled into the pond, you wouldn't sink far. The water is only 6 inches deep. This illusion comes from a black fiberglass lining that darkens the water and makes it look deeper.

Carol resisted the temptation to cram the pond with plants. Doing so would have obscured its lines. Instead, several pots of water iris and cattails—two plants adapted to shallow water—grow in the pond's sunny end. Ornamental koi glide through water cleaned and swirled by a filtration system.

As this garden demonstrates, creating a unique water feature needn't require a lot of space. What's needed most of all is imagination.

Steve Bender

Autumn's rich, warm colors are captured in this informal arrangement assembled using native goldenrod, bamboo fronds, and seedheads clipped from ornamental grasses.

Autumn's Golden Days

You just don't expect a place like this. Not after driving past the manicured lawns and shrubs that front most homes nestled beneath the live oaks and pines along the Mississippi Gulf Coast. Tom and Gale Singley's property, tucked next to a marsh fed by the Pascagoula River, is a glorious exception to the norm.

The golden days of autumn are especially beautiful here. At a time of year when most gardens are faded memories of spring's azaleas or filled with stewed and stringy summer annuals, Tom and Gale's place is going full tilt.

Mexican firebush bears tubular, coral-red flowers from summer to frost. The foliage of this tender perennial turns a copper-red with the onset of cooler weather.

The wide, brick walk to the front doors narrows to a turnstile of flowers and foliage. Low, purple clouds of wild ageratum float next to sky-high native sunflowers, shining on pink clusters of pentas, crowding in with the cosmos, zinnias, and other plants. Bees, butterflies, hummingbirds, and other busy-buzzy critters dive, dart, and flutter among the flowers. To the casual observer, this is a show produced and directed by Mother Nature.

Gale (alias Mother Nature) would be flattered that you thought so. There is a message in this playful "mess," an order to the apparent disorder. Instead of bulldozing back the natural surroundings, Gale took advantage of the setting, using both native and introduced plants. Following are a few time-taught lessons Gale has learned to make a fall garden flourish. Many of these tips aren't limited to one season, but they are all reminders of what makes a garden great.

NATURE'S HUES FOR YOU

"The sunflowers were dug up from a shady area on our property and moved to the walkway," Gale says. Same goes for the wild ageratum and goldenrod, which reseed each year. "And once you've got goldenrod, it becomes a permanent part of your life," says Gale. "But I love the combination of gold and purple in fall."

PLAN FOR FALL FLOWERS

"It's a matter of knowing the plants and when they bloom," Gale advises. "We've lived here for seven years, and I know what plants I can count on for blooms, and what's going to bloom when." (So you don't have to wait that long, we've compiled a list of Gale's fall favorites on the next page.)

Although Gale usually sets out plants or sows seeds in spring, she adds that fall is also a good time to sow wildflower seeds and set out perennials. "Down here, because we have such mild winters, sometimes I'll sow some of the annuals like zinnias and cosmos right after Christmas," she adds. "With the fall salvias, I'll pinch the seed stalks off late in the year, when they stop blooming, and drop them on the ground right where I want the plants to come back."

GOOD SOIL MAKES GOOD PLANTS

To prepare her flowerbeds, Gale adds lots of organic matter to the existing soil and mulches the beds with oak leaves. "Sometimes I get carried away with the mulch, and that's why the cosmos and the zinnias don't reseed very well," she says. Gale will also pile leaves around some of the tender perennials, such as Mexican firebush, when freezes are predicted. To help the plants along during the growing season, she'll sprinkle the ground with Osmocote slow-release fertilizer. "If there's a special event coming up and I want them to look real good, I'll give them a little dose of SuperBloom (liquid fertilizer)," Gale adds. "If the plants are looking a little pale and peaked, I'll give them a boost."

LEARN GOOD BUGS AND BAD BUGS

Gale rarely uses any sort of chemical sprays to control pest problems. "As far as keeping insects down, I'll just handpick them off the plants," she says. "I try and know my caterpillars, because some I thought were damaging are actually the predecessors of beautiful butterflies. For example, I grow lots of milkweed for monarch butterfly caterpillars to feed on."

SHARE YOUR GARDEN WITH WILDLIFE

Instead of fighting what would be a never-ending battle with bayou beasts, Gale literally lays out a spread for them. Her property is an outdoor classroom. She hosts school groups and other interested people and shows them how a garden can be a haven for both people and wildlife. "I'll put out vegetable scraps in a particular spot. Frankly, my busiest customers are box turtles. They hear me drop the food and come up from under the deck and out of the woods. I once saw one up on his hind legs, reaching up to eat a low-hanging tomato on one of my plants. I figured if he wanted it that bad, he was welcome to it!"

RELAX AND ENJOY YOUR GARDEN

Have you gathered by now that Gale isn't overly fussy about making sure her garden is perfect? She does what pleases her and complements her surroundings. "My garden palette changes all the time," she adds. "I'm not a very structured gardener, and I never know what's going to come up from one year to the next."

Perhaps Gale knows the changing seasons so well, she doesn't have to think about them. You might even say gardening has become second nature to her. *Mark Stith*

GALE'S NO-FAIL FALL LINEUP

PLANT	COLORS	TYPE
Goldenrod (*Solidago canadenis* and its selections)	Yellow	Annual
Wild ageratum (*Eupatorium coelestinum*)	Bluish purple	Annual
Fall salvias (*Salvia leucantha, S. coccinea,* and other types)	Purple, red	Tender Perennial*
Pentas (*Pentas lanceolata*)	Pink, purple, white	Tender Perennial*
Mexican firebush (*Hamelia patens*)	Red	Tender Perennial*
Sunflowers (*Helianthus angustifolius* and other types)	Yellow	Annual
Ginger lily (*Hedychium coronarium*)	White	Tender Bulb*
Ornamental grasses (various types)	White/parchment	Perennial

Note: All of these plants can be set out or sown from seed in spring; gardeners in the Coastal and Tropical South can sow seeds or set out plants in fall. In addition to these plants, fall asters, mums, Autumn Joy sedum, and coneflowers can be valuable additions to the late-season garden and can be planted in fall or spring throughout the South.

* Tender perennials and bulbs are not hardy in colder regions of the South (where winter temperatures drop below 20°) and should be grown as annuals.

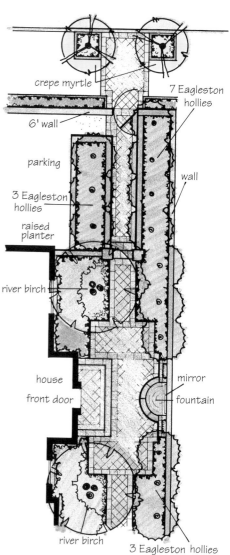

crepe myrtle

6' wall

parking

3 Eagleston hollies

raised planter

river birch

house
front door

7 Eagleston hollies

wall

mirror

fountain

river birch

3 Eagleston hollies

The paving pattern makes this straight walkway distinctive. One-foot squares of lilac Pennsylvania stone, laid diagonally, are bordered by 9- x 18-inch stones.

An Elegant Side Yard

Like most New Orleans lots, this one doesn't have an inch to spare. The parking area is in front of the house; the front door is on the side. To add interest without wasting space, landscape architect René Fransen converted the long, narrow side yard into an elegant entry court.

He designed a walkway that leads straight through the side yard to the door. Eagleston hollies, planted just 6 feet apart in raised planters, frame the walk with a solid green wall of foliage. The hollies' lower branches were removed to expose 4 feet of silvery trunk. Beds beside the walk are edged with clipped boxwood and filled with cool, white caladiums.

The walkway steps up to a landing at the front door. "Any change in elevation in New Orleans is significant," says René. "Steps to the front door landing are more ceremonial than the original ramped walkway."

Though the landing is only slightly wider than the walkway, the shape of the paving gives it the presence of a courtyard. A small fountain tucked against the fence creates an accent.

From the formal planting to the detailed paving pattern, this entry court makes every inch count.   *Jo Kellum*

(Below, left) *A mirror directs attention to the fountain instead of another house just behind the fence.* **(Below, right)** *Crepe myrtles grow well in confined spaces. Two 4- x 4½-foot cutouts in the sidewalk were enough room for a pair of them.*

By February, when the first garden daffodils have bloomed, they can be picked and placed (in water picks) among the dormant bulbs.

In the Middle and Lower South, paperwhites can be grown outdoors, even in a container. Planted near the door, they welcome guests with flowers and fragrance.

Paperwhite Winter

Bulbs have arrived at nurseries and garden centers, but you don't have to endure a winter of waiting before you see blossoms. Among the new arrivals are paperwhite narcissus, little bundles of immediate gratification. You can plant paperwhite narcissus in a pot now, and they'll be in bloom in two to six weeks, depending upon the selection you choose. And if you buy enough bulbs, you can stagger the plantings to have them in bloom all winter long.

Forcing paperwhites to bloom indoors is nothing new. The sweet fragrance of potted bulbs is becoming a holiday tradition in many households. And gardeners in the Lower and Coastal South have grown them outdoors for generations.

The new and exciting prospect for paperwhites comes from narcissus expert Brent Heath of the Daffodil Mart in Gloucester, Virginia. He suggests storing them on top of, rather than inside, the refrigerator. "You can force paperwhites all winter if you store them properly," Heath explains. "They want to be at about 70 degrees. This keeps them from sprouting. We store them right up until spring." That means that gardeners who just don't seem to ever have enough winter flowers can buy a quantity of bulbs *now* and plant a potful every two weeks for the next four or five months.

FORCING IS EASY

■ **Buy the right selection.** Ziva, the the most common selection, can be planted right away. If grown with some heat beneath the pot, it will bloom in as little as two weeks.

■ Other selections need to be stored until after Thanksgiving for best results. The yellow selection called Grand Soleil d'Or can take five to six weeks to bloom. Others are intermediate in bloom time and offer white and bicolored flowers.

■ **Store them properly,** at about 70 degrees. To prevent them from drying out, Brent suggests covering with dry sphagnum moss, plastic foam "peanuts," or vermiculite.

■ **Choose a pot with drainage.** If you plan to display the container, be sure it is decorative or the right size to fit inside a basket or cachepot.

■ **Fill the pot** to three-fourths of its depth with potting soil. Set the bulbs on top, shoulder to shoulder. Pour gravel up to the necks of the bulbs to hold them in place. Water well, and repeat whenever the soil feels dry.

■ **Give the roots warmth** by placing the pot on the television or refrigerator. This ought to hasten root growth.

■ **Move to bright light** as soon as leaves and buds begin to appear. If the bulbs do not get enough light, the stems and leaves will stretch and flop over.

■ **Plant them 4-5 inches deep in the garden** when they finish blooming. If you live in the Lower and Coastal South, they will come back and bloom outdoors next year.

Linda C. Askey

BLUE-LAVENDER BLEND
1. *Majestic Giants White*
2. *Melody Light Blue*
3. *Crystal Bowl True Blue*
4. *Crystal Bowl Purple*
5. *Imperial Purple and White*
6. *Imperial Frosty Rose*
7. *Majestic Giants Blue Shades*

Mix Your Own
PANSIES

Traditionally, gardeners who plant pansies have had a choice between solid colors or contrasting blends of primary or pastel colors. But a visit with Jim Steeves last year unveiled a fresh approach to fall pansy planting. He makes custom blends for his customers at DJ's Greenhouse in Birmingham.

Drawing a dominant color from the house or garden, Jim fills empty trays with a few of this or that, drawing from the wide variety of pansy selections he sells.

"I'll be getting together some flats for one person, and before I know it, someone else has picked them up and bought them," says Jim. The quick sale of his custom blends reveals the level of interest they generate. And best of all, anyone can put them together. You may need only one tray containing three or more selections, or you can buy whole trays and blend them as you plant. The effect is the same.

Jim frequently uses Imperial Antique Shades as a foundation for his blends. "You can throw Crystal Bowl Orange in with Antique Shades, and it adds a lot of pizzazz," he says. "Or if you want to tone down Antique Shades, you can add cream. If you want to make it more alive add yellow or rose."

Imperial Frosty Rose with shades of blue and purple are excellent. Jim even developed a brick-red blend based on a wall adjacent to his nursery. Red brick presents a difficult, but common, background for flowers.

BRICK-RED BLEND
1. *Padparadja*
2. *Crystal Bowl Yellow*
3. *Maxim Sunset*
4. *Maxim Orange*
5. *Maxim Red*
6. *Majestic Giants Red and Yellow*

WARM COLOR BLEND
1. *Imperial Antique Shades*
2. *Maxim Sunset*
3. *Crown Rose*

MAUVE-ROSE BLEND
1. *Accord Rose with Blotch*
2. *Imperial Pink Shades*
3. *Crystal Bowl White*
4. *Imperial Purple and White*
5. *Imperial Frosty Rose*

His plays off the colors in the brick and includes the selection called Black Prince (not shown) in the best use of this novelty selection I've ever seen.

Bored with the same old thing, yet torn between the many selections that are available? You can now choose several.

And if you think they look good in the garden, just wait until you pick miniature bouquets to bring indoors.

Once you've selected just the right color blend at the nursery, you need to take good care of the plants after you get them home. Fall planted pansies provide a lot of color for a little effort.

■ Be sure to set out transplants at least four weeks before the first frost so they have time to get established.

■ Before you plant, loosen the soil in a sunny location, and mix in a 2-inch layer of compost.

■ Mix a slow-release fertilizer, such as Osmocote (14-14-14) or Bulb Booster (9-9-6), into the soil at the rate recommended on the label.

■ Space plants 6 to 12 inches apart and water them when the garden is dry.

■ Mulch after the soil has cooled and a freeze is in the forecast.

■ Fertilize again in late winter (several weeks before spring freezes end) with about ½ pound of 5-10-10 per 25 square feet.   *Linda C. Askey*

November

Winged euonymus

CHECKLIST FOR NOVEMBER

BULB FOOD
Fertilize beds of daffodils, hyacinths, Spanish bluebells, and other spring-flowering bulbs with Bulb Booster or a complete, slow-release formula, such as 5-10-20. Because bulbs are growing roots now, this is a better time to fertilize than in the spring. If you are planting new bulbs, mix the fertilizer into the bed. Putting it into the hole directly beneath the bulb will burn developing roots.

BOSTON FERNS
These ferns are wonderful in summer, but make a terrible mess in winter. Unless you have a garden room where you don't mind the leaflets shedding, give ferns to the compost pile and buy new ones next spring.

CITRUS
In Central Florida, water trees weekly during extended dry spells. This will prevent fruit from splitting later. If a tree becomes too dry, it may soak up too much water when it rains, which can cause fruit to swell past the breaking point.

COLOR
Plant annuals and perennials now to brighten your Florida garden. Set out transplants of dianthus, pansies, and snapdragons throughout the state. Add petunias and spider flower in Central Florida, and add pentas, shrimp plant, and firespike in South Florida.

CONTAINERS
Water evergreen shrubs and cool-season annuals in containers; they dry out even when the weather is cool. Terra-cotta pots need to be brought indoors for the winter to prevent cracking. Concrete containers can remain outside.

COOL-SEASON ANNUALS
In all areas except the Upper South, pansies, snapdragons, kale, stock, ornamental cabbage, and other cold-tolerant bedding plants can be set out now. Plant them in rich, well-drained soil in sunny locations.

DAFFODILS
When planting your spring-flowering bulbs this month, remember that daffodils need at least a half-day of sun on their foliage. Although a bed appears to be sunny during this time of year, it may be shaded after the trees leaf up.

FIRE ANTS
They look like regular ants, but fire ants build unsightly mounds and sting aggressively if disturbed. To eradicate, set out fire ant bait, such as Amdro or Affirm, for the worker ants to take into the mound to the queen. Though slow to work, baits are more effective than direct contact sprays.

HOLIDAY PLANTS
To prolong the show of poinsettias, gloxinias, Jerusalem cherry, forced azaleas, ornamental peppers, paperwhites, and amaryllis, keep these plants away from your forced air vents, fireplaces, and other heat sources. Check them daily to see if they need watering. Removing the spent flowers and foliage will keep them looking good.

HOSE STORAGE
In the Upper South, drain garden hoses and store them in a protected area. Elsewhere, coil them in special "hose pots" with drainage holes.

LAWNMOWER CARE
If you have a warm-season lawn that's gone dormant for the winter, use this time to service your mower. Make sure you drain the gas tank and let the engine run dry. Remove the spark plug (disconnect the wire first), squirt a little oil in the hole, and crank the engine a few times. Replace the spark plug (with the wire disconnected), and store for winter. There are special gas additives available if you don't drain your tank.

LAWNS
Feed cool-season lawns again for good growth and rich color. Apply a fall formulation, such as 20-9-9, where available. This feeding promotes good roots and ensures early growth next spring. In the Middle and Lower South, sow seed of cool-weather grasses, such as fescue, now, or overseed dormant warm-season lawns with annual or perennial ryegrass. Apply 4 to 7 pounds of fescue seed per 1,000 square feet; use the higher rate for establishing new lawns. Ryegrass can be seeded at 5 to 10 pounds per 1,000 square feet. Water thoroughly until the seed becomes established.

PARSLEY
In Florida, for a crop that thrives during cooler weather, soak parsley seeds for about six hours before planting them to speed germination. Sow soaked seeds about 1/8 inch deep. Be sure to keep the soil moist and seedlings should appear in about two weeks.

PERENNIALS

Transplant your spring- and summer-blooming perennials, such as columbine, daylilies, hosta, phlox, and iris, now. Cut back chrysanthemums, asters, and other fall blooming perennials to the ground when they have finished blooming.

ROOT CROPS

In Florida, thin beets, carrots, radishes, and turnips as soon as seedlings have true leaves. After two thinnings several weeks apart, final spacing should be 4 inches for beets and carrots; 1 to 2 inches for radishes; and 4 to 6 inches for turnips. Turnips that are grown for their greens will prosper about 3 inches apart.

ROSES

Winter winds can tear at tall hybrid teas, such as Queen Elizabeth, Mister Lincoln, and Tiffany, and cause damage to the roots. Wait until later this month (when they are dormant) to cut them back to about 3 feet. If any shoots grow prematurely during a warm spell, it won't matter. The plants will get pruned again in late spring anyway. Plant container roses now in Central and South Florida. For the best nematode resistance, choose plants grafted on Rosa fortuniana rootstock. Don't order from out-of-state catalogs because these plants may be grafted on other rootstocks that would have a short lifespan in your state.

SHRUBS

Now is a good time to plant container grown trees and shrubs. Be sure to mulch thoroughly and water generously after planting. Don't forget to water again as needed during dry spells.

SPANISH MOSS

Before using it in holiday decorations, treat gathered moss to eliminate insects. Simply soak moss in very hot tap water for about a half hour and lay it in the sun to dry.

SPIDER MITES

As the rainy season ends in Florida, mite damage increases. Yellow speckles on leaves and curling new foliage indicate the presence of these tiny parasites. Webbing may be visible during large infestations. To control, spray with an insecticidal soap, such as Safer's. Be sure to spray the undersides of leaves.

SPRING BULBS

Plant daffodils, grape hyacinths, and Dutch iris now. Tulips and hyacinths should be pre-chilled in the lower bin of the refrigerator for four to six weeks before planting.

SWEET PEAS

In the Middle and Lower South, sow sweet peas this month in a bed that has been enriched with compost or manure. Plants need this head start to come into full flower before the weather gets hot next spring. In the Upper South, plant sweet peas in spring as early as a month before the last frost. In Central Florida and South Texas, sow seeds at the base of a fence or trellis to give these colorful vines a place to climb. Pick a spot that has good soil and receives about a half-day's sun. Thin seedlings to about 4 to 6 inches apart when they are a few inches tall.

VEGETABLES

In the Lower South, start seeds indoors or set out the transplants of cool season edible greens, such as spinach, lettuce, and collards. Use a fabric row cover to protect plants from cabbage loopers and other leaf-eating insects; fabric row covers also provide a good source of insulation.

November Notes

TO DO:
■ Mark the locations of all newly planted bulbs and perennials so you won't accidentally disturb them while they are dormant
■ Plant and divide perennials
■ To promote heavier flowering next year, prune bougainvillea and hibiscus before you bring them indoors for the winter
■ Store lawnmower—clean housing and filter, disconnect spark plugs

TO PLANT:
■ Trees for fall color, including dogwood, sourwood, sugar maple, red maple, Japanese maple, Chinese tallow, black gum, crepe myrtle, and hickory
■ Fall-blooming camellias

TO PURCHASE:
■ New tools to replace those worn-out over the summer
■ Evergreen shrubs at discount prices

_____

_____

_____

TIP OF THE MONTH

It's impossible to remove the vines of pole beans and cucumbers from nylon netting at the end of the growing season. Rather than throwing the netting away, I take the netting down, vines and all, and store it over the winter. The following spring, I use a rolling pin to mash the vines into small pieces that I can shake out. Then I put the netting in a pail filled with 1 part bleach to 7 parts water for about 30 minutes. When dry, the netting is like new.

R. Roger Dreschler
Baltimore, Maryland

EASY
Embellishments

BY JULIA H. THOMASON
PHOTOGRAPHY EMILY MINTON

How to improve an already attractive houseplant? Just add a creative touch. Both cut flowers and cool-weather annuals can bring color and pizzazz to a plant.

It's easiest to work the flowers into plants that have abundant foliage. Their leaves or fronds easily cover the containers, showing off the flowers to their best effect.

If you use pansies for color, first separate the plastic tray of plants into individual cells. Position the pansies at the base of your houseplant, arranging the leaves to cover the containers. Display the arrangement near a window, or move it periodically to a spot where it receives bright light. With regular watering, the pansies will last two to three weeks. When the flowers begin to fade, plant the pansies outside.

Snapdragons, often sold in 4- to 6-inch pots, require a larger container. First, line the basket with a waterproof trash bag or a plastic liner purchased at a plant shop. Place pots of ivy or philodendron in the basket, arranging the leaves to trail over the edge of the basket. Place the pots of snapdragons behind the philodendron. Display the arrangement by a window, or move it often to a spot where it receives bright light. Water regularly. After about two weeks, plant the snapdragons outside.

Plastic water picks (available from a florist) let you accent a plant with cut flowers. Fill each plastic vial with water, and attach the rubber cap. Cut the stems of the flowers to 4 to 6 inches; then insert the stems through the openings in the rubber caps. Place among the foliage of your plant, arranging the leaves to cover the water picks. Refill the vials with water when necessary. ◇

(**Left**) *Ivy foliage drapes plastic pots, allowing yellow pansies to shine.*
(**Above, left**) *A porcelain bowl serves as a waterproof saucer for pots of bird's-nest fern, button fern, and pansies.* (**Above, right**) *Pink snapdragons add splashes of color to pots of philodendrons in a rustic basket.*

Autumn's Blaze

For many plants, fall color is a sometime thing—brilliant one year, drab the next. If you're the type that abhors such uncertainty, then read on. You're about to meet a shrub that illuminates autumn almost everywhere.

It's commonly called winged euonymus (*Euonymus alata*), but you may know it as burning bush. Each name says something significant about the plant. The first refers to the corky ridges or "wings" that run the length of the twigs. The second speaks of the shrub's resplendent fall color, a cardinal red so saturated and intense that each leaf seems lit from within.

Although classified as a shrub, winged euonymus eventually grows 15 feet tall and wide. A good choice for tall screens (especially because it accepts aggressive pruning), it also works well near ponds and streams, which reflect the vibrant autumn color. If you wish, you can trim off the lower branches and convert it into a lovely, multi-trunked tree.

Is 15 feet too large for your garden? Then check out winged euonymus's little brother, mistakenly named dwarf winged euonymus (*Euonymus alata* Compacta). There's nothing dwarf about it—it's just more compact, growing about 10 feet tall. Dense, boxlike, and less graceful than the species, this form grows into a thick hedge that needs no clipping. Wings are nearly absent, but it atones for this sin with fall foliage redder than glowing coals.

Don't expect a show in the Coastal and Tropical South. Autumns don't get cool enough in these regions. However, everyone else will find that winged euonymus struts its stuff without much assistance.

The plant grows in just about any well-drained soil and in either full sun or light shade. And few pests bother it. Unfortunately, unlike the burning bush of the Bible, this one won't likely talk to you. If at any time it does speak, you'd better hope your name is Moses.

Steve Bender

Before it drops its leaves in late fall, winged euonymus changes from medium green to fiery red.

WINGED EUONYMUS AT A GLANCE

Size: 15 feet tall and wide (species); 10 feet tall and wide (compact form)
Light: Full sun or light shade
Soil: Moist, well drained
Growth rate: Slow
Pests: None serious
Propagation: Cuttings taken during growing season
Range: Upper, Middle, Lower South

(Above, left) *Corky "wings" along the twigs give the shrub its name. Masked by foliage from spring until fall, the twigs become especially handsome in winter.*

(Left) *By trimming away the lower branches, you can convert the large form of winged euonymus into a graceful, small tree.*

Planted shoulder-to-shoulder in pots, these bulbs will make a big display when they bloom.

The Potted Bulb

With the onset of winter, gardeners retreat indoors. Once there, we take delight in a favorite off-season occupation—forcing bulbs to bloom in pots. And even though potted tulips and hyacinths will be for sale soon at the garden center and even the grocery store, it's more sporting to try our hand at this age-old practice of mimicking nature.

The easiest bulbs to force, paperwhites and amaryllis, require no chilling (a period of cold similar to winter). Tulips, hyacinths, crocuses, grape hyacinths, dwarf iris, and most narcissus, however, require weeks of cold temperatures before they will grow and bloom.

TAKE IT EASY

Probably the simplest way to give bulbs the winter they need is to leave them outdoors (provided you live in an area that has night temperatures in the 30s). Set the bulbs shoulder-to-shoulder in the pot. For example, put five tulip bulbs in a 6-inch clay pot. Plant in a well-drained potting mix, water well, and then leave them in an out-of-the-way part of the garden where they will get all the benefits of sun and rain. When they bloom, move them to positions of prominence indoors (see page 232).

Bobby McCain, production manager at Georgia's Callaway Gardens' Sibley Center, recommends covering the pots with hardware cloth if chipmunks, voles, and such are apt to dig them up during winter. "We stretch it over the top of the pots and weight it down," Bobby says.

He also recommends double-layer planting. When you use a container that is deep enough, you can fill it partially with well-drained potting soil, put down a layer of bulbs, put in a shallow layer of potting soil and another layer of bulbs. "For three or four years we have been mixing tulips and daffodils in the same big whiskey barrels," says Bobby. "They sit outside all winter long. In many cases, those tulips are superior because they get better chilling than those in the ground." For gardeners in warmer areas of the South, such as Charleston and Savannah, growing bulbs in pots may be the only way to give them sufficient exposure to cold temperatures.

WHERE WINTERS ARE MILD

Gardeners in the Lower and Coastal South may not have cold enough temperatures for the bulbs to bloom. "After I buy hyacinths, tulips, and crocuses around the first of October, they go right into the refrigerator," says Sally McQueen Squire of Houston, who buys bulbs from her garden club's annual fall sale called the Bulb and Plant Mart. "They come from Holland in an air-cooled container at about 49 degrees, and I buy them and get them back in the refrigerator as fast as possible."

This quick transfer into cold storage is essential. Try to buy bulbs at your garden center soon after they arrive and put them in the vegetable bin of the refrigerator. Leave them there for about four to six weeks, and then plant them in pots with a commercial potting soil. Put as many bulbs in a pot as it will hold for a finished pot full of flowers.

But you aren't finished yet. Bulbs need three to four more weeks of cool temperatures (around 40 to 45 degrees) after they are planted. This allows time for the roots to grow, just like they do in the garden during fall and winter. A big, empty refrigerator is ideal. A more practical alternative may be to put them in an unheated garage, basement, or crawlspace. Light is not important, but occasional watering is. When you see growth beginning, move the pots of bulbs to a sunny spot outdoors. They will bloom in a few weeks. Then bring them indoors where you can see them, which is the reason you went to all this trouble.

THE PITFALLS

Those who grow forced bulbs professionally follow precise recipes of time and temperature, and these vary with the species and selection of bulb. With no control over how the bulbs are handled before you buy them and without refrigerators dedicated to potted bulbs, you can only plant and hope for the best. It's fun to try—and when you succeed, you'll relish those winter flowers.

Linda C. Askey

For advice on using potted bulbs in your home, turn to "Indoor Bulbs," on page 232. ◇

The yellow berries of nandina offer the sparkle of the unexpected in the winter landscape.

Winter Gold

Although striking in their color and diversity, yellow berries remain a rarity in the home landscape.

"Homeowners are not as turned on by yellow-berried plants as nurserymen and writers are," confides Plato Touliatos of Trees by Touliatos in Memphis. "But I don't think birds see yellow like they see red, so the berries last longer."

Garden designer Sara Groves of Oxford, Georgia, agrees. "The birds aren't attracted to them, so these plants are showy a lot longer. And the berries add sparkle to all that green and red you usually have. They give the garden highlights."

Initially they are overpowered by the golden foliage of autumn. But when the leaves are done, the berries turn up the volume of color. Silhouetted against evergreens as they often are, these golden berries are much more amiable in combination with the flowers of the season. The pink and crimson blossoms of sasanquas and camellias meld beautifully with yellow and gold.

Many of our old Southern favorites can surprise us with their yellow forms. For example, *Nandina domestica* Alba bears creamy-white to pale-yellow berries. Just like the red-berried forms, these plants will reseed. You can separate the reds

Framed by glossy evergreen foliage, the berries of Ilex cornuta D'Or *abound at Callaway Gardens in Pine Mountain, Georgia.*

from the yellows before berries appear by the color of the new growth: The Alba nandinas will have no red pigment in their new growth. Other selections found in nurseries are Yellow Fruited and Lutea.

Two of our largest shrubs have golden-berried forms. The evergreen yaupon holly *(Ilex vomitoria)* has several golden selections, the most available of which are Yellow Berry and Sandy Hook. One of the South's deciduous hollies, possumhaw *(Ilex decidua)*, has a selection called Byer's

Golden that has unfortunately been difficult to propagate. But a new selection called Finch's Golden is easier to root and a better grower.

Most of the hollies that have red berries also have yellow-berried forms, including two selections related to the popular red-berried Burford holly. They are called *Ilex cornuta* D'Or and Avery Island. Other holly species with yellow-fruited forms are *Ilex x attenuata* Alagold, *Ilex cassine* Yellow Fruited and Lowei, *Ilex cassine* var. *myrtifolia* Yellow Fruited, and *Ilex verticillata* Winter Gold.

The holly with the most yellow-fruited forms is the native American holly *(Ilex opaca)*. Examples include Blayden Maiden, Calloway, Cecil Yellow, Fallaw, Fruitland, Galleon Gold, Goldie, Morgan Gold, Susan Gregory, and Yellow Virginia Giant. While not all are commonly stocked at local nurseries, be sure to ask for them. They probably won't have them until available customers say they want them.   *Linda C. Askey*

For a list of mail-order sources of these yellow-berried plants, send a self-addressed, stamped, business-size envelope to Yellow Berries, *Southern Living*, P.O. Box 830119, Birmingham, AL 35283.

The ABC's Of Apples

If our story about heirloom apples in the October 1994 issue of *Southern Living,* page 78, has you itching to plant this fall, you'll be glad to know that apples are just about the easiest fruit to grow. Here are some tips to get you started.

Site and Soil: Two things apple trees absolutely require are lots of sun and excellent drainage. They tolerate clay or sandy soils surprisingly well. But if you're planting in nearly pure clay or sand, backfill the hole with a mixture of equal parts excavated soil and sphagnum peat moss or composted bark. Make sure the graft union (the notch near the base of the trunk) sits several inches above grade. If possible, plant on a north- or east-facing slope. This reduces the chance of frost damage to spring buds. Also, never plant in low spots. Areas of Texas with strongly alkaline soil are generally unsuited to apples due to the prevalence of cotton rot disease.

Size: Apple trees come in three basic sizes—standard (20 to 35 feet tall), semidwarf (10 to 20 feet), and dwarf (6 to 10 feet). Most gardeners prefer dwarf and semidwarf trees because they take up less space and bear fruit two to three years earlier. Dwarf trees aren't recommended for very sandy soil because the root systems are too compact to firmly anchor the trees.

Pollination: Some apples, such as Golden Delicious and Grimes Golden, are self-pollinating. But most apple trees require cross-pollination with a different apple variety to produce fruit.

Basic Training: Proper pruning at planting is critical. Prune the tree so the branches alternate up and down the trunk at a spacing of 3 to 12 inches (see sketch). Branch crotches

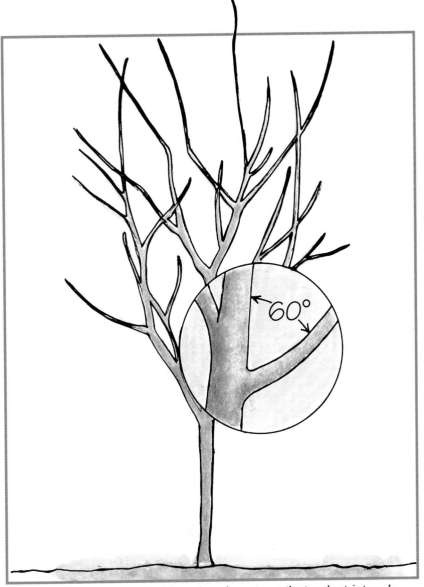

Prune young trees so that branches alternate up the trunk at intervals of 3 to 12 inches. Branches with crotches of about 60 degrees are stronger and produce more fruit.

should be at roughly 60-degree angles. You can gently pull young branches into the proper position with a cord tied to a stake. Then, after one growing season, remove the cord and stake.

Yearly Pruning: In late winter, prune an established tree to open up the center. This allows air to circulate freely and sunlight to reach every leaf, which greatly lessens disease and insect problems. Also remove suckers growing from the base of the tree and branches growing toward the center.

The Big Chill: Most apples require about 1,000 hours of chilling (temperatures between 32 and 45 degrees) in order to set fruit. This poses big problems for folks in the Coastal and Tropical South, where winters vary between 100 and 600 chilling hours. However, certain low-chill apples do well there. In the Tropical South, try Anna, Beverly Hills, Dorsett Golden, Ein Shemer, Fuji, Gordon, and Winter Banana. Gardeners in the Coastal South can try these plus Adina, Blairmont, Granny Smith, Mollies Delicious, and Yellow Bellflower. (Note: No apples are recommended for Florida south of Fort Myers and West Palm Beach.)

For Beginners: If you've never grown apples before, try one or two of the newer pest-resistant trees that need little spraying. They include Dayton, Enterprise, Freedom, Liberty, Prima, Priscilla, Sir Prize, and William's Pride.   *Steve Bender*

INDOOR BULBS

As winter settles upon the garden,

spring unfurls indoors. Pots of

bulbs are fresher than cut flowers

and easier to arrange.

G ardeners cheat. If we can grow a plant that's not hardy, we do. And if we can grow a plant out of season, so much the better. Perhaps that's the perennial fascination we have with forced bulbs.

But remember, "forced" is a term we use to flatter ourselves, implying that we can make a plant do anything against its nature. If we have at least one season behind us, we know better. Honestly, bulbs are cajoled—not forced—into bloom, persuaded that their time has come. And our reward for this effort? The sweet sight and scent of flowers indoors while winter keeps outdoor bulbs quiet for months to come.

Whether we grow our own potted bulbs (see page 229) or buy them from the local market, we face the same challenge that we do with cut flowers. What should we do with them once we have them? The solution lies in simplicity.

Clay pots combine an earthy character and familiar shape with rustic charm. Although bulbs are seldom grown and shipped in heavy, breakable pots, they can be easily slipped out of a plastic pot and into a clay one. For greater fullness, you can

BY LINDA C. ASKEY
PHOTOGRAPHY VAN CHAPLIN

Tete-a-tete narcissus beneath a ficus tree mirror the daffodils that spring up under oaks outdoors. This arrangement required one tray of bulbs forced in 4-inch pots.

(**Above**) *The freshness of white and green dispels the grays and browns of winter outdoors. White hyacinths, white primulas, maidenhair fern, and Granny Smith apples complete a coffee-table composition.* (**Left**) *Dwarf iris appear grand in ornate drinking cups. Placing the flowers in front of a mirror doubles their impact.*

put several single hyacinths in a larger clay pot and fill in the gaps with potting soil.

Once you start thinking of displaying a flowering bulb in a pot different from the original container, anything is possible—from baskets and hand-thrown pottery to fine porcelain and moss-lined glassware. Display them alone or in combination with houseplants.

Most of the bulbs that are easy to force are the early ones, and they are generally small. That means that the most effective display may be next to a favorite chair or on a bedside table. Place them where you will see them—whether that's on the kitchen counter or atop the bathroom vanity.

And once you've placed them, enjoy their cheery color through the cold days ahead. ◇

TO HELP FLOWERING BULBS IN YOUR HOME

■ Buy potted bulbs in bud so you can enjoy watching them open.
■ Water carefully. Do not let them dry to the point of wilting. But if you use a container without drainage, be careful not to overwater, creating soggy soil.
■ Some flowering bulbs do not bloom very long. In fact, dwarf iris will only last a few days, so don't buy them for a party a week in advance.
■ Pinching off individual flowers that have faded will freshen the appearance of the entire plant.

December

Evergreen garland and trees

CHECKLIST FOR DECEMBER

AUCUBA BERRIES

Though best known for their foliage, some aucubas also have red berries useful in holiday decorations. If your plant fails to produce berries, it's either a male plant or a female that needs pollinating. The selection Variegata (commonly called Gold-dust plant) is always female, while the Picturata plant is always male.

ANNUALS

For Florida gardeners, now is a good time to add color to your landscape. Dianthus, wax begonia, petunia, pansy, and snapdragon are good choices throughout the state. In North and Central Florida, include viola, delphinium, and stock. Gardeners in South Florida can also add impatiens, ageratum, salvia, and nasturtium.

BIRDS

Birds add interest to your winter garden. However, once you begin feeding them, they will depend on you. Continue to refill your bird feeder regularly.

BROMELIADS

When grown indoors, bromeliads should be planted in soil that is allowed to dry slightly between waterings. However, when grown outdoors or in a greenhouse, the plant survives nicely on a piece of driftwood where aerial roots hold it

in place. In this case, fill the cup formed by the circle of leaves at the center of the plant with water.

CHRISTMAS TREES

Buy your tree early, while it's still fresh. When you bring it home, cut 1 to 2 inches off the end of the trunk to open clogged water channels. You can mix your own tree preservative by adding 1 cup of Sprite® per gallon of water. A large tree will absorb as much as a quart of liquid daily, so replenish the mixture in the tree stand frequently. Consider a living Christmas tree to enjoy indoors, and plant it outside after the holidays.

CITRUS

In Central Florida, keep materials on hand to wrap trunks of citrus trees during a freeze warning. Buy a commercial trunk wrap, or devise your own from double-sided fiberglass batting, old carpet, or blankets. Wrap the entire trunk, taking care to cover the bud union where the tree was grafted (usually 6 to 8 inches above the ground). Don't let the wrap get warm or wet; remove it as soon as freezing weather has passed.

FISH

Use an outdoor thermometer to check the water temperature in your garden pool. Stop feeding fish when the water temperature drops to 45 degrees.

GIFTS

Consider a present you won't have to wrap. The gardener on your list will appreciate a gift certificate from his favorite catalog.

HOLIDAY PLANTS

For longer lasting displays with amaryllis, poinsettias, and other festive indoor plants, keep them away from drafty locations and heat vents. Allow potting soil to dry out slightly before watering. Cool nighttime temperatures can prolong their blooms.

HOUSEPLANTS

Now that you've brought them all indoors, prune overgrown plants by removing entire branches. Set small pots on top of the soil beneath potted trees. Use big baskets with other containers to combine several separate plants into a temporary garden.

LAWNS

Though it is still necessary to mow lawns in Central and South Florida, you can let the grass grow taller between mowings. Raise the mower blade, and allow St. Augustine lawns to grow about 3 to 4 inches high. Overseeded lawns in North Florida and Bermuda lawns throughout the state should be mowed when the grass gets about 2 inches high.

LIRIOPE

Now is a good time to divide overgrown liriope. It isn't necessary to mow thick clumps. Instead, pierce the clump with a sharp shovel and separate into smaller plants. Divided liriope can be temporarily planted in a shallow hole until you give it away or plant it elsewhere.

MISTLETOE

Prune mistletoe from mesquite, oak, hackberry, and other susceptible trees. Mistletoe is a parasitic plant; heavy infestations can weaken the host tree.

MULCH

Gardeners in the Middle South should remember to mulch tender bulbs such as elephant's-ears, gloriosa lilies, and agapanthus. Although normally considered hardy only in the

Lower South, these flowers may survive if planted deeply and mulched.

ORCHIDS

Of the gift plants available at this time

of year, phalaenopsis orchids may be the most economical buy. Plants may cost $25 or more, but the flowers last 3 to 4 months. Look for plants with branched stems or more than one stem per plant. The blooms can last for several months with proper care. Place them where they receive a couple of hours of direct morning or evening sun. Water sparingly; use a liquid houseplant fertilizer every other time you water.

PESTICIDES

Clean out your pesticide storage now. Discard containers that have lost their labels. Wrap the containers of unused material in several layers of newspaper, and put them in the garbage. Do not pour chemicals down the drain, and do not recycle pesticide containers. Move remaining chemicals to a place where they will not freeze this winter.

SALAD GREENS

In the Texas panhandle, start seeds of spinach, Chinese mustard, bok choy, lettuce, and other leafy vegetables indoors or in a greenhouse. Transplant outdoors or to a cold frame when seedlings are several inches tall; use a row-cover fabric in the garden to protect them from pests and cold weather.

SPRING BLOOMS

Till the soil thoroughly; then sow seeds of larkspur, poppies, bachelor's button, and sweet peas directly in the garden. Water afterward, and apply a thin layer of mulch. Thin seedlings 4 to 6 inches apart when plants are a few inches high.

SPRING BULBS

Set out daffodils, grape hyacinth, Dutch iris, amaryllis, tulips, and hyacinths now in the Lower South. Remember that tulips and hyacinths must be prechilled before planting.

TREE PRUNING

Remove the damaged or diseased limbs on shade trees now. Dangerous or low branches should also be taken off. Make final pruning cuts close to the trunk or large branch; never "top" (remove the uppermost branches) a shade tree.

TREES AND SHRUBS

Don't forget to water newly planted or transplanted trees and shrubs. Dry roots are more susceptible to damage from cold temperatures. Apply several inches of organic mulch around the base of the plant to conserve moisture and to insulate the roots.

VEGETABLES

Seed catalogs will begin arriving soon. Look for selections that offer disease resistance, earlier yields, or better flavor. Gardeners in the Coastal South can begin to plant asparagus, onions, English peas, leeks, cabbage, and rutabagas by midmonth. In Florida, plant radishes, carrots, beets, lettuce, broccoli, and onions statewide. Central Florida gardeners can also start parsley, cauliflower, and celery. Add tomatoes, kohlrabi, lima beans, snap beans, eggplant, and spinach to South Florida gardens.

WINTER BERRIES

Consider adding a shrub with colorful berries to brighten up your winter landscape. Yaupon holly is a native Texas plant with pearl-like, red fruit. Nandina, pyracantha, and other types of hollies also produce attractive berries. Most of these shrubs need a sunny to partially sunny location. Be sure to ask at the garden center about the plant's ultimate size.

TIP OF THE MONTH

When purchasing a clay pot at either the local garden center or a neighborhood garage sale, give it a good tap on the rim with your fingernail. If you hear a ringing sound, buy it. If instead you hear a dull thump, don't buy it. It has a hairline crack that will only become worse with use.
Elaine Irvin
Miami, Oklahoma

GARDENING
PLANTS AND DESIGN

GARLANDS
from the
GARDEN

BY JULIA H. THOMASON
PHOTOGRAPHY EMILY MINTON

*This season, decorate your
home with luxurious swags made
from evergreen foliage.*

I magine the scent of freshly cut
fir, pine, and boxwood drifting
through your home this holiday
season. You can easily make an
evergreen garland to frame a doorway or to swag across a mirror or
mantelpiece. Take cuttings from your
backyard, or purchase them from a
Christmas tree lot.

Refer to our photographs for easy
instructions on assembling trees
and garlands. Use a tape measure to

(Left)
This pine garland
expresses a garden
theme that's beautifully
appropriate for a
sunroom. To make your
own, cut pine into 12-
inch-long pieces; then
wire them together to
form the garland. Wrap
wide raffia ribbon
around the pine for an
easy accent. Wire
garland to nails
inserted in the door
molding. On each side,
allow for an extra yard
of garland to spiral to
the floor. Once it is
securely in place, a
collection of garden-
related items—
miniature baskets filled
with moss and bulbs,
small grapevine
wreaths, and tiny clay
pots—can be attached
with strands of raffia.

(Far left)
Boughs of Fraser fir,
purchased from a
Christmas tree lot, were
used to create this
sumptuous garland. To
make your own, cut
boughs into 12-inch-
long pieces. Then
overlap pieces, and
bind the stems with
wire. Wiring the
garland to long nails
inserted in the
underside of the mantel
adds support. The
treelike shrubs are
junipers purchased
from a garden center;
green sheet moss wraps
the containers. (Hint: If
the junipers are kept
watered, they can be
planted outdoors after
the holidays.) Candles,
fresh lemons, ivy, and a
bark-covered birdhouse
complete the rustic
arrangement.

Long boxwood garlands are wired to the banister, then spiraled around the newel posts. The containers at the base of the miniature boxwood trees are attached to the top of the newels with wire.

MAKE A GARLAND

Cut boxwood into 8-inch pieces. Use flexible florist wire to join stems. Wrap wire around the stem of the first piece. Place a second piece of boxwood over the first, but move the stem an inch down from the leaves of the previous piece. Wrap both stems with wire. Continue adding greenery until the desired length.

CREATE A TREE FROM BOXWOOD

Place a block of saturated florist foam in a plastic dish. Use florist tape to strap the foam to the dish if it doesn't fit snugly. Trim the corners from the block of foam to form the shape of a tree.

Beginning at the base, insert pieces of boxwood horizontally into the florist foam. Continue adding boxwood until the foam is covered; gradually angle the pieces toward the top of the foam. Insert the last pieces vertically. Keep the tree looking fresh by adding water to the dish.

estimate the length of garland you'll need. A long garland will be more manageable if you make it in several pieces, and then assemble the pieces in the room you are decorating. Use a continuous spool of florist wire to strengthen the garland and help it stay together when hung.

To prolong the freshness of cut greenery, apply an antidesiccant according to label directions. You can purchase spray cans of antidesiccants, such as Wilt-Pruf and Cloud Cover, at a garden center. But once applied, these products seal the greenery and mask its fragrance. ◇

TIPS FOR PRUNING EVERGREENS

As you cut foliage from plants, remember that you are actually pruning the plant. Though late winter is the best time to prune, mid-December, when evergreens are dormant, is not too early. And by making garlands and other holiday decorations, you have the opportunity to use the foliage you prune, instead of discarding it.

The way that you make a cut will determine how a shrub or tree will regrow. Study the plant to determine where to prune to leave it looking well-balanced. When cutting a boxwood, snip away a little here and a little there to open up the plant so that sunlight will filter down through the leaves. Try not to cut a major branch from any plant. Before using the foliage, condition it by soaking in water overnight.

Top to bottom:
cast-aluminum hand fork ($8),
wood-handled hand fork ($11),
spring-toothed weeder ($11),
standard trowel ($11-$18),
planting trowel ($8)

Waterworks:
Three-ply, reinforced garden hose ($40
for 50-foot hose, premium quality),
oscillating sprinkler with adjustable
spray width and length ($45),
galvanized watering can ($20),
spray wand with Water Breaker ($15)

LETTERS TO OUR GARDEN EDITORS

Amaryllis bulb: Last year, we ordered an amaryllis bulb. The foliage was pretty, but it didn't flower. This year, we tried again with the same result. What went wrong?

Francis Michel
Waurika, Oklahoma

Amaryllis bulbs are usually easy to force indoors in a sunny room, given moist soil and temperatures between 70 and 75 degrees. However, it appears that in your case the bulb had not yet formed a flowerbud when you bought it. From now on, be sure to order only top-size bulbs (28-34 cm. diameter) of named selections that will force well indoors, such as Sun Dance (red), Aphrodite (pink picotee), Lady Jane (salmon pink), and Wedding Dance (white). Or go to a local greenhouse and purchase only bulbs whose flower stalks are already emerging.

Azaleas: Many of my azaleas have branches bent and frozen under deep snow. Will they recover on their own? What can I do to help them heal?

Nancy Green
Crownsville, Maryland

First, brush off snow to reduce the number of broken branches and allow bent ones to straighten up. But wait until spring growth begins to do major pruning. Cut dead, split, and broken branches back to healthy wood; then spread azalea fertilizer around the base of your plants at the rate recommended on the bag. Unless the damage was severe, your plants should perk right up.

Balsam: My grandmother grew a flower that developed a fat seedpod. When touched, the pod popped and seeds flew everywhere. Do you have any information on it?

K. O'Sullivan
Midlothian, Virginia

The plant you describe is an old-fashioned annual called balsam (*Impatiens balsamina*). A cousin to the popular garden impatiens, its exploding seedpods distribute seeds away

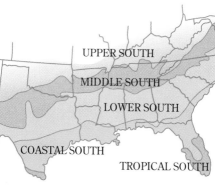

UPPER SOUTH
MIDDLE SOUTH
LOWER SOUTH
COASTAL SOUTH
TROPICAL SOUTH

from the mother plant. Thus developed the plant's other common name, touch-me-not.

Bartlett pear: The Bartlett pear we planted three years ago is nice and healthy, but it still refuses to bloom. We live near the Mississippi coast where the winters are mild with only an occasional frost. Do you have any suggestions for me?

Carolyn Koerner
Diamondhead, Mississippi

It's likely that your Bartlett pear isn't getting sufficient winter chilling. You need to plant a pear with a low chill requirement, such as Twentieth Century, Ya Li, Orient, Shinseiki, or Pineapple. Plant two or more different selections for cross-pollination. For a list of mail-order sources, send a self-addressed, stamped, business-size envelope to Pears, *Southern Living*, P.O. Box 830119, Birmingham, AL 35283.

Beech: We'd like to plant a nice shade tree at our vacation house in northern Florida. Is an American beech a good choice?

Sara S. Pepper
Stone Mountain, Georgia

Not really. The American beech (*Fagus grandifolia*) grows slowly and will take years to shade your house. In addition, its dense shade and surface roots make it nearly impossible to grow grass beneath. Better candidates for your yard would include Drake Chinese elm (*Ulmus parviflora*

Drake), red maple (*Acer rubrum*), Japanese zelkova (*Zelkova serrata*), Chinese pistachio (*Pistach chinensis*), Chinese tallow (*Sapium sebiferum*), and Chinese goldenrain tree (*Koelreuteria bipinnata*).

Bird-of-paradise: My bird-of-paradise is 5 years old and has never bloomed. Can you help?

Mildred A. Stewart
North Port, Florida

This tropical plant often refuses to bloom until it is potbound and more than 5 years old. To encourage flowerbuds, give your plant bright light. Be sparing with the fertilizer: When you do feed it (about once a month during spring and summer), use a "bloom booster" fertilizer higher in phosphorus than nitrogen. Let the soil go slightly dry between waterings.

Bulbs: How can I plant spring bulbs, then continue to use that same space later for annuals and perennials?

T. Gail Warren
Cornelius, North Carolina

It's usually no problem to plant on top of tulips, hyacinths, lilies, and daffodils. That's because you plant these bulbs at least 6 to 8 inches deep. However, "minor bulbs," such as crocus, snowdrops, and starflowers are planted so shallowly (1 to 2 inches deep) that you'd likely dig into them. We use golf tees to mark where to plant minor bulbs in the fall. Then plant perennials around them now or annuals and perennials around them next spring. The flowers will cover any gaps left when the bulbs die down.

Cannas: My cannas have stopped blooming and are starting to look ratty. Can I cut them back? Also, can I safely move them now?

Helen Gallucci
Titusville, Florida

Once cannas stop blooming and the foliage begins to wither, it's okay to cut them back. Fall is also a good time to divide and move them. Use a garden fork to lift a clump from the ground. Then break apart the thick roots. Replant each piece 4 to 5 inches deep, spacing them about a foot apart in fertile, well-drained soil.

Carpenter bees: We're having a real problem with carpenter bees. They drill round holes in the wood siding of our house and deposit eggs there. What can we do?

Robert L. Willard
Carriere, Mississippi

We suggest you spray exposed, exterior wood surfaces with an insecticide called Dursban when the bees appear in spring. Be sure to follow label directions carefully. You may have to do this several times during the year. You'll find it easier to reach high up on a wall and under the eaves if you use a pressurized tank sprayer. Be sure to wear rubber gloves, goggles, and protective clothing while spraying.

Cats: How can I keep cats from digging in my flowerbeds? I have placed bricks around my flowers, tried different sprays, but nothing seems to work.

Laura M. Ramsey
Gastonia, North Carolina

In response to your letter, we surveyed our staff. Here are their suggestions.
■ Place pinecones on exposed soil.
■ Place rose canes on the exposed soil.
■ Try mothballs.
■ Dust the soil with cayenne pepper.
■ Sprinkle Ortho SCRAM Dog & Cat Repellent over the soil.
■ Buy a ravenous Rottweiler.
Hope this helps.

Chinese goldenrain tree: Last fall I saw what I thought was a beautiful goldenrain tree. But its seedpods were pink instead of brown. What was it and where can I buy one?

June Hiter
Nashville, Tennessee

The tree you describe sounds like Chinese goldenrain tree (*Koelreuteria bipinnata*), a lovely cousin of the more familiar goldenrain tree (*K. paniculata*), but with seedpods that are a striking pink. Order it from Forest Farm, 990 Tethrow Road, Williams, OR 97544-9599.

Clematis: I have a white-flowering clematis called *Henryi*. Can you tell me how to root it?

Dot Nuckolls
Newport, Arkansas

Take a 1- to 2-inch cutting in early spring when the flowerbuds are expanding but haven't yet opened. Cut just above a node (the point where leaves join the stem), dust the cut end with rooting powder, and stick the cutting in a pot filled with moist vermiculite or perlite. Enclose the pot in a clear, zip-top plastic bag to retain humidity. The cutting should root in four to five weeks.

EDITOR'S NOTEBOOK

Want to know why your newly bought annuals shrivel and die unless you water them twice every day for the first three weeks? It's a question of balance. A plant growing naturally of its own accord produces top growth in direct proportion to its roots. But flowers grown in greenhouses are products of a totally unnatural situation. They get all the sunlight, humidity, water, and fertilizer they ever want. So they grow much more flowers, leaves, and stems than their roots could support if they weren't so pampered. Sure, they look fantastic in the garden center. But plant them in the ground and you soon discover you've taken home a pack of "water junkies." You can avoid this by doing two things: First, never buy annuals already in bloom. Buy healthy, but less advanced plants instead. Second, if someone gives you water junkies, remove all the flowers and about half the foliage. Then plant. Within two weeks, your plants will be back in balance. Plus, they'll bloom much longer and fuller than coddled, greenhouse plants. *Steve Bender*

Crepe myrtles: The leaves of our crepe myrtles have turned black like they've been burnt. When this started we had a light on at night right beside where they grew. Did the light do this?

Linda Banks
Luthersville, Georgia

No. The culprits are aphids, which secrete a sticky honeydew; then black mold grows on the honeydew. To control, spray your crepe myrtles three times this summer at two-week intervals. Use malathion, Diazinon, horticultural oil, or insecticidal soap according to label directions. If you use malathion or Diazinon, don't spray the flowers or you'll also kill bees. Neither horticultural oil nor insecticidal soap harms bees.

Daffodils: Can you tell me how to grow daffodils from seed? What do the seeds look like?

Sidney A. Murray, Jr.
Vidalia, Louisiana

According to Becky Heath of the Daffodil Mart in Gloucester, Virginia, very few of the large hybrid daffodils produce seeds because they have no nectar to attract pollinating insects. However, most miniature daffodils and other narcissus species do form seeds. After pollination, a green seedpod forms on the end of the stem. The pod turns brown when the seeds, which look like shiny, black BBs, are ripe. Sow them soon after gathering in a flat filled with moist potting soil. Barely cover them. The first year, seedlings will look like single blades of grass. Transplant them to the garden in spring. The second year, they'll look like two blades of grass. By the fifth year, they should be big enough to bloom.

Epsom salts: I've been told that Epsom salts is good to use on flowers and shrubs. Is this true? What time of year should I use it?

Carey Ray
Glen Allen, Virginia

Epsom salts is another name for Magnesium sulfate. Magnesium aids photosynthesis. If you're using a general-purpose fertilizer that contains magnesium, you probably don't need to add Epsom salts. However, if it doesn't contain this element, mix a tablespoon of Epsom salts into a gallon of water. Pour this around the base of a plant or spray on the foliage once a month during the growing season. In winter, use it to keep your houseplants green and happy.

Fertilizer: You stated a while back that the best time to fertilize warm-season grass is in spring. Here in San Antonio, it's highly recommended to feed in October and November for an early spring green-up. Which recommendation is right?

Les Lande
San Antonio, Texas

We hate to disagree, but we're going to anyway. Feeding warm-season grass in November may cause it to delay dormancy and not harden off in time for winter—especially if you use high-nitrogen fertilizer. So for most readers with warm-season grass, we recommend fertilizing twice a year—once in spring and once in early summer. If you insist on fertilizing in fall, we recommend a winterizing formula low in nitrogen and high in potassium, such as 8-8-25.

Figs: When should I prune a big fig tree?

Ann Sturdivant
McComb, Mississippi

Late winter is a good time, just before the new growth starts. Most fig trees produce two crops of figs per year in the South, so you'll lose some of the early crop. But the new growth encouraged by pruning will compensate you with fruit later in the season.

French drain: Standing pools of water collect in our yard. The mud and fungus are killing our Bermuda grass. Someone suggested we install French drains. Can you tell us something about them?

Susan R. Noble
Tuscaloosa, Alabama

A French drain usually consists of a trench, gravel, and perforated PVC pipe. Dig the trench where you want to drain problem water, and line the bottom with gravel. Place the pipe in the trench, and wrap the pipe in filter fabric to prevent clogging; then cover the pipe with more gravel. The pipe needs to drop at least ¼ inch every 10 feet to carry away excess water. French drains aren't that expensive to install. But for them to work properly and not detract from your garden's appearance, consult a landscape architect or contractor before installing one.

Funginex: Can you please give me some information about a spray called Funginex?

Selma Singer
Dunwoody, Georgia

Funginex, a systemic fungicide that controls many plant diseases, is the brand name of a chemical called triforine. Its most popular use is on roses to prevent black spot, powdery mildew, and rust. You can buy it at most garden centers, nurseries, and hardware stores. Be sure to follow the label directions carefully.

EDITOR'S NOTEBOOK
Droughts happen almost every summer. Weeks go by without a drop of rain. Sometimes it gets so bad that cities have to ration water. And what uses up the most water? Lawns, of course. Wouldn't it be great if there were a way to keep the grass green without watering so much? There is. It's called (drum roll, please) *not mowing.* That's right. Every time you cut your grass when it's hot and dry, you must water it immediately or it turns brown. Then it turns green and grows some more, so you have to cut it and water again. If this sounds like a waste of time and water, do what I do. When an extended drought hits, vow not to cut your grass until it rains two days in a row. Water no more than once a week. Last year, my Zoysia lawn went from July 15 to September 1 without being cut. It grew to 4½ inches tall, looked thick and lush, and I watered hardly at all. Once the rains resumed, I gradually shortened the grass until I returned it to its customary 2 inches. I saved water, I saved gas, I saved time, and I saved money. Saving is good.

Steve Bender

Grass alternate: My yard has 10 to 12 tall pines growing in a small area. This provides nice, mottled shade for our picnic area, but doesn't allow grass to grow. What can I plant instead?

Debra Burgess
Conroe, Texas

Try planting an evergreen ground cover. Good choices for your area of southeast Texas include Algerian ivy, common periwinkle, liriope, mondo grass, holly fern, Japanese ardisia, and Asian jasmine.

Gully: I have a natural drainage gully at the back of my property that is being overrun by weeds. Can you recommend a type of ground cover or flower that would like very moist, sandy soil?

Debra D. Hutcheson
Fairfax Station, Virginia

Two flowers you might try are forget-me-not (*Myosotis sylvatica*) and cardinal flower (*Lobelia cardinalis*). Forget-me-not is a reseeding annual with beautiful blue flowers in spring. Cardinal flower is a perennial that produces bright-red flower spikes in late summer. As far as ground covers go, try a newcomer called chameleon plant (*Houttuynia cordata*). Its gaudy, heart-shaped leaves combine colors of red, cream, gold, and blue-green. Be warned, however, that in moist soil this plant multiplies faster than Dustin Hoffman did in *Rain Man.*

Hyacinths: The grape hyacinths I planted early this fall have sprouted foliage. Will cold weather hurt them?

Jane S. Christiansen
Denton, Texas

Don't worry. Grape hyacinths, dwarf narcissus, and some other minor bulbs naturally sprout in the fall. This way, they get a head start on absorbing energy from the sun. When freezing weather comes, the foliage will wither. But fresh foliage will appear in spring, accompanied by blooms.

Lacebugs: Can you suggest a solution for lacebugs on my azaleas—something that doesn't involve a chemical?

Regina Gallia
Hollywood, Maryland

Lacebugs are small, winged insects that feed on the undersides of leaves of azaleas and other plants. By midsummer, the leaves look light green and speckled. A good, nonpoisonous control for these insects is an organic pesticide called insecticidal soap. You can find it at most garden centers. Spray it on the leaf undersides, following label directions carefully. Because it has no residual action, you'll have to spray more often than if you used chemicals. Begin spraying one week after the bloom; then spray every other week until midsummer. Another way to reduce lacebugs is to plant azaleas in the shade. Lacebugs prefer to attack azaleas in hot sun.

Magnolia: Someone recently told me that healthy magnolias don't bloom, and a good way to make them bloom is to drive nails into their trunks. Is this true?

Evelyn R. Lammons
Shreveport, Louisiana

Absolutely not. And anyone who says so ought to be reported to the SPCST (Society for the Prevention of Cruelty to Shade Trees). Fact is, most Southern magnolias are naturally slow to bloom, often waiting 10 years or more after planting to start. Deliberately injuring them only increases the likelihood that they'll fall victim to insects, disease, or environmental stress. The best way to obtain flowers on young trees is to plant selections that bloom while the tree is still young, such as Goliath, Little Gem, Majestic Beauty, and Saint Mary. Save the nails for a loose board.

Magnolia seed: Could you give me some advice on how to germinate the seeds of Southern magnolia?

Francyne M. Wells
Montgomery, Alabama

First, collect the seedpods when the berries are bright red. Pull the berries from the pods; then scrape off the red coating from around each seed. Place the seeds in a zip-top plastic bag filled with moist potting soil. Seal the bag, and store it in the refrigerator for about three months; then transfer the seeds to individual pots and plant them ½ inch deep in moist soil. Place in a warm, sunny spot, and they should sprout in a week or two.

Maple tree: I have a 4-year-old maple that is 12 to 15 feet tall. The upper part of the tree appears to be wilted. The leaves are dry to the touch, half-curled, and hang limply.

The lower part looks normal. What could be wrong?

Linda Fish
Goldsboro, North Carolina

It sounds like an attack by Verticillium wilt, a soil-borne disease. If the situation is ignored, it will kill the tree. We suggest you ask a local tree service to root-feed your maple with a high-nitrogen fertilizer this spring. This will encourage the production of corky cells that may help in walling off the infection.

Morning glories: A neighbor planted morning glories two years ago.

EDITOR'S NOTEBOOK

Think you've seen everything? Then order some bulbs of autumn crocus (*Colchicum* sp.) and see what a sheltered life you've led. True to their name, autumn crocus bloom in fall, not spring. So anxious are they to flower that if you forget to plant them this month, they'll bloom anywhere you leave them—in a bag, in an ashtray, or atop your VCR. However, to keep them coming back year after year, plant them in the ground, 3 to 4 inches deep, in fertile, well-drained soil.

Many different species and selections exist, ranging in height from 3 to 8 inches. Colors include violet, rose, lavender, pink, and white. Specialty garden shops occasionally carry them, but we find the best selection in the McClure & Zimmerman catalog (108 W. Winnebago St., P.O. Box 368, Friesland, WI 53935-0368 ([414] 326-4220).

Don't put off ordering. Jogging, aerobics, and golf can wait. But autumn crocus won't.

Steve Bender

Now they have taken over my flower gardens. How can I get rid of them?

Sharon Bobier
Williamstown, West Virginia

Don't dig up your flowerbeds. All that would do is bring more morning glory seed to the surface to germinate. Instead, pull up all new vines before they flower. This will keep them from producing additional seed. Then apply a pre-emergence herbicide, such as Dacthal or Treflan, around your established plants to stop morning glory seed from germinating. Follow label directions carefully. Also, try mulching around your flowers to discourage unwanted seedlings.

Mosquitoes: For the last two years, it has been impossible to enjoy my backyard during the summer because of mosquitoes. Help!

Susan Sherrill
Atlanta, Georgia

To repel mosquitoes you need a product that contains DEET. For your backyard, use an aerosol fogger to drive mosquitoes away from your yard for an hour or two to permit outdoor entertaining. Direct the fog into bushes, hedges, and other thick vegetation where mosquitoes rest during the hot part of the day.

Moss: We'd like to build a brick patio under some large shade trees. But we're afraid the shade will cause the brick to become slick with moss. What can we do to help prevent this?

Billie Rogers
Selma, Alabama

Brick placed in a moist, shady spot provides a happy haven for moss. One way to combat moss is to treat the brick with a chemical sealant to keep it from absorbing water. If this doesn't work, you can kill the moss by periodically spraying the brick with Safer Moss & Algae Killer, following label directions. Or you can spray the brick with a solution of chlorine bleach and water. If you opt for the latter, be sure the bleach doesn't touch the leaves or reach the roots of desirable plants.

Nandina: I am in a quandary as to when and how to prune nandinas. If they're not trimmed, they become tall and leggy. If they are trimmed, they have no red berries in the fall.

Mrs. Larry D. New
Asheville, North Carolina

To help preserve the berries, each year prune one-third of the total number of canes. Make each selected cane a different height, cutting it back to just above a tuft of foliage. This prevents legginess, while maintaining the shrub's natural form. Prune any time from late spring to midsummer. Don't do it later in the year or you may encourage late growth that won't harden off in time for winter.

Nandina: I'm considering planting nandina in my garden. Could you tell me what kinds of birds are attracted to its red berries?

Floyd Beach
Powhatan, Virginia

Nandina makes an excellent winter food source for birds because it holds its berries all the way to spring. In Birmingham, we've noticed the berries attract mockingbirds, cardinals, sparrows, catbirds, and juncos. These birds should visit nandina in your area, too.

Nasturtiums: Why don't my nasturtiums bloom? They have lots of foliage, but no flowers.

Katherine Dodd
Front Royal, Virginia

Our guess is that you've been too generous with fertilizer. Nasturtiums thrive on neglect. Next time, plant them in a sunny spot with rather poor soil and don't feed.

Oleander: When should you cut an oleander back? When is a good time to fertilize?

Elbye A. Toole
Graceville, Florida

You can prune an oleander in very early spring before it starts growing or in summer after it finishes flowering. But be sure to keep the irritating sap off your hands. Oleander tolerates poor soil, so it doesn't need much fertilizer. You might just sprinkle a few handfuls of cottonseed meal or 5-10-5 around the base of the plant this spring.

Parsley: I have a parsley plant in my garden, full of black swallowtail caterpillars. Will my plant survive?

Michael Adler
Memphis, Tennessee

First, let us congratulate you for not wiping out the caterpillars. Without caterpillars, you wouldn't get butterflies. As to whether your parsley will

come back next year, that depends on how old it is. Parsley is a biennial, meaning it lives as a tuft of foliage the first year, then flowers, sets seed, and dies the second. If yours has set seed, you'll have to start a new plant from seed next spring.

Pecan trees: My pecan tree usually produces well, but in the fall the hulls don't open. And there are always worms inside the shells. What do you suggest?

Olivia Iverson
Graham, Alabama

Your tree is infested with weevils. To control them, do three things. First, if possible spray your tree with carbaryl three to four times at two-week intervals beginning in August. Second, collect and destroy all infested nuts that drop to the ground. Finally, treat the soil beneath the tree with Dursban granules to kill the grubs. Be sure to follow the label directions carefully.

Peonies: I love peonies. Are there any varieties that thrive in my area?

Lisa Carter
Albany, Georgia

Certainly. In fact, there are several. For your area, single-blooming and Japanese types generally perform better than the doubles. Recommended singles include Imperial Red, Le Jour (white), Sea Shell (pink), and Sparkling Star (dark pink). Japanese types to try include Do Tell (pink), Shaylor's Sunburst (white), Ama-no-sode (dark pink), and Comanche, Mikado, Dignity, and Nippon Brilliant (all red). The best double peony for the South is the Festiva Maxima (white).

Pine straw: You recommend pine straw as a mulch, and I wonder why you don't also recommend it as a soil additive?

R. E. Clapper
Prattville, Alabama

In fact, we do. Pine straw adds lots of organic matter to the soil as it decomposes. We find it easier to work with if we chop it up with a mulching mower before tilling it in.

Poppies: When should you plant poppies? Will they bloom next year?

C. Samuel Scott
Piney Flats, Tennessee

Fall is a good time to plant poppies, either transplants or seed. Select a spot with well-drained, fertile soil that receives plenty of sun. Space transplants 6 to 8 inches apart. If you sow seed, first rake the soil to loosen it, and remove any surface debris. You'll get better germination on bare soil. Mix the seed with sand for a more even distribution; then sprinkle the mixture over the soil. Both transplants and seedlings should bloom next spring.

Quaking aspen: My parents in Pennsylvania enjoy the quaking aspens on their property. Would these trees grow for us in Florida, 75 miles south of Melbourne?

Drucille Conrad
Fort Pierce, Florida

Quaking aspen (*Populus tremuloides*) is perhaps the most beloved tree of the Rocky Mountains. Each fall, it turns whole forests bright gold. Unfortunately, it naturally favors the cooler weather of higher elevations, which doesn't sound like any part of Florida we know. Sentenced to the heat and humidity of your climate, the tree would likely croak rather than quake. But if you want to give it a try, go ahead. Just don't spend a lot of money.

Queen Anne's lace: I've tried transplanting Queen Anne's lace from the wild to my garden, but have had no luck in getting it to grow. What do you suggest?

Marva Jacobs
Mitchellville, Maryland

Queen Anne's lace is difficult to transplant successfully once it develops beyond the seedling stage because it has a root like a carrot. Our advice is to collect seed from the withered flowers in summer and fall. Sow the seed in fall onto bare garden soil, and don't cover them. Seedlings will sprout the following spring. If they don't come up where you want, move them while they're still small.

Redtip: We've lost 20 large redtips to a disease that attacks the leaves and causes them to drop. What, if anything, can we use to halt its spread?

Robert L. Willard
Carriere, Mississippi

Redtips, also called photinias, suffer greatly from a disease called Entomosporium leaf spot. This fungus attacks the shrubs' young, reddish foliage. Once leaves mature, they become resistant. To control leaf spot, spray your plants just as the new leaves emerge in spring with a fungicide called Daconil. Be sure to follow label directions carefully. Spray three more times at intervals of 10 days. Rake up and destroy any diseased leaves that fall to the ground.

Rubber plant: I have a beautiful rubber plant, but the limbs keep rotting off. What am I doing wrong?

Ethel Duvall
Kannapolis, North Carolina

Our guess is that you're overwatering it. Rubber plant (*Ficus elastica*) likes

its soil to go slightly dry between thorough waterings. Make sure the pot has a drainage hole, so that excess water escapes.

Sedum: Why does our Autumn Joy sedum rot off at the ground after blooming?

W. C. Hardee
Loris, South Carolina

Soggy soil is the likely culprit. All succulents demand excellent drainage or they rot. Try planting it in a raised bed that sits 6 to 8 inches above the existing grade. Fill the bed with a

My neighbor worries about everything, from comet fragments smashing into Jupiter to whether she'll someday be reincarnated as an animal. So when she sees the leaves of her azaleas turning colors in fall, she gets so nervous you'd think she was a jelly doughnut being eyed by Elvis Presley. "Relax," I tell her. Some azaleas, particularly those with red, orange, or purple flowers, sport bronze winter foliage every year. Of course, if older leaves drop after turning red or yellow, it could be a sign that your azaleas need a little nitrogen. Try sprinkling a cup or so of cottonseed meal around the base of each plant this month. This inexpensive, organic fertilizer will release nitrogen over a period of months and also acidify the soil. "But whatever you do," I remind my neighbor, "don't panic. Jupiter is a long way away, your azaleas aren't going to die, and even if you come back as a pooch in the next life, you'll probably have a nice owner and your own water bowl." *Steve Bender*

soil mix consisting of equal parts of topsoil, sphagnum peat moss or compost, and coarse builder's sand. If the problem persists, drench the soil around the sedum with a fungicide called Funginex, mixed according to label directions.

Tomatoes: I planted tomatoes last year. Is it all right to plant them in the same spot this year or should I plant some other vegetables there?

Susan L. Church
Hampton, Virginia

It's not a good idea to grow tomatoes in the same spot year after year. Doing so encourages the buildup of soil-borne wilt diseases, as well as other pests. For the next two years, plant something different in the spot where you're growing tomatoes now. But don't choose peppers, eggplants, or potatoes. These three are close relatives of tomatoes and susceptible to some of the same pests.

Tulip poplar: I have a tulip poplar about 20 feet tall. It's never bloomed. What's wrong?

Betty Hooker
Lufkin, Texas

Probably nothing. One of the tallest-growing of our native trees, tulip poplar (*Liriodendron tulipifera*) usually bides its time before beginning to bloom. Yours may not be old enough. Another possibility is that the flowers it has produced have been in the top of the tree, partially obscured by foliage, where you can't easily see them.

Weed-and-feed: My lawn looked good in early summer. Now it's overgrown with all kinds of weeds, even though I used a weed-and-feed. What should I do?

Jane Dwight
Clarksville, Tennessee

Unless you follow directions carefully, weed-and-feed products can make a weed problem worse. The weedkiller can become ineffective and the fertilizer can make the weeds grow faster. What can you do now? For broadleaf weeds—dandelion, clover, chickweed, plantain, etc.—spray according to label directions with Weed-B-Gon or 33-Plus. For grassy weeds, such as crabgrass and goosegrass, do nothing. These grasses will die with the first frost. To keep them from returning next year, apply a pre-emergence herbicide, such as Balan or Dacthal, in early spring.

Index